Obama's Bank

The Obama administration aims to lay a sound foundation for growth by investing in high-speed rail, clean energy, information technology, drinking water, and other vital infrastructures. The idea is to partner with the private sector to produce these public goods. An Obama government bank would direct these investments, making project decisions based on the merits of each project, not on politics. This approach has been a cornerstone of U.S. foreign policy for several decades. In fact, our government-led reinvestment in America is modeled explicitly on international public banks and partnerships. However, although this foreign commercial policy is well established with many successes, it has also been deservedly controversial and divisive. This book describes the international experience, drawing lessons on how the Obama Bank can forge partnerships to promote a durable twenty-first-century New Deal.

Michael Likosky is a Senior Fellow at New York University's Institute for Public Knowledge, and formerly a tenured law professor at the University of London. He has held visiting professorships at Fordham University Law School and University of Wisconsin–Madison Law School. Likosky has been Markle Foundation Fellow at Oxford University and Global Crystal Eastman Research Fellow at New York University School of Law. He is an expert to the United Nations and Organization for Economic Cooperation and Development. He has published four books on law and finance: *Law, Infrastructure, and Human Rights*; *The Silicon Empire*; *Privatizing Development*; and *Transnational Legal Processes*. Likosky has twice contributed to the Oxford Amnesty Lectures, and his work has been supported by the Arts and Humanities Research Council, Ford Foundation, Institute for a New Reflection on Governance, and World Affairs and the Global Economy. He actively advises intergovernmental organizations, governments, investors, major broadcasters, public interest groups, and labor unions.

Obama's Bank

Financing a Durable New Deal

MICHAEL LIKOSKY

Senior Fellow

Institute for Public Knowledge, New York University

CAMBRIDGE UNIVERSITY PRESS
Cambridge, New York, Melbourne, Madrid, Cape Town, Singapore,
São Paulo, Delhi, Dubai, Tokyo, Mexico City

Cambridge University Press
32 Avenue of the Americas, New York, NY 10013-2473, USA

www.cambridge.org
Information on this title: www.cambridge.org/9780521147118

First published 2010

Printed in the United States of America

A catalog record for this publication is available from the British Library.

Library of Congress Cataloging in Publication data

Likosky, Michael.
Obama's bank : financing a durable new deal / Michael B. Likosky.
p. cm.
Includes bibliographical references and index.
ISBN 978-0-521-19754-0 (alk. paper)
1. Infrastructure (Economics) – Government policy – United States.
2. Public-private sector cooperation – United States. 3. Fiscal policy – United States. 4. Economic crisis – United States – History – 21st century.
I. Title.
HC110.C3L55 2009
363.60973–dc22 2009032486

ISBN 978-0-521-19754-0 Hardback
ISBN 978-0-521-14711-8 Paperback

For Joy

Drink Deep, or taste not the Pierian spring;
There shallow draughts intoxicate the brain,
And drinking largely sobers us again.

– Alexander Pope (1711)

True Axioms must be drawn from plain experience, and not from doubtful.

– William Rawley (1627)

Publicity is justly commended as a remedy for social and industrial diseases. Sunlight is said to be the best of disinfectants; electric light the most efficient policeman.

– United States Supreme Court Justice Louis Brandeis

Leverage is Everything.

– United States Supreme Court Justice
Oliver Wendell Holmes

Contents

Acknowledgments

This book has been influenced by many colleagues and events.

Over the last several years, I have been an expert to international organizations on public-private partnerships (P3s). Since 2007, I have worked closely with the United Nations Conference on Trade and Development as a regular contributor to its *World Investment Reports* and *World Development Report* as well as to Board Meetings. Much of this work has focused on providing policy advice tied to the role of P3s within infrastructure, oil, gas, and extractives to low- and medium-income countries. I am particularly thankful to Torbjörn Frederiksen. More recently, I have begun work with the Organisation for Economic Co-operation and Development (OECD) on these issues in Africa as a Member of its Working Group on Infrastructure and Extractives. I have also similarly benefited from my ongoing collaboration with the Ford Foundation on both international and domestic P3s; my work with Lisa Jordan helped shape the material on international infrastructure banks, and Katherine McFate read the bulk of the manuscript and provided insightful comments. The underlying research for this book has also been helped along in important ways by grants from the Arts and Humanities Research Council and the Center for World Affairs and the Global Economy.

The ideas for this book have been tested out and refined at many public lectures and events. I would like to single out several of them.

I convened three New York University (NYU) panels with the OECD as part of a series – Reinvesting in America – with support from the Ford Foundation. I am thankful to the panelists for their insights: John Adler (Director of Private Equity, Capital Stewardship Program, Service Employees International Union), Samara Barend (Executive Director, New York State Commission on State Asset Maximization), Phineas Baxandall (Senior Analyst for Tax and Budgetary Policy, United States Public Interest Research Group), John Buckley (Tax Counsel, House Ways and Means Committee, United States Congress), Tony Dutzik (Senior Analyst, Frontier Group), Karen Hedlund (Chief Counsel, Federal Highway Administration, United States Department of Transportation), Bob Helwig (Deputy Director, Office of the Secretary of Defense, United States Department of Defense), Emilia Istrate (Senior Research Analyst, Metropolitan Infrastructure Initiative, Brookings Institution), Aaron Klein (Deputy Assistant Secretary, Policy

Coordination, United States Department of the Treasury), Kris Kolluri (Chief Executive Officer, New Jersey State Schools Development Authority, and former Head of New Jersey Department of Transportation), Peter Rosenblum (Leiff, Cabraser, Heimann & Bernstein Clinical Professor, Columbia University Law School), Susan Rose-Ackerman (Henry R. Luce Professor of Law and Jurisprudence, Yale Law School), and Dan Zeitlin (Senior Legislative Staff, Office of United States Congresswoman Rosa DeLauro).

The book benefited from public lectures and debates including: a public talk within the International Development Policy Series of the International Affairs Council of Yale University (sponsored by the International Affairs Council, African Studies Council, and The MacMillan Center and also financed by the Edward J. and Dorothy Clarke Kempf Memorial Fund); a keynote talk to the American Society of Civil Engineers; a keynote talk to the Common Core of European Private Law at the University of Trento; an official presentation to the United Nations Conference on Trade and Development Board Meeting; an International Project Finance Association panel debate on private participation in public works sponsored by Fulbright & Jaworski LLP; and a Masters Class at the Project Finance International Annual Meeting in Paris.

The book was also shaped in important ways by presentations at the Social Science Research Council, Kyushu University, Law and Society Association annual meetings, New York University Law School, University of Wisconsin

Law School's New Legal Realism Conference Celebrating the twenty-fifth anniversary of the Feminist Legal Theory Project, Columbia University Law School, a meeting on Civil Society Intervention in the Reform of Global Public Policy organized by the Ford Foundation and the Institute for a New Reflection on Governance, the School of Oriental and African Studies (SOAS) Law School, Oxford University Law Faculty, Max Planck Institute for Social Anthropology, American Association of Anthropology, Center for State Innovation's State Chief Financial Officers' Roundtable, American Society of Civil Engineers New York Metropolitan Section Infrastructure Group, University of Wisconsin–Madison Law School Outreach Workshop on International Finance and Taxation, World Free Zone Convention, Project Finance International, and the International Institute of Communications.

Many colleagues and institutions have helped this book out in substantial ways. I am particularly thankful to Matthew Craven and Lynn Welchman, sequential heads of the Law School at SOAS, as well as Dean Stephan Chan and SOAS Director Paul Webley. Each made sure that scholarship and its real-world application were highly valued in their leadership. Thanks are also due to Craig Calhoun for his generous support as Director of NYU's Institute for Public Knowledge, where I completed the last leg of this project from 2008–2010. During the spring of 2009, I was also a visiting professor at Fordham University School of Law; conversations with Gráinne de Búrca there also helped the book along in important ways, as did teaching international trade law and international banking law as the crisis and stimulus unfolded. In 2007–2008, I spent a productive year exchanging views on ethnographic approaches to law and the New Legal Realism at UW Law School that informed the book, largely through exchanges with Stewart Macaulay, David Trubek, Beth Mertz, and Victoria Nourse. In addition, I had the luxury to read widely and flesh out the concept of free market statism that underpins the book as Global Crystal Eastman Research Fellow at the NYU School of Law within the Hauser Global Law School Program during the 2006–2007 academic year. I am particularly thankful to Joseph Weiler, Eleanor Fox, Benedict Kingsbury, Judge Dennis Davis, Philip Alston, Dick Stewart, and Kevin Davis.

As can be imagined, this book has benefited from ten or so years of conversations with colleagues and friends about the role of government in the economy in times of both growth and crisis. I would like to thank (in alphabetical order) some of the main protagonists in the book's writing, in addition to those already mentioned: Richard Abel, Jose Alvarez, Fred Aman, Bill Angelo, Upendra Baxi, Charles Berry, Richard Buxbaum, Lan Cao, Peter B. R. Carey, Sam Carter, Michael Cernea, Aileen Cho, Allison Christians, Jerry Cohen, Yves Dezalay, Laura Dickinson, Catriona Drew, Richard Falk, Jonathan Fanton, Martha Fineman, Stanley Fish, John Flood, Sheila Foster, Bennett Freeman, Marc Galanter, Bryant Garth, Joshua Getzler, Matthew Gibney, Linda Greene, Ken Hansen, Andrew Harding, Jim

Harris, Godfrey Hodgson, Rob Howse, Josh Ishimatsu, Christian Joppke, Harold Koh, Jonathan Koppell, Philip Lawton, Vaughan Lowe, Ugo Mattei, Bill Maurer, Sally Falk Moore, Joe Norton, Laura Rival, Joel Rogers, Peter Rosenblum, Jack Salzman, Saskia Sassen, Richard Scholar, Joanne Scott, Francis Snyder, Richard Story, David Sugarman, Ruti Teitel, William Twining, Stefaan Verhulst, Don Wallace, Immanuel Wallerstein, Horatia Muir Watt, Bill Whitford, Ngaire Woods, and Jay Zukerman. I benefited greatly from Shar Habibi's insights into the stimulus act bonds. I am indebted to Laura Wilmot of Cambridge University Press not only for her skilled editing but also for patiently accommodating my significant late-stage revisions. Jack Berger provided excellent research assistance.

Particular thanks are due to Susan Rose-Ackerman for both her ongoing support and encouragement and fruitful collaboration on two publications, one in the *Guardian* and the other in *Engineering News-Record*, on public-private partnerships in the United States. The start of Chapter 9 draws from this work heavily. I would especially like to thank John Berger, Senior Law Editor at Cambridge University Press, not only for the exceptional care taken with the usual publishing duties, but also for his intellectual support and friendship.

As happens with my books and all other endeavors, I am grateful to single out Joy Mooberry, who ensured that this book did not wither on the vine through her constant encouragement, loyalty, and intellectual energies.

1 Introduction

I started researching this book in 1997 as I watched the East Asian currency crisis unfold. I was writing my doctoral dissertation at Oxford University on the role of Silicon Valley firms and the United States government in that regional crisis. At the time, I saw the crisis across the Pacific as, in part, an American crisis. We had contributed to the East Asian Miracle, while at the same time creating a brittle economic and social environment both in Asia and at home. In turn, our subsequent policies addressed, prolonged, and ultimately deferred aspects of the crisis itself. Since the early 1980s, we had progressively divested from our own real economy in America. In doing so, we had redirected our financial and political energies overseas, promoting globalization. We benefited some and disadvantaged others, both at home and abroad.

When the dot-com boom/bust cycled through the United States, I was in San Francisco. My first spurt of writing happened as I watched our underlying crisis deepen. We razed communities to create dot-com paper wealth. Although many Silicon Valley firms continued to produce real value, the boom cultivated paper wealth as a mix of readily available finance for business plans, resulting in stock market growth. That crisis and its aftermath continued to erode the foundations of our national economy while financing production abroad to meet steroid-induced consumer demand at home.

Matters after the dot-com bust only grew more serious. Our foreign policy squandered the global goodwill, resiliency, and solidarity that emerged in the face of 9/11; we had demonstrated our national mettle and quickly rallied without losing sight of the gravity of living with the reality of terror, while our leadership steered us elsewhere. We found ourselves mired in an unpopular war. Spending on destruction and consumption overtook productive investment not only in America but abroad. With the subprime mortgage crisis and the engineering of a growing middle-class opportunity, our government and financial institutions debased the American Dream by remaking it into a Ponzi scheme.

Until this year, though, it had mainly been a book about perpetual deepening crisis without a clear prospect for recovery. It had attempted to explain, with some exasperation, how the Great Depression had been caused by a partnership between government officials and well-placed private commercial interests. This partnership had impeded rather than advanced the public interest, ultimately resulting in systemic crisis. At the time, the drivers called the pre-crisis economy laissez-faire to downplay the role of government. In a related manner, today we talk about a free market or globalization to play down the role of public policy during our boom time. We blame the crisis on deregulation, the retreat of the state from the economy. However, just as in the early twentieth century, an activist state underpins our economy in good times and bad, in boom and bust.

My own hope with the Obama approach to the crisis is not that we vilify government-industry relations or quixotically aim to do away with them. Instead, the purpose of writing this book is to advocate bringing to the fore their justification. In other words, why should we use companies as policy organs? Moreover, *public-private partnership* (PPP or P3) is now a term very much in vogue. Yet, this and similar terms are catch-all words with little meaning, except in reference to ways specific partnership-based programs or projects are structured. This book focuses on how to model partnerships so as to advance their public interest aims.

Furthermore, partnerships have been used extensively throughout American history, from the railroads to the Second World War, from the Internet to the Iraq War. They were central to the East Asian Miracle and regional crisis. The European Union has pursued them to integrate Central and Eastern Europe into the expanded union. As these varied examples demonstrate, in practice partnerships both solve and cause problems. They can advance or retard the public interest. With our recovery, reinvestment, and growth strategies premised increasingly on partnerships, the stakes are high in modeling them appropriately. This means not only clothing them in high purpose but also making sure that the financial and corporate, civil and political plumbing are well thought through and attuned to meeting actual need. Partnerships invariably claim to produce public goods, but in practice their benefits can be reduced to profits and their gains privately held and largely short lived.

One of the most important institutional mechanisms for conceiving and directing partnerships has been government investment banks. In the United States, such banks were used during the First and Second World Wars. In foreign policy, we established the Export-Import Bank during the Great Depression and then the Overseas Private Investment Corporation in the early 1970s. These public financial institutions aim to use private firms as foreign policy organs, sometimes with success and other times causing damage. And, perhaps largest in scale and subject to much controversy has been the World Bank, founded by the victors of World War II to lay the foundation for postconflict economic stability and growth. Since the 1980s, the World Bank has redirected its efforts away from promoting government projects and toward partnerships. A similar timeline of support has occurred within public regional development banks representing every continent, the African

Development Bank, Asian Development Bank, European Investment Bank, and Inter-American Development Bank.

The Obama Infrastructure Bank idea and the Clean Energy Bank proposals now on the table are essential for devising effective partnership-based growth. They base themselves explicitly on the international infrastructure banks. The idea is to turn this foreign policy model inward to reinvest in the American economy. However, thus far we have spoken about these international banks in unrealistic terms, focusing more on how their most un-self-reflective advocates understand them, rather than on how they function in practice. We have compounded this distortion by doing the same with public-private partnerships. We must learn from international experience and take the issue of institutional design much more seriously than we have thus far. This book advocates for a single mega-bank combining traditional infrastructure sectors along with clean energy in far greater depth than currently envisaged. The Obama Bank should gather together all bond- and subsidy-financed federal projects. We should expect the bank to produce public goods, to solve real-world problems, and to coordinate and reintegrate our national economy.

The book starts on the campaign trail with then-Senator Barack Obama's speech in Janesville, Wisconsin, introducing the Infrastructure Bank. The third chapter turns to the origins of partnerships and a bank within the Democratic Party as a response to Reagan Revolution–led privatization. The next chapter returns to President Obama's economic philosophy, placing it within the context of twentieth-century views on the appropriate role of government in the economy.

We then turn, in Chapters 5 through 7, to discuss how P3s evolved internationally since the 1980s to become a cornerstone of American foreign policy. Chapter 8 focuses specifically on how to approach transparency within P3 projects. It draws on the work of Supreme Court Justice Louis Brandeis aiming to make Gilded Age P3s more accountable.

Next, in Chapters 9 through 11, we turn back to the international experience with P3s, focusing on the role of contracts in catalyzing projects. Partnership contracts were essential for turning the page away from unequal colonial bargains. However, more recently, countries have sought to rebalance many of the enduring inequalities associated with extractives and infrastructure contracts through renegotiations. A series of lessons are drawn from three decades of experience with P3 contracts for the United States.

Lastly, drawing on domestic and international experience with P3s, a series of specific recommendations are advanced for modeling our national infrastructure bank so as to promote effectively the public interest. Attention is paid to institutional design, the modeling of P3 projects themselves, and also how to build upon the successes of our recovery to date.

2

The Janesville Plan

I. Obama's Axioms

On February 13, 2008, then-Senator Barack Obama delivered a speech that marked a turning point in his candidacy, one that helped propel him into the presidency and came to define at least his first year in office. On the factory floor of the General Motors assembly plant in Janesville, Wisconsin, Obama pivoted away from being the sole candidate to have opposed the Iraq War and toward positioning himself as the forceful champion of America's economic recovery. In this landmark speech, Obama argued for redirecting our energies away from reconstructing Iraq and toward reinvesting in America, proposing a national infrastructure reinvestment bank to direct these efforts.

By the time Obama took office as president roughly a year later, our national ailment had became synonymous with a financial contagion originating in the subprime mortgage sector. In line with this diagnosis, our economy was undergoing a course of capital injections initiated under the previous administration into blue-chip financial institutions and the market-dominant insurance firm AIG. Obama's apparent decision not to disrupt this treatment predominated the twenty-four-hour news cycle. However, despite the exasperation caused by bipartisan bailouts, non-performance-based bonuses, and Washington–Wall Street teamwork, it is nonetheless useful to take a Copernican view of things. The subprime mortgage crisis, although disastrous, is a symptom of a much larger, graver chronic illness.

The Obama capital infusion was a stimulus package, not an extension of the Bush administration bailouts. It marked a sharp break. Viewed through the lens of the Janesville speech, which would become a template for his inaugural address, Obama's handling of the banking crisis looks different than typically portrayed by pundits. The infusion, while still worthy of debate like much else, is not designed to restore the Wall Street status quo. Instead, it should be viewed as an attempt to redirect lending practices. The argument here is that Obama has been recapitalizing the banks so that they can serve specific public policy purposes, namely financing a new approach not only to our domestic economic renaissance but also to our foreign commercial policy.

For this reason, the bank and AIG stimulus should not be dismissed outright as restoring the pre-crisis Wall Street status quo. Instead, we should be engaging in a debate over the public policies that actually underpin them with an eye toward whether the capital infusion itself is the appropriate means to accomplish the intended aim. In other words, we must determine what these policies actually are and ensure that public and private tools are in place that are tailored to advancing them. This is a prerequisite to devising appropriate accountability measures.

The Janesville Plan set forth the basic axioms of the Obama administration's approach to recovery and reinvestment. Obama prefaced his Janesville speech by stating, "What I really want to do is talk from the heart about where I want to take this country."[1] Thus, one might look to Janesville to give definition to that enigmatic Obama principle of empathy.

Obama began by telling the audience not to expect the rousing speech delivered a day earlier to a full-capacity audience of nearly twenty thousand in Madison, the capital city of Wisconsin and a university town, at the Kohl Center, the University of Wisconsin's sports stadium, which was named for the state's U.S. senator and department store magnate. Instead, Obama would "take it down a notch," giving "a little more detail." On *Hardball* that night, Chris Matthews described the speech this way: "He's saying: I better move from the great speechmaking to the nuts and bolts to show the beef here to mix the metaphor."[2] It was no accident that

Obama chose to deliver his speech, assessing our economic predicament and proposing a policy agenda to lead us out of it, on a factory floor in the Rust Belt. In fact, his competitor at the time, then-Senator Hillary Rodham Clinton, the next day waved boxing gloves above her head on the factory floor of another General Motors assembly plant a couple states over in Lordstown, Ohio, saying, "We need a fighter and a champion in the White House again for the American people."[3] With sports utility vehicles behind him, Obama spoke to an audience of around six hundred autoworkers.

Obama dispelled the still-persistent and prevalent myth that the subprime mortgage meltdown caused the crisis. Instead it was "the straw that broke the camel's back." In fact, the crisis was "the culmination of decades of decisions that were made or put off without regard to the realities of a global economy and the growing inequality it has produced." As a result, the central job of government was to restore equal opportunity. Obama spoke compellingly about how the root of our crisis lay in government decisions to advance domestic and international policies that privileged corporate profits and the interests of the wealthy over worker jobs and fair wages. In other words, the crisis was not caused by the government passivity associated with the commonplace idea that it was the absence of government, its retreat through deregulation, that alone allowed the market to grow out of control. Moreover, it was not simply a banking crisis, arising in the financial sector and destined to be solved there. Instead, the government actively promoted policies driving a form of globalization that advantaged the few over the many. The Janesville speech explained how government policies driving both domestic and foreign commercial investment are inextricably entwined. The Council on Foreign Affairs included Obama's Janesville speech in its *Essential Documents* collection, devoted to seminal foreign policy pieces.[4]

As Obama diagnosed our underlying illness, he turned to the infrastructure crisis, telling a story of neglect, decay, and a collapsed bridge in nearby Minneapolis. Although he made no mention of Hurricane Katrina, the decision by the executive branch to ignore the human cost of infrastructure failure was still fresh. With this diagnosis, Obama proposed a solution that sought to redirect our foreign reconstruction policy inward: "It's time to stop spending billions of dollars a week trying to put Iraq back together and start spending the money on putting America back together instead,"[5] an effort organized through the Infrastructure Reinvestment Bank, the topic of this book. Thus, the Obama Bank itself is the central institution for reenvisioning our domestic and foreign commercial policy in order to address the root causes of our financial crisis and to chart a durable twenty-first-century New Deal for America.

Through the bank, Obama would address the broken political system's inability to devise policies that advance the public interest, moving decisions over infrastructure policy away from the earmark system and instead toward being made on the merits of the projects themselves. In other words, the bank would choose projects "not by politics" but instead "by what will maximize our safety and homeland security; what will keep our environment clean and economy strong." It would be capitalized by sixty billion federal dollars over a ten-year period. This relatively modest sum in the face of astounding need, Obama asserted, "will multiply into almost half a trillion dollars of additional infrastructure spending."[6] Importantly, as we shall see in the course of this book, the financial institution and insurance firm stimuli are key elements in this strategy. Speaking at a factory, which would not survive to see his inauguration, Obama presciently explained that the bank would create two million new jobs, which could not be outsourced.

The Obama Bank arguably came into being with the stimulus act, before being officially constituted and prior even to its inclusion within the 2010 budget. On behalf of the president, his chief of staff Rahm Emanuel inserted ten billion dollars into the American Recovery and Reinvestment Act for high-speed rail. It was, according to Emanuel, Obama's "signature issue in the bill, his commitment for the future." Emanuel explained, "High-speed rail is the infrastructure bank."[7] In other words, as this book describes, although the Obama Bank itself obviously refers to an institution, it also is a stand-in for an approach to recovery. This approach combines a set of public purposes with a partnership-based means to deliver them. The second half of the stimulus bill devotes itself mainly to this bond-driven, subsidy-based reconstruction, as does our clean energy strategy. The high-speed rail itself is such a partnership, aiming to create a new foundation of a clean energy economy, one that, in the words of Obama's inaugural address stressing the importance of infrastructure, "binds us together."[8]

II. "That's My Basic Philosophy"

As Obama's Bank evolves and as his administration mobilizes massive financial capital and political will to reinvest in American infrastructure, his axioms are already under attack. Rush Limbaugh first popularized the opposition messaging. The day after the inauguration, on Fox News Network's *Sean Hannity Show*, the host asked Limbaugh whether he wanted Obama's plans to fail. In his own inimitable way, Limbaugh answered, "I want him to fail, if his agenda is a far-left collectivism, some people say socialism, as a conservative heartfelt, why would I want socialism to succeed?"[9] Shortly thereafter, a *New York Times* reporter drew fire for reinforcing the right-wing messaging when he asked the president in a one-on-one interview whether he was a socialist. The *Times* reporter subsequently justified his question by saying that he innocently wanted to know how the "new president defines his political philosophy."[10] Neither Limbaugh's remarks nor the reporter's question gets us any closer to the essential task of understanding what the president sees as the appropriate role of government in the economy.

Socialism is a boo word. We use a "boo" to express disapproval, to show contempt or derision, to end a conversation, to get the performer off the stage. In the 1970s, NBC brought the boo word idea to television with the *Gong Show*, hosted by Chuck Barris, in which a panel of professionals ended mediocre amateur contestants' performances by striking a gong.

Before taking office, Obama explained in an interview with John Harwood on a CNBC special entitled *Your Money, Your Vote: McCain vs. Obama*: "Look. I am a pro-growth, free market guy. I love the market. I think it is the best invention to allocate resources and produce enormous prosperity for America or the world that's ever been designed." He continued, articulating the basic inequalities inherent in the globalization model pursued over the last several decades. To address this lack of balance, he prescribed, "Let's make sure that we are investing in what's required for long term growth." Obama said flatly about this pro–free market position coupled with a balance achieved through the government playing the role of investor: "That's my basic philosophy."[11]

President Obama's inaugural address reinforced this vision of the free market that is compatible with government activism. First, he lauded the market as a "force for good" that has an "unmatched" "power to generate wealth and expand freedom." At the same time, he underscored the need for a watchful government eye to prevent "the market from spinning out of control." Ultimately, the yardstick for judging market performance is the promotion of the public good: "The success of our economy has always depended not just on the size of our gross domestic product, but on the reach of our prosperity; on the ability to extend opportunity to every willing heart – not out of charity, but because it is the surest route to our common good."[12] Thus, Obama's vision of government is not only as a regulator, setting out and umpiring the rules of the game, but also as a proactive promoter of market characteristics that advance the public good.

Moreover, Obama's speech in Janesville underscored the idea that government policy choices have directed the market over the last twenty-five years, albeit poorly, shortsightedly, and irresponsibly. Thus, government has two roles – in good times and bad – regulator and promoter. The performance of both the government and the market must be judged by the yardstick of the common good.

In contrast, the socialism attack on Obama assumes that a free market can exist even independent of the government. In doing so, critics take the position that, postcrisis, Obama has newly introduced an activist government into the American political landscape. Moreover, many Republicans, and some Democrats, presume that the crisis was not caused by government policies. Instead the root of the crisis was deregulation or simply market excesses. Their prescriptions too argue in the language of the free market. However, it is the contention of this book that the Republican free market approach in practice involves the government advancing a certain set of interests. The counterfactual assertion of government passivity or retreat from the economy over the last several decades runs counter to Obama's Janesville diagnosis. It also rests on faulty empirical ground. As Obama observed, globalization was a government policy choice that advantaged some while structurally disfavoring many others.

The bank is premised on this economic philosophy, which underpins much of his administration, including the departments of State, Education, Energy, Transportation, Treasury, Housing and Urban Development, and Defense: the government acts in partnership with market actors to produce public goods. Chapter 5 sets forth Obama's economic philosophy, putting it into the context of a long-standing American tradition of what I term "free market statism," referring to the active role played by government in our economy. Government creates much of the free market, allowing corporations to exist and operate. It also maintains the market, actively intervening to promote certain public values by using corporations as policy organs.

In making his argument about the nature of the crisis and his prescriptions for remedying it, Obama echoes earlier calls made at the beginning of the twentieth century about the laissez-faire economy that resulted in the Great Depression. At the time, a group of Legal Realists argued that the crisis itself was caused by the public-private partnership–based economy that actually underpinned laissez-fairism. Moreover, these Realists argued that the answer to this government-industry-driven crisis was to take back control over the public interest and ensure that the partnership itself advanced it. Thus, the New Deal reforms were a reconfiguring of the government-industry partnership, rather than an insertion of government into an out-of-control, stateless economy.

Despite accusations of socialism, President Obama does not even intend to rebuild our economy through government vehicles like the self-liquidating public corporations of the New Deal era. Instead, the government will form public-private partnerships (PPPs or P3s), using private companies as policy organs to re-lay the foundations of our economy with a large-scale network of infrastructure projects including roads, bridges, high-speed railways, clean energy, telecommunications, and other vital areas. The financial institution stimulus package is designed to facilitate these partnerships. Obama's New Deal is mainly premised on partnerships rather than government vehicles.

These partnerships, and the bank itself, are modeled on our foreign commercial policy of the last twenty-five or so years. Thus, if we want to know more about the Obama New Deal, it is best to look at the formulation of this foreign policy. Our foreign affairs–driven partnerships were the engine of economic development throughout Asia, in post-Soviet Central and Eastern Europe, and elsewhere. As we emulate this model, looking to China, for instance, it is useful to learn lessons from what has been an uneven experience in order to replicate and adapt the good. At present, when we discuss this overseas model, it is through the lens of the service providers, consultants, lawyers, and bankers who drove it, rather than from the perspective of the citizens who experienced it.

Moreover, although the term *P3* is used as an umbrella concept to refer to wide-ranging policies and practices, a glimpse at our foreign commercial policy shows the heterogeneity of partnerships in practice. That is, P3s mean different things in Asia, Europe, and Latin America and vary according to sector and specific project. As we redirect this policy toward the domestic economy, it is also essential to understand which types of partnerships have worked in practice. Just as with our own two main domestic experiments with partnerships – nineteenth-century railroads and twentieth-century military buildup – this experience abroad offers many lessons for crafting partnerships that not only promise to promote the public good but also deliver.

III. A Foreign Affairs Model

The inclusion of the Obama speech within the Council on Foreign Affairs series is a recognition that an active, not permissive or passive, government drove the financial crisis; it did so through foreign affairs policies that reinforced domestic ones. This synergistic policy program, which advanced the interests of a few for several decades, was not simply an instance of lax or overly permissive regulation. Government created globalization. Our banking and insurance firms contributed to this coordinated approach to foreign and domestic affairs and, in doing so, undermined not only the durability of our domestic economy but also their own competitiveness. Nonetheless, they are now vital partners in our reinvestment plans. The government underpinning, however, also means that we can reshape our foreign and domestic commercial policies so as to advance a broader concept of the public interest and tailor accountability mechanisms appropriately to ensure its realization.

For example, the overseas call center system long credited with outsourcing American jobs would have been unthinkable several decades ago. Without massive U.S. government investment, it would have been physically impossible and certainly not competitive with U.S. call centers. Although call center outsourcing is generally presented as arising from an unregulated globally integrated economy, it has been facilitated by specific tax laws, securities regulation, and lax enforcement of labor regulation. The cables that call centers rely on to work and transmit information around the globe did not exist before globalization. They had to be financed and laid.

The U.S. government played an instrumental role in making this happen. Without these cables, globalization could not exist, financial markets could not integrate, and labor markets could not become internationally flexible. Just as the cost of weaning ourselves away from foreign oil by creating a clean energy–based domestic economy is prohibitively high for the private sector to do on its own, over the last twenty-five years, government put out the financial capital to create globalization and to make it a financially lucrative proposition. In fact, if we look at the basic staple of U.S. foreign commercial policy over the last several decades – power, water, telecommunications, health care, energy, extractives, and transportation – we see the blueprint for our domestic reinvestment. One way the U.S. government invested abroad was by helping to lay the global information infrastructure, itself a precondition to globalization. This government investment made U.S. companies free to outsource domestic jobs. It also contributed to the rapid growth of many U.S. sectors, including high technology. For this reason, although trade agreements should be revisited, the North American Free Trade Agreement's approach to labor is not at the heart of our economic predicament.

In 1995, US West finalized an agreement for the construction of the Fiber Optic Link Around the Globe (FLAG). This $1.5 billion project would run a fiber-optic cable from the United Kingdom to Japan. In the process, it would link up twenty-five political jurisdictions. It contributed to a series of interlacing global information infrastructure projects. Although underwater telegraphic cables had been laid at the close of the previous century, this project represented the first ever privately initiated and financed transnational communications link of this size and scale. FLAG was only as strong as the public guarantees of the twenty-five licensing authorities involved in legitimizing the project. In other words, it was a transnational public-private partnership.

Although private actors would benefit commercially from this undertaking, governments were heavily involved in ensuring its success. Not only would each jurisdiction along the way have to grant valuable licenses to run cable through their sovereign territories, but also insurance would be provided by the Export-Import Bank of the United States of America (Ex-Im Bank). The licensing system would grant private companies the right to sell their products to consumers. These licenses thus represented a state cessation of public property to private actors. Governments had offered their respective citizenry up as consumers to private companies.

Regardless of whether FLAG was ultimately advantageous to citizens of the participant nations, its success depended on the ongoing political acquiescence of each government and its population. To mitigate risk that a government would grant a license and then repeal it, perhaps as a result of domestic agitation by citizens (democracy risk), the private companies sought insurance from the U.S. government through its Ex-Im Bank against political risk. As licensing approval by many states, under customary practice, involved not responding to faxed applications to licensing authorities, such risk was palpable.

The feared volatility of this endeavor was acknowledged by A. Jay Baldwin, the vice president and chief financial officer of FLAG, who, when asked about what the company would do if a constituent country revoked its license, responded, “Let’s hope we never have to find out.”[13] The fear expressed by Baldwin derived from the reliance on popularly attenuated states; in other words, basic planning determinations are made by institutions that do not incorporate citizens into decision-making processes. To ensure further that American firms would not be deterred by such political risks in emerging markets, securities law was revised, specifically SEC Rule 144A, which reduced the reporting requirements by firms making overseas infrastructure investments in risky environments.

Moreover, FLAG transformed international labor markets. Not only did it make outsourcing profitable, FLAG made much of globalization possible. The government's role in this project was reinforced by countless contemporaneous state-sponsored projects carried out through dozens of other U.S. public entities including the Overseas Private Investment Corporation (OPIC) and a series of international infrastructure banks. We played a central role in creating these banks and participate actively within them, including the World Bank, the Asian Development Bank, the African Development Bank, the European Investment Bank, and the Inter-American Development Bank. These government agencies and intergovernmental infrastructure banks promoted globalization through wide-ranging subsidies including loans, insurance policies, guarantees, and feasibility studies. Since the 1980s, they have actively subsidized P3s as a means for creating basic infrastructure.

Governmental and intergovernmental banks over the last several decades used companies as foreign policy organs to produce the basic infrastructure that made globalization – and a profitable proposition – possible. The world factory system resulted from our eagerness to help pay for power plants to keep the lights on, roads and rail lines to get goods to overseas markets, and water systems essential to operating shop floor equipment all over the world. The bulk of these factories are located in what are called free zones, hived-off territories within countries wherein a set of rules apply distinct from the rest of the nation-state. In fact, they are heavily subsidized zones in which all the basic infrastructure is co-financed by the U.S. government and its allies. It is this public subsidy that underpins the free market abroad.

At times, our government facilitated the public infrastructure of these zones by providing below-market-rate loans, political risk insurance policies, or guarantees to infrastructure companies to build roads or lay water pipes. At other times, we gave money for feasibility studies to see if projects could turn a profit. We even agreed to top up payments to an overseas road company if not enough drivers used it to ride to work. With our allies, we paid to set up and maintain parallel justice systems to resolve disputes between governments and companies in which a private legal order was formulated and applied. More often than not, U.S. subsidies for overseas development were tied to the participation of American firms in carrying forward projects. Although the Reagan Revolution divested from American domestic infrastructure, it massively subsidized our companies and banks in their efforts to create public goods abroad. Of course, this countercyclical investment pattern could have instead been a more equitable and durable one. In other words, we could have contemporaneously invested in the domestic real economy rather than in consumptive capacity.[14] When oil-rich countries and the Chinese government recycled dollars back into the American economy, we could have channeled it toward productive investment rather than mortgage and consumer credit.

At times, these subsidies advanced the public interest. Generally, however, we spent little effort making sure that projects were accountable to the public good of the country that got the road, for example, or whether overseas transportation projects promoted the U.S. public interest. In fact, many citizens protested the roads and power plants in East Asia that we celebrate as unqualified successes, models for our own reinvestment. We specialized in ensuring that government agencies were accountable when it came to delivering on profitability promises to private market actors. We gave our own firms money to build these things for other countries. Our government also paid potential overseas customers to buy American goods. Globalization is our dependent; moreover, as the financial crisis highlights, it requires ongoing government assistance to maintain itself. The domestic and intergovernmental infrastructure banks are now being capitalized by our government alongside our own private banks in an effort to resuscitate the economy. In other words, we are rescuing overseas public-private partnerships through international infrastructure banks. It is unclear who benefits from these international rescues of projects with TARP bank and AIG sunk investment. It is simply a topic that we do not discuss.

The Obama Bank is an effort to turn the most appealing aspects of this foreign affairs model inward. The bank itself is modeled on our U.S. export infrastructure banks and the intergovernmental ones. Just as these banks use companies as foreign policy organs to accomplish specific goals such as social and economic development, we will use our own bank to create incentives for companies to accomplish policies promoting the common good. In fact, the Obama Bank aims to do for ourselves what we have been doing for others over the last twenty-five years.

Obama has spoken about emulating China's infrastructure-driven economic growth. For example, in a campaign trail speech in Chester, Pennsylvania, with the Olympics under way, Obama said,

> Everybody's watching what's going on in Beijing right now and the Olympics. Think about the amount of money that China has spent on infrastructure. Their ports, their train systems, their airports are all vastly superior to us now, which means if you're a corporation deciding where to do business, you're starting to think, Beijing looks like a pretty good option.[15]

Through the U.S. Ex-Im Bank and OPIC, as well as our participation in the various international infrastructure banks, we have ourselves co-financed the infrastructure and factory system that make China far more attractive to our firms. Or, as then–Vice President Al Gore put it in 1998 in the midst of the Asian currency crisis: "After all, we are the nations that, together, created an economic miracle for Asia and the whole Pacific-Asia region."[16] In other words, we have helped create the basic infrastructure in Southern China that has fueled outsourcing. In doing so, overseas markets have become increasingly more attractive financially and our own comparatively more expensive. Furthermore, as the toy safety scare demonstrates, our partnership-oriented investments do not always effectively ensure the public interest at home and abroad. Decisions about how to model public and private partnership tools so as to advance the public interest must be appropriately thought through at the front end; hidden costs are not just financial.

Is it sensible then that we should do unto ourselves what we have done for others? In other words, are our globalization promotion policies worthy of reproducing domestically? The contrast between our attempts at reconstructing Iraq and our partnership in the Asian miracle is a stark reminder that not all infrastructure-promoting activities are created equal. We might want to emulate some, while learning cautionary tales from others. Moreover, even the so-called infrastructure-driven economic growth stories such as China require serious qualifications. The U.S.-subsidized Three Gorges Dam in China is an exemplar. Furthermore, infrastructure banks have financed large numbers of environmentally damaging projects. We must take care to ensure that our own bank does not undermine the very principles that justify its existence. The Obama Bank must not copy other banks; it must adapt models and learn lessons from what has been an uneven experience with partnership-driven infrastructure-led growth.

Our economic recovery depends on not only rehabilitating our national infrastructure but also on large-scale investment in state-of-the-art new projects. Infrastructure investment is a precondition to robust economic growth. America benefited from this insight during the New Deal and through Cold War–period investments into our information infrastructure, which created the Internet. The United States has long advocated this strategy abroad, contributing to the East Asian Miracle and jumpstarting the postwar European economy through Marshall Plan infrastructure investments in Europe.

Support for infrastructure-induced economic growth draws on U.S. experiences as well as on international ones. Modernizing and importing successful models is paramount. The techniques for carrying out projects now circulating among policy-makers invariably are public-private partnerships. From Illinois to Florida to California, all recognize that limited government budgets necessitate private-sector co-financing to meet dire needs. Governors Arnold Schwarzenegger (California) and Ed Rendell (Pennsylvania) and Mayor Michael Bloomberg (New York City) advocate P3s in their subnational Building America's Future plan.

Although the argument for making use of the large pools of private capital now forming and the increasing political will accumulating is sound, we must take care to avoid the Wild West mentality that has often undermined P3s abroad, leading to large numbers of failed projects and renegotiations. Arguments that we must learn from China or emulate the UK's railway privatization must be viewed with skepticism.

Internationally, too often P3s are carried out in the shadow of government regulation. P3 planners consistently advocate lessening government oversight and bypassing government agencies. The idea is that the private sector can itself re-create the good aspects of government and shed the bad. The result of this parallel private government has produced many low-quality projects, public outcry over unaffordable toll roads, undrinkable water, and uneven electricity. Moving projects off the government balance sheet has reinforced this accountability deficit.

In introducing P3s, we must maintain America's strong public civil engineering culture to ensure that infrastructure quality will be not only profitable but of a high standard. Our tradition of participatory planning will ensure that projects meet public needs and are accountable to citizen users. In our national economy, we must also guarantee that our government planning coordinates local, regional, and national levels. Importantly, although we must partner with international allies, we must employ our undercompensated, highly skilled American workers to carry out these projects. We must encourage the use of U.S.-manufactured equipment and technological know-how. If we build American labor into our infrastructure investment, then projects will not only stimulate economic growth but will also create the high-quality jobs we so sorely need.

The Obama Bank must take the lead in reinvigorating our economy through strategic public investment that not only benefits Americans tomorrow but also gives them jobs now. Infrastructure should be the cornerstone of this strategy; however, the means for achieving economic renaissance – finance and private firms – should not overwhelm the ends in shaping our policies and approach to accountability. Just like our nineteenth-century railroads, infrastructure bank–created P3s abroad have often cycled back and forth between the private sector and government because of insider dealings, mismanagement, and failure to deliver on public good promises. The East Asian infrastructure-driven miracle that was largely carried out through P3s was followed by the East Asian crisis, during which many projects either went under or had to be rescued by state pension funds.

We have many concrete challenges to overcome with reinvestment in the United States. Our country is best served by learning real lessons from our foreign policy model, rather than promoting an imaginary one. Increasingly, investment bankers and private construction firms are seeking out partnerships that offload risks on government and ensure privatized rewards that would be unthinkable abroad. In other words, one of the main appeals of the American market for private actors is its low-risk environment. Furthermore, many of the same banks and private firms advocating the introduction of partnerships on a large scale within America are the same ones that promoted the inequality-producing globalization model. Although we are all capable of learning from our mistakes, we must nonetheless stop circulating private equity power points and figures as if they were objective statements of fact. They are sell-side documents with substantial potential service fees attached to their translation into action.

This fact does not discount their worth. However, we must be critical consumers of the information. For example, on the government or industry conference circuit, UK rail privatization is often presented as a model for the United States to emulate. Even if we control lobbying abuses in this sector, something that does not seem likely at the time of this writing, if we uncritically accept these figures and prescriptions, then the influence is nonetheless already exercised.

Furthermore, the institutions carrying out this economic philosophy, both our own agencies and the international ones in which we are key stakeholders, have themselves been roundly criticized, often even from within, sometimes for the damage caused by their projects and other times for internal governance problems. Infrastructure banks have been highly controversial, and their track records mixed.

Also, these banks over the last several decades have mainly carried out their projects through P3s.

American public interest groups have been key figures in ensuring accountability both within the governance structures of these international banks and in the specific partnership projects that they facilitate. These banks have evolved over time and have become more transparent and participatory because of public interest campaigns. We should thus not only learn lessons from these campaigns but also view our Obama Bank as itself a dynamic institution that will evolve over time not just as a result of the economic context but also to ensure accountability. Furthermore, many basic institutional features that have evolved over time to make these banks and their partnership projects more accountable have not made their way into the U.S. infrastructure bank discussions. Instead, the bond structures of the European Investment Bank along with a range of universal infrastructure bank corporate subsidies have been the main appeals of the foreign affairs models. A central lesson of the international banks has been that a failure to incorporate transparency, accountability, and participation into projects only makes infrastructure more costly and less durable. It simply pushes the costs off to the future.

At the same time, it is also important to recognize that P3s themselves in foreign affairs emerged as an emancipatory contractual form, a reaction against colonialism. They were an attempt to rebalance grossly unfair unequal treaties in the extractives sectors that were negotiated in the context of conquest. Although most agree that the partnerships were a marked qualitative improvement on the colonial concessions, it is also nonetheless widely thought that they too have produced great inequalities not only through the related process of divesting from the United States, but also in their impact abroad. They have come to be viewed as an instance of neo-colonialism, part of the Washington Consensus. As this book shows, arguments both for and against P3s are more often than not asserted rather than based on reliable evidence. If we are to promote the common good with our Obama Bank, then we must learn lessons from our own experience of using companies as foreign policy organs.

3

A Bank of Our Own

Prior to his nomination to the post of secretary of energy, Nobel Prize winner Steven Chu, then the director of Lawrence Berkeley National Lab and also professor of physics and molecular and cell biology at the University of California, was a member of the Council on Competitiveness's Energy Security, Innovation and Sustainability Initiative Steering Committee. The Council on Competitiveness is a group of CEOs, university presidents, and labor leaders devoted to America's prosperity. As a committee member, Chu helped to draft *A 100-Day Energy Action Plan for the 44th President of the United States*.[1]

The initiative was launched in July 2007 "with the belief that the crucial role of private sector demand in driving energy system transformation has gone largely unrecognized and unaddressed in prior policy initiatives."

Moreover, in line with the idea of free market statism, the initiative asserted, "The government has the power to greatly strengthen the business case for investment and innovation in sustainable energy solutions."[2] Among the recommendations put forward for the incoming president was to "jumpstart Energy Infrastructure Investments" by turning the U.S. foreign policy model discussed previously inward to the domestic economy.

The initiative recommended establishing a national clean energy bank. It would be capitalized to the tune of two hundred billion dollars, which it would use to leverage much larger sums of private capital, "provid[ing] debt financing and driv[ing] private investment." The council called for charging the secretaries of energy and treasury with formulating the legislation. Importantly, the recommendation explicitly called for basing the bank on free market statist foreign affairs institutions, indicating that it should be

> modeled on the U.S. Export-Import Bank and Overseas Private Investment Corporation, to provide long-term financing – including loan guarantees, lines of credit, equity investments and insurance – or the market deployment of breakthrough energy efficiency and clean energy products, technologies, services and projects that reduce, avoid or sequester carbon.[3]

Although these institutions have concrete attractions in their ability to mobilize capital, engage in planning, and centralize decision-making to ensure swift focused action, their track record in foreign affairs has been mixed. If we decide to model our own domestic infrastructure bank and P3s on them, then we should learn from experience.

For example, the U.S. OPIC, a government entity that Secretary of Energy Chu argued was a model for a domestically focused American clean energy bank, promotes development abroad through a range of corporate subsidies. OPIC has been subject to controversy since its legislation was first introduced.

At the time, a House report cautioned that the means, that is, the use of companies as foreign policy organs, might hinder more than help development goals. Instead, it argued, "Before the U.S. Government enters the business of supporting the export of American capital, it should assure itself that each project is both commercially feasible and beneficial to the long-range development goals of the country." These members of Congress were skeptical, believing that the purpose of development would be eclipsed by the desire to subsidize companies, and that OPIC would "be guided by business motives." Moreover, they argued that business interests "are not necessarily congruent with the needs of developing countries or with U.S. interest." Continuing with important cautionary words applicable to the domestic environment, they worried, "Additional problems will arise through an increased identification of the U.S. government with business interests."[4] Furthermore, members of the Senate Committee on Foreign Relations, upon considering the bill, argued "that the free enterprise system was subverted when the Government, in effect, underwrote foreign investment risks."[5] This book looks at the actual practice of these institutions and the international infrastructure banks on which the Obama Bank is based.

On February 17, 2009, shortly after Obama's inauguration, the federal government settled a lawsuit with Friends of the Earth; Greenpeace; Boulder, Colorado; and three California cities. This landmark global warming settlement was brought against OPIC and its sibling executive agency, the Ex-Im Bank, both of which offer subsidies, for example, loans and insurance, to American firms investing overseas in infrastructure, oil, gas, and energy projects. The plaintiffs argued with some success that these agencies were subsidizing companies pursuing projects that dramatically aggravated global warming.

The settlement means that the Ex-Im Bank will now take projected carbon emissions into account when deciding whether to subsidize American firms. OPIC agreed to a goal of reducing the emissions of the projects that it finances by 20 percent before 2019. The incorporation of carbon concerns into their decision-making represents a broadening of what is considered in the American public interest.[6]

These are significant settlements. Our government has subsidized companies for ages with these agencies without such environmental oversight. The Ex-Im Bank was created by FDR during the Great Depression as a way of promoting international commercial engagement at a time when nationalistic protectionism reigned. Although OPIC came into being in 1971, its origins lay in the Marshall Plan government insurance policies that helped encourage American companies to reconstruct Europe. This postwar public insurance policy was the brainchild of a committee chaired by the head of Chase Bank.

However, it was not until the 1980s and 1990s that these agencies became so important in devising how our firms would pursue foreign policy goals. It was the onset of privatization and its worldwide promotion under President Ronald Reagan and his bipartisan successors in response to the so-called Third World Debt Crisis that put the wheels into motion. They have only accelerated since. As we helped governments transfer public services – roads, rails, ports, airports, power stations, oil, and gas – into the private sector around the world, these agencies helped American firms compete for the new opportunities to deliver these services. Unlike within the United States, where privatization was about constricting the money invested in public services, in foreign policy, the idea was to use privatization as a means of promoting large-scale investment in public infrastructure. It is this privatization as investment that is appealing now within America.

From Latin America to Asia to Africa, we subsidized our firms to promote development abroad, which is rightly in the American public interest. However, although our government agencies excelled at ensuring that our companies competed effectively for these opportunities against foreign firms, we often did not scrutinize carefully enough whether the opportunities themselves were in the public interest. Nor did we closely monitor whether our subsidized companies carried out their mission effectively. Instead, we focused mainly on bankability, that is, ensuring that our firms found it profitable to pursue these opportunities abroad.

Importantly, the recent carbon victory points to the central role that public interest groups have played in holding American firms and our government accountable to the public interest – that is, the principles that justify the government subsidies in the first place, the advancement of foreign affairs goals such as overseas development. For the last twenty-five years, public interest groups have carefully monitored these subsidy programs. When companies have displaced communities, harmed indigenous groups, or undermined wages, public interest groups have campaigned to encourage our government to live up to our public interest ideals. As a result of their persuasive powers, we now have rules in place to limit damage to vulnerable groups and the environment. This book details these public interest strategies and their role not only in transforming projects, from transportation to clean energy, but also in ensuring that international infrastructure banks are accountable. These international banks have transformed dramatically over their lives, becoming more transparent and participatory institutions as a result of civil society campaigns.

For this reason, with a new administration, it might be useful to debate the ways in which our corporate subsidies should be designed to advance the public interest. As we create an infrastructure bank modeled on these and related agencies for the domestic market, it is imperative that we advance a concept of accountability that not only promotes revenue transparency but also ensures civil society participation in the Obama Bank's decision-making.

The use of an infrastructure bank as a vehicle to meet large-scale needs is not new. The United States has been a key player in establishing a number of international banks. In 1944, the World War II Allies formed a basic pillar of the postwar economy, the World Bank, which devoted itself to infrastructure. The institution itself recognized that international peace, development, and prosperity depended on a robust public infrastructure in countries around the world. In the second half of the century, America helped found similar banks in Africa, Asia, and Latin America. Moreover, when the United States reconstructed postwar Europe through the Marshall Plan, infrastructure was a central plank. As the European Union has emerged, infrastructure-premised regional integration and national growth has continued on the Continent through the European Investment Bank and the European Bank for Reconstruction and Development. These European banks have been central to expanding the EU eastward through transportation and energy networks.

Although the idea of international banks and also domestic use of P3s has a long history within the United States, they together hit the national stage forcefully in the late 1980s as a policy prescription for the domestic economy. In the late 1980s, Democratic Party presidential candidates began to argue that the Reagan Revolution had put us en route to financial crisis by divesting from infrastructure. Within the private sector, the bank idea was associated with two investment bankers, Joseph M. Giglio Jr. and Felix G. Rohatyn. Giglio had founded the public finance division at Bear Stearns and Rohatyn was chairman of the Municipal Assistance Corporation (and Lazard).[7] The bank has been popular with a succession of Democrats running for president, including Gary Hart, Jesse Jackson, and Bill Clinton.[8] A look back at the financial figures that at times accompanied the proposals from these politicians is striking, because the figures quoted then are nearly identical to those quoted today.[9]

The idea for the bank, as well as the emergence of P3s as a policy prescription among Michael Dukakis and others, had two parts. First, it was a reaction against President Ronald Reagan's tenure. An argument was made that his presidency had divested from public infrastructure. As a result of this neglect, infrastructure began to deteriorate. This, in turn, undermined national competitiveness, putting us on a road toward eventual crisis, the argument presciently went. A second part was an attempt to remake the Democratic Party, moving away from an economic model that relied on government to produce public goods and toward one that leveraged private-sector pools of finance such as pension funds.

Although the federal bank and leveraging were mainly associated with the Democratic Party in the late 1980s and 1990s, it is nonetheless important to stress that President George H. W. Bush's compassionate conservatism also incorporated the partnership idea, recognizing some of the hidden costs of Reagan's tenure. In fact, economists such as Milton Friedman were publicly critical of Bush for departing from Reaganomics in his promotion of social welfare programs.[10]

President Clinton, however, came closest to establishing a federal infrastructure bank. It was a campaign promise, along with partnerships in telecommunications, transportation, and clean energy. However, the bank was subject to much controversy when William Kristol, then with Project for a Republican Future, leaked a budget proposal memorandum prepared by Alice Rivlin, the director of the Office of Management and Budget, to the *Wall Street Journal*. The memorandum was titled "Big Choices" and advocated the bank as a way of raising financial capital for projects without increasing taxes.[11]

Of course, the more recent history of P3s and the infrastructure bank is better known. President George W. Bush championed P3s, particularly in transportation. And the bank idea reemerged as a bipartisan effort spearheaded not only by Congresswoman Rosa DeLauro, a longtime champion of infrastructure bank–led reinvestment (she introduced such legislation first in 1994), but also notably by Democratic Senator Christopher Dodd and Republican Senator Chuck Hagel, who together introduced legislation to establish a bank that then-Senator Obama sponsored. In addition, a bipartisan group of governors and mayors, called Building America's Future, organized by Governor Rendell (one of the longest-standing advocates of an infrastructure bank), Governor Schwarzenegger, and Mayor Bloomberg with seed money from the Rockefeller Foundation, has been a main proponent of the bank. From the private side, leading figures from the 1980s, such as Rohatyn, remain main drivers of today's bank.

Importantly, the Obama Bank will necessarily evolve over time. Although his bank was initially formulated to address the transportation sector, many have argued persuasively that it should encompass additional sectors. For example, when senators Dodd and Hagel proposed their bank in 2007, they included both water and housing. On May 22, 2009, on *Meet the Press*, Governor Rendell urged an expansive umbrella-like concept of infrastructure, saying that it was "so much more" than just transportation. In speaking of the country's infrastructure crisis, Building America's Future has repeatedly referenced not only the collapse of I-35 in Minneapolis, but also the broken levees in New Orleans and New York's power outages.[12] Moreover, when President Clinton considered establishing a bank during his first term, the idea was to include traditional infrastructures as well as clean energy and telecommunications. Congresswoman DeLauro's introduction of bank legislation at the impetus of the Obama administration also took such an expansive approach with the support of a broad-based group of politicians, unions, investment bankers, and civil engineers.[13] This book too argues for such an expansive approach. In fact, it goes several steps further and argues that the Obama Bank should expand to encompass all federal infrastructure-based subsidy programs that involve innovative financing techniques. Furthermore, it makes the case for combining the national infrastructure bank together with the clean energy bank.

President Obama aims to promote national economic strength, a transition to clean energy, and homeland security through his infrastructure policy. These goals are achievable only when infrastructure policy itself is holistic and integrated. In line with this recognition, invariably, international infrastructure banks finance projects across sectors including transportation, oil and gas, energy, telecommunications, water, and housing. A main reason for adopting a holistic integrated vision of infrastructure policy is that the sectors are interdependent. Moreover, although much of our infrastructure policy is balkanized across executive agencies, with proper planning, projects should be mutually reinforcing. Because the infrastructure bank aims to make regional and national policy, it must engage in careful planning that coordinates projects across sectors, overcoming tendencies toward projects that serve mainly local needs.

For this reason, the Obama Bank should progressively expand its province to include increasing numbers of sectors and projects. Areas in which the Obama administration presently provides arrays of government subsidies to stimulate innovation and growth, such as clean energy and telecommunications, should move more deeply within its jurisdiction. Moves to create a separate clean energy bank would reinforce the balkanization of infrastructure policy. Clean energy itself depends on careful coordination and planning with other infrastructures to progress efficiently and effectively. It is much better to create a super-bank, rather than dueling banks. In addition, existing subsidies for infrastructure across these wide-ranging sectors should themselves be gathered within the Obama Bank. This will not only promote more effective planning, but will also ensure greater accountability, providing a central node of coordinated decision-making.

Moreover, Obama aims for the bank to promote homeland security, much as Eisenhower's national road system did in its emulation of the German Autobahn. To promote security effectively, our physical infrastructure must also be integrated at the policy level in order to promote effective interagency coordination with the Department of Homeland Security and also to ensure that weak links or poor investment decisions do not compromise our safety.

Furthermore, a single institution is best able to build capacity regarding how effectively to craft P3 subsidies to achieve specific public purposes. This capacity building promotes an ability to understand the risks and rewards associated with tapping international financial markets and foreign direct investment into the sector. Regardless of our aim to buy American products and to employ citizens for projects, at present this is nothing more than an aspiration; a clear realistic plan suggesting otherwise is as yet unavailable. Infrastructure is not just about pouring concrete. It is also about designing clean energy. We must ask whether the decision to wean ourselves away from foreign oil also applies to various areas of infrastructure dominated by overseas firms. If our public goals are too general and our subsidies not transparent, then we will likely face an accountability deficit.

Also, establishing a bank that promotes regionalization as well as national integration means reconsidering the intended institutional structure now developing. This book argues that the bank itself should have representation from state government within its decision-making structure. Every international infrastructure bank incorporates participation of the constituent governments that will carry out projects within their territories. Even though citizens have a say in federal infrastructure policy through presidential and congressional channels, state and city governments will often be a central node of decision-making. Success in promoting regional and national projects depends on making infrastructures appealing to local and state constituencies. Formalizing representation will promote this goal. Given the unwieldy number of states in the union, a representative rotating system is best suited. Devolution of power is often an effective strategy internationally as a means for promoting transjurisdictional goals.

4 Leverage

In Janesville, Obama said that his infrastructure bank would take a government commitment of sixty billion dollars over ten years and turn it "into almost half a trillion dollars of additional infrastructure spending." This multiplying investment will produce "nearly two million new jobs."[1] For those who complained that the initial stimulus package undercapitalized infrastructure, these figures in the pipeline might be reassuring. Along these lines, Secretary of Transportation Ray LaHood related a core benefit of the Obama Bank: "Some of us that have been thinking about it believe you can raise a pretty good chunk of money."[2] At the same time, how does this mathematics work?

In October 1988, Governor Michael Dukakis of Massachusetts was running for president against Vice President George H. W. Bush. During the campaign, Dukakis introduced a partnership-based model that would supplant traditional Democratic Party economic policy. The *Wall Street Journal* explained the approach:

> Mr. Dukakis's campaign hinges in large part on his ability to redefine liberal Democratic social policies so they become more affordable. Instead of giant federal social programs, the Massachusetts governor proposes government-led "partnerships" with the private sector and the states to provide such things as health care, housing and student loans – in short, leveraged liberalism.[3]

This concept of leverage at the heart of partnerships is a cornerstone of today's proposed infrastructure policy. In fact, during the Dukakis campaign, the two terms were used interchangeably.[4] Moreover, *leveraged liberalism* was defined at the time as "the use of government leverage to direct the energies of the private sector toward achieving public goals";[5] "government as the engine for creating services, rather than paying for them outright";[6] or, in the words of Dukakis's director of economic development, Alden Raine, "catalytic government."[7] Frank Keefe, his secretary of administration and financing, explained, "It's activism, but measured activism and, most of all, inexpensive activism. . . . We leverage by leading the way";[8] in other words, what is being called here "free market statism."

Dukakis's chief economic adviser was Lawrence H. Summers, then a thirty-four-year-old professor in Harvard's

Economics Department. Summers at the time described himself as an "eclectic Keynesian":

> I believe in "leveraged liberalism." That is, I believe we should try to achieve social objectives with minimal government spending. I think we should help the private sector do the tasks, rather than direct the private sector. In that sense, I think there is a role for a cooperative effort to increase private investment. The student-loan program, which was slashed by the current Administration, is a good example of the kind of leverage you can produce in the private sector with small amounts of government money. The same type of leverage can be applied to economic, scientific and technological development, as well as to infrastructure repair.[9]

He continued, "I think government has that ability as long as we realize that the ideas have to bubble up rather than bubble down." In other words, the job of government is not to raise investment dollars. Instead, Summers argued, "[g]overnment money should only go where substantial sums of private money are available. The government should only lever private-sector responses."[10] A *Los Angeles Times* feature article explained the rationale for this approach at the time:

> But the party's fundamental problem today remains not much different than it was on the morning after Jimmy Carter's landslide defeat in 1980: Democrats still need a way to affirm a positive role for government in the economy,

> without validating Republican charges that they ache to return to the policies of tax and spend.[11]

Alternately, Dukakis explained it in the language of P3s, "I'm somebody who believes that the thing that works these days in the country is very strong and vital public-private partnerships, in which public resources and private investment combine, especially in communities and regions that need economic growth and new jobs."[12] In today's parlance, *leveraged liberalism* is no longer in vogue, so we simply use *public-private partnerships*.

Dukakis aimed to apply leveraged liberalism in other sectors, including low-income housing.[13] Also, then-Senator Al Gore Jr. of Tennessee was urging investment in an information superhighway. The rationale was in part national competitiveness, addressing a Japanese advantage. Gore thus argued for a more expansive definition of infrastructure: "Infrastructure has to be redefined . . . because transportation is no longer the principal determinant of national competitive advantage." Instead he stated: "Our ability to handle knowledge is."[14] Thus, in the late 1980s, in response to Reagan's presidency, the Democratic Party reconfigured its approach to financing, embracing P3s and adopting an expansive infrastructure-led growth strategy.

The idea of a federal infrastructure bank reemerged during President Bill Clinton's tenure, advancing leveraged liberalism. The continuity made sense, as Clinton had placed Dukakis's nomination in and, along with a small group of governors, was credited during the Dukakis campaign as part of a "Democratic effort to rethink the role of government in this era of scarce resources."[15] During his campaign, Clinton promised large-scale infrastructure investment. *Pensions and Investments* newspaper explained,

> As part of his campaign, Mr. Clinton proposed the "Rebuild America Fund," which would invest $20 billion annually for four years in new federal money into infrastructure needs and projects to enhance America's competitiveness. Besides highways, bridges, airports, water and sewage plants, the Clinton team envisions investing in a high-speed rail network, new environmental technologies and a national telecommunications network.[16]

Like Dukakis, Clinton focused on the power of leveraging: "His fund would be leveraged by investments by public and private pension funds, state and local governments and private investments, and backed by user fees, such as toll road charges. But little other detail is available." Two bank models were on the table, one that would be based on user fees and another one backed by the gasoline tax. Importantly, as with today's infrastructure investments, pension fund money was thought essential for driving the market forward.[17]

An infrastructure bank premised on leveraged liberalism was the subject of controversy during Clinton's first term. In 1994, the Rivlin memorandum was leaked by Kristol, then with the Project for a Republican Future, to the press, where it ended up on the front page of the *Wall Street Journal*.[18] In line with the appeals of leveraging, the memorandum sought to "cut [the budget] and invest" at once. As Dow Jones explained in late December, the leveraging purpose of the bank was not universally welcome: "the idea of using government funds to 'leverage' private markets is controversial – it reminds some in Washington of the savings and loan deposit guarantee institutions that caused scandal and budgetary concerns in the 1980s."[19] Leveraging, in other words, involves increased debt liability, albeit off–balance sheet.

The idea of using off–balance sheet financing to meet vital infrastructure needs in a time of acute financial crisis was central to its use as a response to the so-called Third World Debt Crisis. It solved a concrete problem for investment banks as well as governments. For example, if a country owed a bank a large amount of money, the country was unlikely to service the debt effectively. This, in turn, created a disincentive to lend to the country. Because countries had large-scale infrastructure needs that promised to produce generous economic returns as well as development, leveraged financing was introduced. Through this financing mechanism, investment banks would front money to build infrastructures, expecting returns directly from the user charges of completed projects. In other words, the money from the user charges would not mix with the government balance sheet, so banks would not be forced to stand in line behind themselves to recoup costs. Furthermore, if the infrastructure project did not pursue returns as anticipated, often both the local government and intergovernmental banks or U.S. government entities would step in and top up payments.

This particular mode of leveraged financing coupled with government guarantees was a feature of the Roosevelt-era self-liquidating infrastructure companies. However, the Roosevelt agencies were governmental, not private firms. Quasi-public entities such as turnpike authorities spread like wildfire in America after the war. The features of these quasi-public entities that made them appealing, for example, the ability to move quickly to raise capital and solve problems, also led to accountability deficits, perhaps most famously connected to the Robert Moses development strategy in New York.

This use of government leveraging agencies also occurred initially in developing countries in response to the financial crisis. However, there too, the nature of the shift in practice was not entirely clear. For example, when government corporations were privatized, some agencies persisted and simply partnered with private firms, but at other times private companies came to dominate. Importantly, even in the pre-privatization period, some degree of partnership with private firms, often foreign, happened necessarily because of technological know-how capacity and other issues. Thus, public-private partnership has been used to apply to wide-ranging arrangements. However, typically, partnerships involve the strategic use of public and private entities to advance specific interests by planners.

The 2007 Dodd-Hagel bill envisaged a bank making the most of leveraged liberalism. The bank would have "a preference for projects which leverage private financing, including public-private partnerships, for either the explicit cost of the project or for enhancements which increase the benefits of the project." In March 2008, Senator Dodd chaired the U.S. Senate Committee on Banking, Housing, and Urban Affairs hearing on infrastructure. Chairman Dodd introduced the hearing by explaining the leveraging concept underpinning the proposed bank, which

> would establish a unique and powerful public-private partnership. Using limited Federal resources, it would leverage the significant resources and innovation of the private sector. It would tap the private sector's financial and intellectual power to meet our nation's largest and most critical structural needs.[20]

Senator Hagel went on to explain to the hearing:

> The Infrastructure Bank – a public entity similar in nature to the Municipal Assistance Corporation – would have the ability to leverage private capital to supplement current levels of public spending. A public entity that can focus private sector investment onto public infrastructure could help provide the necessary investment for 21st Century Infrastructure in America.[21]

Likewise, when Representative John Yarmuth of Kentucky's 3rd Congressional District wrote a letter that April to Speaker of the House Nancy Pelosi urging support in the House for such a bank, he also spoke in the language of "leverage liberalism": "It would leverage public and private capital to create government-backed financing packages that could include a variation of direct subsidies, low-interest loans, tax credits, and infrastructure bonds."[22] Governor Rendell, on *Meet the Press*, made the point too: "There's so many innovative ways to, to use the tax code to get private investment."[23]

The ability of the Obama Bank to multiply a sixty-billion-dollar federal commitment over ten years into nearly half a trillion more is rooted in the concept of leveraging. Shortly after the new president took office, a carefully crafted lobbying document was presented, entitled *Benefits of Private Investment in Infrastructure*. Kearsarge Global Advisors, a government affairs and communications firm, produced the document in coordination with a group of leading law firms (Allen & Overy LLP, Chadbourne & Parke LLP, Debevoise & Plimpton, Freshields Bruckhaus Deringer, Fulbright & Jaworski, Mayer Brown, and McKena Long & Aldridge LLP), private investors (Babcock & Brown, Barclays Capital, Carlyle Infrastructure Partners, Citi Infrastructure Investors, Credit Suisse, Merrill Lynch, Morgan Stanley, RREE, RBC Capital Markets, Scotia Capital, and UBS), and the Spanish transportation firm Abertis. Many of these professional service providers have already benefited greatly from the nascent market for partnerships. Some of the more active law firms have taken on a role of promoting partnerships.

Beyond this lobbying document, Ned Neaher, a White & Case partner, made a typical statement to the *National Law Journal* in an article entitled "Growth of Privatization Deals Nets Big Fees for Firms": "This is a market that is expanding and will continue to expand. . . . It's here to stay, even though politically it takes some education to bring people around to the concept that private-equity investment in public infrastructure is a good thing."[24] Stroock & Stroock & Lavin LLP, a major medium-size U.S. law firm, issued a brief in March on Obama's proposal for the bank within the budget. In line with this advocacy approach, the bulletin's author, Richard Madris, who heads the Infrastructure Group, and Brian Greene, a firm associate, indicated, "Too often, government (and especially the legislative branch and certain of their constituencies) has been fearful of private investment in infrastructure." The firm went on to praise Chicago mayor Richard Daley, an active proponent of private participation, for "his bold experiments in privatization of public assets."[25] A notable amount of circulation by professionals between government, on the one hand, and banks and law firms, on the other, happens.

Many of these lawyers and other professionals have international partnership experience prior to working on the U.S. projects. For example, Neaher pointed out, "This is one of the few examples where you take expertise and knowledge gained outside the U.S. and apply it inside the U.S."[26] Moreover, UK firms with partnership specialism like Freshfields are dominant players in the law firm sector. Also, Carlyle Group's partnership practice took care to hire a Bechtel executive with substantial experience in UK privatization to co-head its practice. KPMG has also valued UK track records in its senior-level hiring. The dominance within the U.S. infrastructure market of American and UK law firms mirrors the international P3 sector, in which these firms dominate even in Western European deals.

At the same time, firms with close regional ties have also benefited. This too mirrors the international P3 market, in which foreign firms often partner with local ones, which act as gatekeepers and offer privileged access to domestic markets. Mayer Brown, a firm with close ties to Illinois, has played a key role in advising the government of Chicago in partnership deals. John Schmidt, a leading partner for Mayer, claims that after a successful P3 for Chicago's Skyway, the city's mayor turned to him and said, "What else?" Likewise, firms such as KPMG have established regional offices to take advantage of market opportunities.

The market strategy being pursued by a number of firms of establishing or taking advantage of regional offices also involves establishing an integration of both domestic and international offices. For example, tenders in one locality are prepared by multiple offices working together. As a result, the market itself begins to rationalize with regard to contract structure, pricing of assets, and government policies as a result of increasingly internationally integrated service providers. Furthermore, pricing of assets may seem irrational because offers may be tied to attempts to assert monopolistic power over a sector or region whereby losses are taken in the short term in anticipation of market-dominant deals later.

The *Benefits of Private Investment in Infrastructure* document asserts that almost $200 billion now sits in privately managed infrastructure funds devoted to the American market. When pooled with the government cash, these two pots of money can create upward of the $450 billion referenced by Obama. Moreover, if the private equity money with a thirst for the clean energy market is combined and potentially leveraged by the Obama Bank, the numbers grow enormously.

On *Meet the Press*, fresh from a bullish meeting with the president, Bloomberg, Rendell, and Schwarzenegger tied the leveraging idea with public-private partnerships and the Obama infrastructure bank. Mayor Bloomberg explained, "Yes, the amount of stimulus in the – the amount of money in the infrastructure package is a small amount. But Governor Rendell – who deserves all the credit, I think Arnold would agree with me, to putting this organization together – has talked about how we can leverage that money." Rendell asserted that the Obama Bank could be the lever: "You could finance – for $30 billion a year, which these days is not a lot of money, you could finance almost $400 billion to put up front in an infrastructure repair program administered through something like the infrastructure bank."[27] He did not mention the fact that the stimulus act itself already included generous tax incentives to promote this leveraging. In fact, these tax incentives have been downplayed by all involved and are exempt from many of the accountability rules in the stimulus act itself.

As the Obama Bank moves toward encompassing an increasing number of infrastructure sectors in greater depth, it is important to take account of the fact that the financing, regulatory, and contractual structures differ markedly from one sector to another. As a result, when we speak of the use of P3s in stimulating clean energy technology, we may mean something qualitatively different from when we use the term in transportation. Little progress has been made in coming up with a workable definition of P3s capable of being used across sectors for the purpose of the bank.

As this book argues, leveraging is not simply about the amount of money the government puts in the pot. In fact, the numbers themselves necessary to attract foreign capital into the market have been somewhat elastic. Instead, private investors are also looking for the government to signal its willingness to engage in legislative reform on an ambitious scale. In addition, one of the appeals of the U.S. market to investors is the assumption that the courts will not expropriate property. Having the projects backed either implicitly or explicitly by the U.S. government or our states is important.

Furthermore, given the centrality of infrastructure for durable growth, regardless of formal commitments, many understand that the government itself is the practical lender of last resort even if projects are not fully guaranteed by the state. As we move away from a mortgage-backed economy and toward an infrastructure-backed one, it is important to recognize that it is not viable for the government to let water systems fail. As a result, an unstated assumption is that the government will by necessity step in to rescue key troubled infrastructure projects. Such a presumption was more explicit during the Roosevelt era, when it was understood that a certain percentage of self-liquidating government projects would fail and require rescue. For this reason, in our assessment of the costs of partnerships, it is important to soberly reflect on hidden costs.

Looking to international experience with partnerships and infrastructure banks is one way to do this. Off–balance sheet financing has too often been an excuse for not realistically measuring debt burden. If state subsidies will drive the infrastructure sector forward, then we must assess the back-end costs if there is a possibility that public pension funds will rescue essential services. Fiduciary duty requires pension fund managers to take this cost into account. Such costs are not hidden when due diligence is conducted. Nonetheless, the fact that the countercyclical quality of infrastructure projects as an asset class depends on public subsidy in this way does not mean that investments should not happen. Instead, such real costs must be factored into investment decision-making. Due diligence by fund managers in this area has been too narrowly defined. The record of international experience with infrastructure projects is too readily available to substitute the word of external advisors for due diligence.

A bank's central task is to achieve a public purpose, for example, economic growth, environmental sustainability, regional integration, poverty alleviation, or homeland security. It does so in part by using private firms as policy organs. Infrastructure banks have a toolbox to do this that is mainly filled with carrots, for example, loans, insurance policies, and guarantees. Thus, from the bank's perspective, a P3 is useful defined as a substantial mixing of public and private sectors over a project's life cycle from financing, to construction, to operation. Ascertaining the appropriate mix is a public policy question – to achieve the public purpose is the job of an infrastructure bank. Thus, the bank looks at projects differently than does a private-sector partner.

A P3 is a project that includes substantial private and public participation in the financing, construction, or operation stage. For example, a privatized project might be financed by a private investment bank and carried out by a quasi-public entity. Likewise, a government might finance a private company's participation in a project. In practice, most projects include a mix of public and private financiers. Furthermore, a consortium of public and private companies might construct a project. Thus, this definition focuses on shared ownership and control over the project's life cycle.[28] Furthermore, most large-scale P3s are transnational as well.

This definition is intended to include certain transportation projects carried out through service contracts under its umbrella. It does so because a series of well-crafted service contracts can produce a P3 structure. For example, if a private firm is contracted by the government to design, build, and operate a project through a series of agreements, then only an overly formalist definition of P3s would exclude it. This ability to replicate the P3 structure through service contracts is prevalent in the Iranian oil sector, where limits on foreign participation in the sector have resulted in such schemes in order to take advantage of foreign firms in arrangements that function like production-sharing agreements. The use of the word *P3* instead turns on the degree of ownership or control.

Moreover, a focus on the ownership and control mix over a project's life cycle helps in crafting policies that address the fact that a typical project is not a bilateral agreement. Instead, P3s are created through large numbers of contracts and subcontracts among parties that might enter and exit the project over its life cycle. Although a general spirit of working together to achieve a common goal might undergird the partnership arrangement writ large, when it comes to modeling a project from the bank side, it is important to anticipate the possibility of a main private-sector partner making a strategic exit. In leveraged arrangements, often a participant's practical importance is not realized until an unanticipated event occurs. Furthermore, defining P3s on the basis of user charges does not clarify this issue, as off–balance sheet financing was a basic feature of the FDR-instigated, quasi-public, self-liquidating entities.

5 Free Market Statism

I. Introduction

Chapter 2 related how a dispute over President Barack Obama's economic philosophy took center stage shortly after his inauguration, as Rush Limbaugh popularized the opposition messaging, which used the word *socialism* as a boo word in an attempt to discredit Obama's policies. It argued that Obama's emphasis on an important role of government in the economy was not incompatible with his adherence to free market principles. In fact, the financial crisis itself was not caused by an absentee deregulatory government alone. Instead, for several decades, government used companies as foreign policy organs to promote a brand of globalization that undermined the domestic health of our economy and eventually resulted in today's systemic crisis. Thus, government plays an active role in our free market economy in both good times and bad. The aim then is to ensure that the government partnerships with private firms underpinning our economy advance, rather than undermine, the public interest. The success of the Obama recovery must ultimately be judged by his own standard: its ability to promote the common good.

Obama explained his economic philosophy as having three basic aspects. First, he is a firm believer in, a champion of, the free market. Second, he also takes the position that government can legitimately make sure that America invests in what is needed for long-term growth. Third, the success of the market must be judged based on its ability to advance the common good. This philosophy is firmly rooted in American economic tradition. This chapter defines it as free market statism. It explains that adherents of free market statism over the last hundred years have not only understood the American economy in similar ways, but they have also voiced a common set of concerns about accountability.

This chapter argues that an understanding of Obama's economic philosophy is essential to break down the fourth wall between the infrastructure bank and the citizenry. Accountability depends on a rich concept of transparency that is closely attuned to the specific role that Obama intends the government and the bank to play in our economic renaissance. Important and unprecedented pledges have been made to promote transparency within the administration. However, as the final section of this chapter shows, a mismatch exists between Obama's economic philosophy and his policies designed to promote transparency and ensure accountability. The infrastructure bank should be designed to guarantee this accountability. It is well positioned to do so. Thus, it is essential to understand the specific economic philosophy underlying the bank in order to judge how the institution itself and its policies are crafted to accomplish a set of goals. Here, *transparency* means making how these policies are formulated and carried out visible and measurable. *Accountability*, in turn, means ensuring that the policies advance the common good.

The socialism messaging that Limbaugh advanced on Sean Hannity's program has legs, at least within the Republican Party, and continues to obscure our understanding of the president's philosophy. On April 21, Representative James Bopp, Republican from Indiana, sent around an email announcing the introduction of three proposed resolutions for consideration at the upcoming Republican state chairman's meeting. Pursuant to Republican National Congress (RNC) Rule 8(b), sixteen members sought to protect the country from "the Democrats' March Toward Socialism," Obama's attempt "to restructure American society along socialist ideals." The proposals called for a renaming of Obama's party, "the Democrat Socialist Party." The email conjured Ronald Reagan and the Cold War: "Just as President Reagan's identification of the Soviet Union as the 'evil empire' galvanized opposition to communism, we hope that the accurate depiction of the Democrats as a Socialist Party will galvanize opposition to their march to socialism."[1] Thus, the insurgent Republicans wrapped themselves in Reagan, resuscitating the Cold War to lead a charge against a foreign un-American threat to the national polity and way of life. The word *socialism* was asked to pack a punch against our president, his policies, and his party.

Shortly after the president's first one hundred days in office, the RNC considered these proposals. RNC chairman Michael Steele was opposed to the renaming. Although the compromise measure that ultimately passed excised this particular aspect of the proposals, it was nonetheless entitled "RNC Resolution Recognizing the Democrats' March Toward Socialism." The resolution began by referencing the *American Heritage Dictionary*'s definition of socialism "as a system of social organization in which the means of producing and distributing goods is owned by a centralized government that often plans and controls the economy." It then went on to claim that various nationalizations had occurred or were planned before turning to the bailouts and ballooning of government spending. The RNC then, quoting directly from a *Newsweek* article, argued that we were in danger of "becoming even more French," or as our members of Congress reiterated, "the American traditions of hard work and free enterprise are at risk as the Democratic Party pushes our country towards European-style socialism and government control."[2] The resolutions had thrown in the kitchen sink.

This chapter takes issue with the Republican line of attack on empirical grounds. In doing so, it does not seek to mount a defense of Obama's policies. Instead, the aim is to present a theory to understand the basic economic philosophy that underpins the Obama approach – free market statism. As this chapter argues, Obama's philosophy has firm roots in American history and tradition. The government invariably plays a central role in creating, nurturing, and directing what we term "the free market." It does so in both good times and bad. As the financial crisis shows, the government may play a more proactive role at certain moments of transition or restructuring. Also, the form and extent of government involvement vary in different times and places, sectors and projects. Nonetheless, the central issue with regard to our economy has always been what values we promote through the public-private partnership that forms the foundation of our economy. In his inaugural address, Obama suggested that the yardstick for judging the economy's success is its ability to promote the common good.

To achieve these goals, the chapter first defines free market statism. It aims to cut through much of the obscuring bipartisan politicizing of decisions over the appropriate role of government. The Supreme Court has itself contributed to this politicizing of the economy. As indicated, the argument of this chapter is that free market statism has been a basic tenet of the economy throughout our history. The chapter thus discusses a number of examples of free market statism. It does not intend to be exhaustive. Moreover, the chapter aims not to provide a list of examples of free market statism but instead to argue that a set of concerns about free market statism preoccupy policy-makers and that these concerns have recurred throughout history.

II. The Concept

Free market statism refers to two interrelated qualities of the economy. First, the government creates and sustains companies even if we fictionalize them as private. As the stimulus-financed jobs make clear, we use companies as policy organs. Second, we have created government institutions and policies that themselves are designed to enmesh with private firms effectively. An example is the subsidies to promote clean energy, which are carefully tailored to ensure that they work effectively to promote specific private-sector technologies. Such subsidies make clean energy itself a public-private partnership. The effectiveness of government lies in its ability to produce specific results. Regardless of the government initiative, invariably the underlying rationale of free market statism is the advancement of the public interest.

The main ideological hurdle that an acknowledgment of free market statism faces is the widespread bipartisan claim that economic stasis means that companies, as individuals, reside free and independent of government support. In its socialism name-calling, the RNC claimed, "history has demonstrated that free markets and free men are the only way to prosperity and have been the bedrock of the United States economy."[3] This claim conjured a long-standing bipartisan understanding we have of ourselves. Although America is by no means the only free market economy on the planet, we are peculiar in our vocal insistence on, and indeed celebration of, a private sector that goes at it alone, often in opposition to the state.

In doing so, we conflate the liberty and independence of the individual with that of the private corporation. Government has always actively participated in our free market economy, and for more than a century we have ignored interventions on behalf of business, focusing instead on antagonisms between government and private firms. The Internet, that intersection where civil liberties meet corporate freedoms, is itself the product of Defense Department contracts during the Cold War. The global information superhighway, those fiber-optic cables linking the world in a civil society without borders, was laid by companies with the help of U.S. government loan and insurance programs, as discussed in the Introduction. Many of our greatest scientific achievements have been incubated through long-term strategic government investment in our world-class universities. In other words, the foundation of our free market economy has always been importantly public.

Corporate executives and the courts have done little to dispel this myth that individual freedoms are one and the same as those of corporations.[4] The Supreme Court has often done more than the political branches to create the foundation for this misconception that companies are anything but our collective dependents. In the landmark Supreme Court case *Dartmouth College v. Woodward*, Chief Justice John Marshall explained the public basis of the private firm: "A corporation is an artificial being, invisible, intangible, and existing only in the contemplation of law."[5] This recognition has not persisted.

In one of the biggest affronts to the U.S. Constitution that has retained status as a good law – *Santa Clara County v. Southern Pacific Railroad* – a creature of government statute argued that it had rights by virtue of the Fourteenth Amendment. In other words, the executives of this private railroad company hired lawyers who argued to our highest court that Southern Pacific was the appropriate beneficiary of a post–Civil War constitutional amendment passed to belatedly acknowledge that former slaves possessed equal rights in America. However, even though Southern Pacific had been granted legal life by a congressional statute written just for it, Chief Justice Morrison Waite declared prior to oral arguments in the case: "The court does not wish to hear argument on the question whether the provision in the Fourteenth Amendment to the Constitution, which forbids a State to deny any person within its jurisdiction the equal protection of the laws, applies to these corporations. We are all of the opinion that it does."[6] Thus, the foundations of corporate freedom were laid.

Nonetheless, despite the fact that this Supreme Court precedent mistakenly presumed that the Fourteenth Amendment aimed to establish equal rights for companies, for more than a century since then we have treated companies like cowboys going at it alone and often in opposition to government. In reality, not mythology, companies are themselves public-private partnerships, creatures of a dominant American economic philosophy of free market statism. The fact that public power parents our corporations is true in good times and bad and does not extinguish the existence of a free market in America. For this reason, arguments that Obama is introducing socialism to America mistakenly assume that the free market has ever stood on its own, that companies are anything more than creatures of the state, ongoing dependents. Corporate privileges thus masquerade as rights. Instead, companies, just like our government, are justified on the basis of their ability to advance the public interest.

Free market statism refers to the public law underpinnings of the free market economy. Here, the government is not just a neutral rule-maker. Instead, it may be an active promoter of certain private commercial interests. The commercial order is political in at least two senses. First, private law is itself political; that is, it is rooted in public law. Second, private commercial actors continue during their legal life to rely on proactive government support. In contrast, proponents of the free market may tend to downplay or deny the existence of government subsidy, preferring instead to argue that commercial actors are going at it alone or at times to focus on government-industry antagonism. Given that the public purse legitimizes and subsidizes private commerce, it follows that corporate activity should be held accountable to the public interest in a way that is sensitive to the nature and extent of the activity under analysis.

III. An American Tradition

In his inaugural address in 1981, Reagan fired the first shot in a revolutionary movement against the New Deal state: "Government is not the solution to our problem. Government is the problem."[7] Bush I conjured FDR himself, suggesting that one of his worst fears had become a reality: the welfare state was now "a narcotic and a subtle destroyer of spirit."[8] During the Roaring Nineties, Clinton took the reins of the Reagan Revolution, famously claiming that the "era of big government is over"[9] as he sought to make the state more efficient and economical – to modernize government. Shortly before the Iraq War deficit budget boom, Bush II honored Milton Friedman, that Nobel Prize–winning beacon of laissez-fairism, at the White House, reminding us: "In contrast to the free market's invisible hand, which improves the lives of people, the government's invisible foot tramples on people's hopes and destroys their dreams."[10] This bipartisan revolution succeeded in dismantling much of the welfare state, moving responsibility for its traditional functions into the nominal private sector.

The impact of the decades-long revolution was clear when President Obama announced his stimulus plan on YouTube. Although Obama was likened by friends and foes to Roosevelt, this was no 1930s-style New Deal. Whereas FDR had created government corporations, such as the Tennessee Valley Authority, to carry out his agenda, Obama related that his own plan would be carried out by private companies. In fact, the Reagan Revolution had successfully moved the staples of the New Deal economy into mainly private hands, including transportation, power, and water. Not seeking to reverse the Revolution, Obama related, "Our plan will likely save or create three or four million jobs. . . . Ninety percent of these jobs will be created in the private sector. The remaining ten percent are mainly public sector jobs we save like teachers, police officers, firefighters and others who provide vital services to our communities."[11]

However, importantly, when Obama announced that these jobs would be retained or created in the private sector, he downplayed the obvious. To call these stimulus jobs private stretched the imagination, unless one adopted a free market statist orientation, which allows that the private is itself substantially public.

Discussions of state intervention in the U.S. economy during the twentieth century generally focus on the rise and fall of the welfare state. However, free market statism has also spanned the last hundred years. It has even extended back to the Gilded Age with its public-private-partnership–based railway projects,[12] to post–Civil War Reconstruction, and to the creation of the monetary system itself. In fact, after the Revolutionary War, Massachusetts experimented with various public-private partnerships, as citizens "found themselves yoked to the high costs of independence" – war debt.[13] In the twentieth century, from the *Lochner*[14] period, during which freedom of contract reigned, to the massive military mobilization for the Second World War,[15] government-company collaborations occupied policy-makers. Similarly, in the postwar period, collaborations pervaded the defense sector as the country did battle in the Cold War. They were also present elsewhere. Most recently, privatization has progressively supplanted the welfare state. Despite contrary representations, privatization itself is premised on free market statism.

This section provides a brief menu of instances of this statism in the United States over the last century. It in no way is meant to be comprehensive. The field is characterized by variation. Importantly, our inquiry does not put all instances of free market statism on an equal footing with regard to the nature and extent of government-corporate collaborations. Instead, the aim is to point to the prevalence of free market statism within the United States during this period and also to identify some common concerns that animate policy-makers who have looked at the relationships between governments and companies.

In the early twentieth century, law, philosophy, and economics professors critical of laissez-fairism pointed to the role of government in fortifying the free market. Diagnoses of today's financial crisis that pin the blame for the downturn solely on deregulation, the recession of government from the economy resulting in the free market growing out of control, seem to assume that the pre–New Deal laissez-faire economy was characterized by the absence of government. That is, FDR brought the government into the economy to solve widespread market abuse. However, the generation that drove the New Deal reforms understood the Great Depression entirely differently.

Instead, they argued that the financial crisis was caused by a government-underwritten laissez-faire system that misdirected the economy by partnering with firms to advance the interests of the few at the expense of the public interest. Any law professor on the street knows this movement as Legal Realism. Until the new legal laissez-fairism, law and economics, remade much of constitutional law in the image of the bipartisan Reagan Revolution, most professors subscribed to its basic tenets.

In other words, the New Deal was not formulated to introduce government into the economy. It was already there. FDR's programs instead redefined the public interest and reforged the partnerships of a free market statist economy. These reformers countered the radical freedom of contract position represented by *Lochner*. Some sought to counter opposition to the social reforms associated with the New Deal.

Three durable insights are important here. The first insight is the observation that companies have benefited from a proactive government. The second insight concerns the public law foundations of private corporate organization. A third insight focuses on the question of how to appropriately guide government-company collaborations. Importantly, they did not presume that free market statism was an unqualified bad. Instead, the aim was to guide such statism so as to advance the public interest.

In two widely read articles, one in 1911 and the other in 1932, City College of New York philosophy professor Morris Raphael Cohen related the first insight that companies are against government intervention in the market selectively.[16] Cohen, a central figure in legal history, argued that "the theory of *laissez faire*, of complete non-interference of the government in business, is not really held consistently by those who frequently invoke it." This "group . . . protests against child labor law, or against any minimum wage law intended to insure a minimum standard of decent living." At the same time, it "is constantly urging the government to protect industry by tariffs."[17] Expressing the third insight of interest, rather than urging a return "to medievalism,"[18] the issue for Cohen is then "what interests should be protected and who should control the government."[19] Likewise, as the economics professor and sometime legal scholar Robert Hale argued, "[s]ome sort of coercive restriction . . . is unavoidable." The issue then is to recognize that "[t]here is accordingly a need for the development of economic and legal theory to guide the process."[20]

In 1935, pointing to the public basis of private contract, Hale put the underpinnings of the second position neatly: "[A]bsolute state power is the background norm upon which private power is exercised."[21] Like Cohen, Louis Jaffe, who served within both the New Deal's Agricultural Adjustment Administration and National Labor Relations Board, urged a greater openness:

> Participation in law-making by private groups under explicit statutory "delegation" does not stand then in absolute contradiction to the traditional process and conditions of law-making; it is not incompatible with the conception of law. It exposes and brings into the open, it institutionalizes a factor in law-making that we have, eagerly in fact, attempted to obscure.[22]

Thus, in focusing on the intermingling of sovereignty and corporate behavior, these reformers urged a more factually based public debate and greater scrutiny of how this mixing operates in practice in light of public values and principles. Moreover, the judicial philosophy that they advanced, based on the Continental European free law doctrine, urged the realignment of government-corporate mixing so as to advance the public interest.[23] This was the legal theory that drove the New Deal state and our staple regulatory agencies and public welfare guarantees. It was about reasserting control over the meaning of the public interest and ensuring that our partnerships advanced it.

Similar concerns were raised by postwar policy-makers. Yale law professor Charles A. Reich argued in 1964 that the Cold War period was characterized by a sharing of "sovereign power . . . with large private interests."[24] He explained how "the impact of government power falls unequally on different components of the private sector." In other words, government did not favor all private firms equally, "some gain while others lose." Also, speaking in what has become today's vernacular, Reich related how "the government largess often creates a partnership with some sectors of the private economy." These partnerships are not antagonistic; the government "aids rather than limits the objectives of those private sectors." And, importantly, Reich expressed an insight now associated with public choice theory and criticism of lobbying: "[T]he apparatus of government power may be utilized by private interests in their conflicts with other interests, and thus the tools of government become private rather than public instrumentalities."[25] This cautionary point about partnerships is often voiced in relation to the large-scale bank bailouts, both by those institutions that did not need bailing out and felt put at a competitive disadvantage as a result and also by critics of the close relationships between firms such as Goldman Sachs and Blackstone with government financial decision-making.

In 1963, Michael D. Reagan made a related critique. He argued against widespread claims that the free market side of the Cold War divide was anything but a mixed economy.

The public and private sectors, according to Reagan, had instead merged. Thus, "[w]hile public attention has largely been directed at conflicts between government and business," this had obscured a more important feature of our economy that had "gone relatively unnoticed." It was "the gradual erasure of long-standing distinctions between private and public activities." This erosion of the wall between government and the private sector meant in practice "the increased amalgamation of the sectors."[26] A decade earlier, Don K. Price of the Kennedy administration, Ford Foundation, and Harvard University, discussing government spending on science research, called the system "federalism by contract."[27] Thus, partnership was a basic feature of even the postwar heyday of the free market.

In 1986, Stewart Macaulay took Reich's point about the private sector taking on government powers one step further. He argued that many companies had become private governments. For this reason, it was important to look at "both harmony and conflict among public and private governments."[28] In practice, the distinctions between the two might be more a matter of assumption than a realistic recognition "that public and private governments are interpenetrated rather than distinct entities."[29] Like the New Dealers, Macaulay was concerned mainly with issues of control and accountability. He argued, "Large corporations may assume functions usually thought of as governmental when they want control and little accountability."[30] Importantly, as with his predecessors, Macaulay argued that we cannot have meaningful accountability without knowing more about how governments and companies mix to accomplish goals in practice; in other words, empiricism is a precondition to accountability.

Many of the Cold War concerns about a partnership-based economy masquerading as a government-less free market focused on the defense sector. The merging of government and private sectors to wage war preoccupied policymakers also during the First and Second World Wars with the First and Second World War Powers Acts.[31] The latter was particularly noteworthy, because the industrial side of the economy had grown so large that its merger with defense created enormous gains. The scale of the wartime effort was unprecedented in America and involved an extensive contract-based effort that persisted after the war and into the Cold War. These partnerships were highly successful, as evidenced by Henry Kaiser's adaptation of private-sector industrial strategies to national defense. Kaiser streamlined and accelerated the production of the Liberty Ships, which were key to the Allies' victory. At the same time, the large number of legal claims arising out of these Second World War contracts was noteworthy.[32] In addition, a number of companies such as IBM traded with the enemy, contributing to their size and strength in ways similar to how oil companies during wartime also fuel both sides of a conflict. After the First World War, the Nye Commission had been formed to address some of the worrisome conflicts that arise within wartime mixing.

However, the landmark free market statist speech about the partnerships in the defense sector came from D-day commander President Dwight D. Eisenhower in his famous statement about what he termed the "military industrial complex." As with the New Dealers, Eisenhower made the three recurring observations about defense mixing discussed previously. It is worth quoting a section of his speech here at length:

> This conjunction of an immense military establishment and a large arms industry is new in the American experience. The total influence – economic, political, even spiritual – is felt in every city, every State house, every office of the Federal government. We recognize the imperative need for this development. Yet we must not fail to comprehend the grave implications. Our toil, resources and livelihood are all involved; so is the very structure of our society.
>
> In the councils of government, we must guard against the acquisition of unwarranted influence, whether sought or unsought, by the military industrial complex. The potential disastrous rise of misplaced power exists and will persist.
>
> We must never let the weight of this combination endanger our liberties or democratic processes. We should take nothing for granted. Only an alert and knowledgeable citizenry can compel the proper meshing of the huge industrial and military machinery of defense with our peaceful methods and goals, so that security and liberty may prosper together.[33]

Thus, in Eisenhower's statement as well as in the work of Michael Reagan and others, we see an echoing of the early critics of laissez-fairism's call for a revisiting of government-company mixing in order to counter false representations and ensure that mixing is judged by the yardstick of the public interest. In 1963, Ernest F. Leathem argued that although the "[d]efense procurement of the United States reaches directly or indirectly into the lives of every inhabitant, young and old, in every state and territory of our nation," "it is one of the least discussed, the least studied and the least understood facets of our national life."[34] Even though many years have gone by since these statements, as we broaden this model within the United States, the empirical record remains sparse.

Michael Reagan fleshed out this claim in his discussion of how the defense-sector partnerships were carried out. He focused on the extensive network of public and private contracts that emerged. It had become so powerful, Reagan argued in 1963, that it could not be reduced to a single industry or product.[35] Frederick T. Moore called the area "diffuse" and "less homogenous than other areas of procurement."[36] Instead, Reagan explained that the government was pursuing policies "through local contracting firms rather than through subordinate layers of government." He explained how, because the bulk of large-scale government contracts went to a small number of firms, even these prime contractors themselves had to set up vast subcontracting systems to execute their tasks. As a result, "private business firms are acting as de facto antitrust administrators under this system." This "decentralization by contract"[37] or in Price's terms "federalism by contract"[38] has been replicated under the Reagan Revolution most publicly with the post–Iraq War reconstruction contracts that concentrated power in prime contractors like Bechtel while also directing them to subcontract out the vast majority of their tasks to Iraqis.

Moreover, Michael Reagan also explained how congressional committees charged with disbursing private-sector contract awards were staffed by members of the private sector. Also, the government financed private-sector lobbying for government defense contracts.[39] High technology is a well-known product of this partnering, and it resulted eventually in the rise of the Internet and the commercial application of myriad other defense-subsidized technologies.

Since the late 1970s, the defense-sector model of free market statism has spread more widely with the onset of privatization.[40] Privatization was first introduced by Prime Minister Thatcher, followed by President Reagan. It has since spread throughout the world. Once again, a similar set of concerns crop up. The welfare state here has been partially dismantled, while free market statism has emerged unscathed. Privatization has witnessed a dramatic extension of federalism by contract and other government-industry synergies into almost all walks of life. Just as with the laissez-fairism of the early twentieth century, the advocates of privatization have downplayed market statism, focusing instead on the introduction of the logic of the free market into public-sector activities.

Nonetheless, in practice, despite the shift away from a public service model toward privatization, the government has often maintained itself as the financier and licenser of many enterprises. For instance, our vast network of privatization within the United States, state after state, at the federal level, involves contracting out services to the private sector. Our roads system, although nominally public, is largely maintained by private companies. For the most part, these companies are paid directly by states and the federal government. Companies may rely mainly on government contracts for their subsistence.

In addition, one of the most popular partnership-based contractual techniques is the Build-Operate-Transfer (BOT) agreement. Although this contract type is widely touted as an exemplar of privatization, in fact, a BOT agreement causes a project to sit within the public sector. The idea is that a private party will build and operate the road. It will do so long enough to collect enough tolls to retire the debt incurred in building the road. After also garnering an agreed-upon profit, control over the road will then transfer to the government. Moreover, as we shall see in the next chapter, even during the building and operating stages, a BOT project involves heavy government participation. In other words, privatization techniques are partnership-based creatures of free market statism.

IV. Conclusion

Without an understanding of Obama's economic philosophy, the infrastructure bank will not function properly. It will not promote the common good. Instead, we will continue to be ensnared by the false socialism versus capitalism trap, the question of whether an active or passive government is the most appropriate response to crisis. Because government is a cornerstone of the free market regardless of the position we take on this issue, it is more important to focus on how we mix government and industry rather than whether we do. All mixing is not equal. Moreover, without careful attention to the actual context, form, and function of mixing, bank policies and projects will be consumed rather than formulated by the American citizenry.

Not all government activism in the market is made visible. Even though President Obama refreshingly acknowledges that the government plays a perennial role in the free market, his policy positions at times obscure this role, frustrating rather than promoting transparency and accountability.

For example, the stimulus package famously included cash grants for short-term shovel-ready infrastructure projects. However, it also provided large-scale tax incentives to promote public-private-partnership–based projects.

Within public-private partnerships, governments and companies share the responsibility for financing, building, and operating projects. This book's subsequent chapters devote themselves to how these partnerships operate in practice, drawing mainly on three decades of international experience. However, first, we turn to how the American Recovery and Reinvestment Act takes a first step down the path toward the embracing of P3s through its innovative bond vehicles.

6

A New Foundation

I. Re-laying the Foundation

We do not invest in infrastructure projects because they are inherently profitable. Instead, a quality portfolio of infrastructure projects is itself a precondition to self-sufficiency and economic development. President Barack Obama views infrastructure and energy projects as a way of re-laying the foundation of our economy, as we saw in earlier chapters. Our physical and social infrastructure is, for Obama, what "binds us together."[1] For this reason, the federal government should adopt a prudent management standard for its investments, as it did within the American Recovery and Reinvestment Act (ARRA), which viewed infrastructure investments as vehicles for preserving and creating jobs as well as providing long-term benefits. Such a standard ensures that the president, officers of the bank, and heads of agencies will view project investments as a holistic portfolio. In addition, attention will be paid not only to the cost of capital and leveraging ratios tied to project delivery, but also to the impact of the infrastructure projects on their intended beneficiaries.

Infrastructure is a foundational right. Professor Louis Henkin defines human rights as: "a *floor*," which is "necessary to make other values flourish."[2] It is the precondition of our shift to an energy-independent twenty-first-century economy promoting equal opportunity. Likewise, laying infrastructure has been the necessary first step toward recovery after most large-scale financial crises, conflicts, and occupations. This was true with the Great Depression, the Second World War, and decolonization in Africa, Asia, and Latin America. Infrastructure was thus the cornerstone of the New Deal, the Marshall Plan, and nation-building among newly independent states.

As a foundational right, infrastructure both solves immediate problems and promotes longer-term progressive values. We see this two-fold purpose within ARRA. It includes two types of infrastructure projects: in the first instance, ones that move quickly to market and are relatively short term in life span. Then, the next wave of projects are more ambitious and might extend for ten to seventy-five years. The former projects are referred to as ready-to-go ones and come under the heading of "Appropriations Division" within the Recovery Act, while the latter comprise the infrastructure bonds in the second half of the Act itself, which is titled "Tax, Unemployment, Health, State Fiscal Relief, and Other Provisions."[3]

Individuals will depend on these bond projects for their pension payments, drinking water, and paychecks. Moreover, these large-scale long-term investments in infrastructure and energy projects are a precondition to moving us toward a more equitable, competitive, and secure America. In other words, the costs of poor bond investments will be felt not only today but are likely to be high and born by future generations. Just as the Liberty Bonds during the Second World War were essential to financing victory in Normandy, so too are these reinvestment bonds key to delivering a sound foundation for an equitable America. For these reasons, appropriately tailored public interest safeguards must be in place to ensure that quasi-public and P3 investment decisions promote the act's purposes. The strict accountability measures set forth by the President to guide ARRA investments explicitly exempts the bond-financed infrastructure and energy projects.[4]

Thus we have two waves to our recovery and reinvestment strategy. The infrastructure bank aims to contribute to this second wave. This two-wave approach is modeled on President Franklin Delano Roosevelt's two-staged New Deal, albeit with substantial departures: we have compressed the time span and rely not just on the Tennessee Valley quasi-publics but also on P3s.

II. Recovery in Two Waves

The first wave of our recovery aims to retain and create additional jobs by financing capital-intensive ready-to-go projects. This wave of projects also intends to promote economic development by beginning to remedy decades of Reagan Revolution–led divestment from clean water, sustainable transportation, and energy independence. This dual purpose of the first stage of our infrastructure-driven recovery strategy – jobs and economic self-sufficiency – also drove the first wave of President Roosevelt's New Deal. By and large, these projects are modest and thus attuned to a short-term business cycle. For this reason, a transition to longer-term projects is essential in order to preserve job retention accomplished by this wave, and to move on to the next stage of recovery.

The second wave of our recovery can be found in the second half of the American Recovery Act, Division B, and related legislation and regulatory action. While mainly promoted as a tax-cutting section of the Act, Division B also comprises reinvestment bond incentives geared toward financing large-scale infrastructure and energy projects. A subset of these bonds finances state-driven projects, for example, what are called Build America Bonds, which are a new class of tax-credit bonds for capital projects.

However, a range of other bond vehicles promote private activity in public works from railroads to drinking water and clean energy. These projects combine public and private financing control and are thus P3s. This second wave of projects aims to lay a foundation for progressive growth, and is reinforced by the more ambitious infrastructure and energy bank agenda commonly associated with P3s or leveraged projects. We see this shift maturing most swiftly within the clean energy sector, with its transition from modest retrofit bond projects to large publicly guaranteed ones carried out through the Financial Institution Partnership Program.

The Recovery Act aims to promote economic recovery and to assist those most impacted by the recession by:

- preserving and creating jobs
- maintaining basic services
- providing long-term benefits by investing in sciences, health, and infrastructure[5]

It seeks to carry out this purpose in two distinct, yet reinforcing, waves.

The first wave includes ambitious short-term shovel-ready grant-based projects, while the second wave provides opportunities to invest in large-scale long-term public works projects through bond vehicles. Each of these two waves is an integral part of the stimulus act. However, while the impact of the first wave has already been felt, the full force of the second wave has not. Moreover, the second wave is far more ambitious than the first, and its impact is likely to be more dramatic and long-lasting. It will impact upon forward-looking planning across all public works sectors, job retention and creation, and savings and pension payments.

Furthermore, the second wave of ARRA represents a new way of financing and carrying out projects focused on innovative solutions to seemingly intractable financial problems. For instance, the Build America Bond program, which introduced an innovative tax-credit approach into quasi-public project financing of public works projects, succeeded in unfreezing the municipal bond market. Moreover, through other vehicles such as private activity bonds, we see a reinforcing of existing trends toward greater private participation in projects including P3s.

Wave One has become virtually synonymous with the stimulus itself, even though it is designed only to be the first stage of ARRA. It stimulates a short-term business cycle, which impacts on the types and duration of jobs retained and created. In other words, it provides a bridge toward an anticipated resuscitation of the economy. In themselves, first-wave projects do not last long enough for firms to think about expanding payrolls through new hiring. Only greater market certainty will facilitate such hiring.

Wave Two responds to this concern and is keyed into a longer-term business cycle, providing a substantial boost to public works financing, thus promoting job retention and creation. Likewise, an Infrastructure Bank promotes a longer-term stabilization of public works. In addition, whereas the first wave is largely remedial in its focus on repairing and renovating existing public works, the second wave is more forward-looking and geared toward large-scale new-build capital-intensive projects.

The second wave thus reinforces Wave One and is essential for building on its contribution toward sustained recovery and growth. While the first wave was made up of grants, Wave Two of the stimulus advances the public interest through a set of opportunities made available to individuals and companies to invest in ambitious public works projects through bond vehicles.

Wave Two projects represent an attempt to move toward longer-term investments in a time of severe financial crisis. For example, the average Build America Bond runs between twenty and thirty years. Also, the second wave includes sweeteners of private activity bonds, which have helped finance the several-decade-long North Tarrant P3 Expressway in Texas. Likewise, within clean energy, we see a transition away from short-lived retrofit projects toward larger projects benefiting from Department of Energy guarantees.

Within Wave One projects the government carries out public works projects either on its own or through private contractors. This mode of carrying out projects continues with the second wave. However, it also includes projects in which private investors and firms play a greater role. The idea with the quasi-public projects is to broaden the investor class to include pension funds and sovereign wealth funds. Similarly, with the private activity projects, such as P3 rails and roads and the large clean energy projects, Wave Two–leveraged projects increase the role of private participants.

At the same time, as with infrastructure projects more generally, the shift is in degree of control, not ownership, which retains within the public.

This second wave has already impacted upon financial markets and the real economy with more than sixty billion dollars of Build America Bonds alone across diverse sectors such as airports, power, utilities, water, transportation, K–12 education, and universities issued by the time of this book's writing. Also, a high-profile and successful wave of cooperative-based clean energy bonds resulted in many retrofitting and related investments.

However, the full force of Wave Two is only starting to be felt. For instance, although Build America Bond projects have been financed, much of the money has yet to be expended. Also, the scale of bond issues is estimated to be larger in 2010. Unlike the first wave that finances projects within a short business cycle to stimulate the economy and retain and create jobs, the second wave finances projects that will last longer. It furthers Wave One's quick substantial infusion of grant money, which is tailored toward stimulating a short-term business cycle. The long-term nature of the Wave Two public works projects encourages forward-looking private-sector planning that allows construction firms to make substantial capital investments and thus also to commit to retaining and hiring workers.

Thus, while, to date, the bulk of attention in the media and policy circles has focused on the first wave of the recovery, before long, Wave Two of the stimulus will take root and command our attention. Given the scale and innovative aspects of Wave Two bonds, these provisions warrant careful attention. For our purposes, the stimulus bonds are particularly important, because an effective infrastructure bank will build on their successes. For example, the book's final chapter makes concrete recommendations for incorporating the bond programs into the bank itself.

Wave Two bonds aim to stimulate investment in projects that will impact upon many sectors, including:

- Education
- Energy
- Development
- Housing
- Transportation
- Water disposal
- Water and sewage

The actual financial impact of the Wave Two bond inducements may be significant. The bond proceeds, combined with other sources of capital, offer governments an opportunity to leverage existing sources of private capital both through increasing the investor base within the Build America Bond program and through the private activity bond-leveraged P3 projects. Moreover, the Build America Bonds are not subject to volume caps, meaning that few restrictions are placed on the number that can be issued. Furthermore, several major changes are under consideration within Congress and the U.S. Treasury Department to supplement the traditional

Tax-Exempt municipal finance bond market with tax-credit bonds and more readily available private activity ones. Consequently, Wave Two stands to have an economic impact that is more long lasting and influential than Wave One.

The second wave thus represents an opportunity to pursue larger-scale, desperately needed infrastructure and energy projects that promote the public interest. The Wave Two bonds are also significant because they provide attractive government-backed investment vehicles in a time of financial uncertainty, which will promote a savings and investment culture rather than a spend and speculate one. Pension funds may be particularly attracted to the promise of long-term projects that are capable of financing retirement schemes, as may sovereign wealth funds, which share a similar risk profile. The bond vehicles also provide an alternative to Treasury Bonds for domestic and foreign investors, one that gears itself directly to productive economic activity within the United States.

The budgetary scale, scope, and duration of the second wave of the stimulus may be far more ambitious than the first. The large amount of public works financing that Wave Two bonds will spur across a wide range of sectors aims to help rebuild the foundation of the country by promoting investment in durable jobs and recovery, long-term public works, and savings. As a result, individuals will depend on Stimulus Act projects for their pension payments, drinking water, and paychecks. Moreover, large-scale long-term investments in infrastructure and energy projects are a precondition to moving us toward a more equitable, competitive, and secure America. In other words, the costs of a poor bond investment might be high and borne by future generations. For these reasons, it is essential to put appropriately tailored public interest safeguards in place to ensure that bond investment decisions promote ARRA's purposes.

Wave Two represents a significant effort to bring together public and private entities to share in the rebuilding of our country's economy and infrastructure. However, ARRA's public interest principles and goals must guide the projects that Wave Two helps finance. Since ARRA bond proceeds will be combined with private capital and leveraged to finance public works projects, it is critical to ensure that there are safeguards that prevent Wave Two from being overleveraged. We must shift away from discussions about the cost of capital and toward identifying and investing in public works projects that promote long-term growth, competitiveness, and equal opportunity.

Given the enormous scope and long-term effect that Wave Two will have, it is of serious concern that public interest guidelines have not been developed to inform decision-making in the issuance of Wave Two bonds and the projects they will finance. These projects, which will change the landscape of our country, will be complicated and require the coordination of multiple public and private parties at the national, state, and local levels. Explicitly defining our public interest priorities is essential to creating projects that have a positive long-term impact on our economy and recovery.

Furthermore, Wave Two lacks the accountability and transparency measures that characterize Wave One. No single agency possesses the jurisdiction or capacity to adequately monitor the issuance and spending of the Wave Two bond inducements. Proper oversight and transparency of all involved parties are critical to ensuring that public interest aims are adequately met.

Without clear federal involvement, guidance, and oversight, public interest responsibilities will devolve to states and localities. Presently, insufficient capacity exists within these entities to guide, oversee, and monitor many bond projects. Moreover, after three decades of privatization, government at all levels is not always well positioned to ensure that large-scale complex projects advance the public interest. For this reason, the final chapter of this book recommends incorporating the ARRA bond program and related initiatives within the Infrastructure Bank.

III. FDR and Obama Compared

President Obama's approach toward bond-driven progressive growth shares common features with the second wave of President Roosevelt's New Deal; however, it also departs dramatically. The second wave of FDR's New Deal also promoted long-term public works projects, rather than simply ready-to-go ones. Like Obama, FDR pursued innovative financing techniques. Early on in the New Deal, FDR had begun to reform existing public corporations and to advocate for new ones in order to carry out his program, notably through Title II of the National Industrial Recovery Act, the Public Works Administration, and the Rural Electrification Authority. This agenda was only partially realized during the first wave of the New Deal.

Just as today's first wave of the Recovery Act has been met with opposition by those viewing the agenda as redistributive and incurring mounting debts, FDR faced concerted opposition to the New Deal along the same lines. Marriner Eccles, FDR's Chairman of the Federal Reserve, wryly summed up this criticism: "Unwise spending seems to be spending for the other fellow."[6] Nonetheless, this criticism led to a scaling back of the New Deal and then a subsequent deepening crisis. At that point, Eccles and Treasury Secretary Henry Morgenthau Jr. advocated further reform to the public corporation system.

The idea was to buttress existing public corporations and to create additional quasi-public entities, what were often referred to as self-liquidating enterprises. These quasi-publics would maintain their public purpose and ownership; however, they would be clothed like private corporations so that they could act quickly, be managed flexibly, and, importantly, raise large amounts of manageable leveraged debt, which was necessary to engage in tremendously expensive much-needed projects. FDR explained the Tennessee Valley

Authority as a "corporation clothed with the power of government, but possessed of the flexibility and initiative of private enterprise."[7] By using leveraged debt, Morgenthau and Eccles sought to economize projects while still catalyzing capital raises attuned to needs.

Mounting criticism of the New Deal reforms and the Tennessee Valley approach to recovery made its way into the courts. The Roosevelt quasi-public corporations met and weathered many court challenges across the country. These quasi-publics were conflated with the Gilded Age projects that drove the country into financial crisis. In fact, although the Roosevelt corporations mixed public and private powers, they included qualitatively greater public control and oversight than the Gilded Age partnerships.

At the same time, the challenges themselves are instructive, because they highlight certain weaknesses that are characteristic of some P3s. For instance, challenges centered around concerns over moving public works decisions into the headquarters of relatively nontransparent government companies, the risks of accumulating large amounts of off-balance-sheet public debt without transparent accounting, and the planning problems that might arise in moving major public planning decisions over public works into a network of corporations insulated from representative and popular government.

The hope for these corporations was nonetheless high and their public purpose sharply defined, so they survived the challenges, subsisted, and accountability mechanisms were put in place to promote transparency, public participation, and sustainable planning. For instance, public corporations were fiscally responsible to the executive branch, and at times the legislative. They also often had government officials sitting on their boards as directors. Moreover, Roosevelt made clear that the primary purpose of these entities was not profit-based.

In fact, with the specter of the Gilded Age for-profit partnerships looming, it was made clear that public works themselves were not amenable to a profit-driven motive. In other words, infrastructure on its own should not be viewed as a for-profit enterprise. Instead, projects must be conceived and run for the public interest. They would take on private features only so as to advance the public interest effectively. In fact, FDR envisaged that the government would have to rescue a certain percentage of strategically significant quasi-public enterprises that would necessarily fail because of their private-sector features. Nonetheless, the use of quasi-publics was deemed essential to recovery and reinvestment. Thus, the too-big-to-fail concept went to the necessity of the project, and any bailout would be attuned to rescuing infrastructure rather than investors.

When Roosevelt advocated the American model for Europe and insurgents mounting anticolonial movements in the wake of the Second World War, he focused on this New Deal infrastructure-driven approach. In his "Four Freedoms Address," the progressive approach toward reinvestment, of which infrastructure was a central plank, FDR spoke of how individuals have a right to "a wider and constantly rising standard of living." According to Roosevelt, this involves "freedom from want, which, translated into world terms, means economic understandings which will secure to every nation a healthy peacetime life for its inhabitants everywhere in the world."[8] We see the same sentiment echoed in the Universal Declaration of Human Rights, which emerged from the ashes of the Second World War. It was a response to fascist Europe, one of the most extremist and damaging forms of public-private partnerships in history: "the peoples of the United Nations have in the Charter . . . determined to promote social progress and better standards of life."[9] Thus, infrastructure is both itself a public good and also a driver and precondition to progressive planning.

President Obama shares the purpose of the Roosevelt New Deal infrastructure commitment in both its short-term and progressive goals. At the same time, while FDR promoted quasi-publics as the vehicle for his forward-looking approach to infrastructure, Obama instead looks also to domestic and foreign companies and financial institutions to serve as complementary vehicles for growth. The argument is that the quasi-public approach is moored too much in public institutions that carry with them inefficiencies and proclivities to insider deal-making. It reflects a growing trend away from quasi-publics domestically and internationally.

With appropriate direction and oversight, the argument goes, P3s – a public-private consortium of government agencies, private banks, insurers, and companies – will be more efficient and able to make decisions based on the merits of projects rather than their own self-interests. Today, we are engaged in an active debate and struggle over which institutions are optimal for advancing the public interest. Important differences can be obscured by the language of public-private partnership, which suggests not only consensus-based approaches but also a homogeneity of the diverse projects included under its umbrella.

Importantly, we must shy away from basing our arguments for P3s and other innovative financing techniques entirely on the cost of raising capital. Our infrastructure crisis rests in a failure to invest in what is needed for long-term growth, competitiveness, and opportunity. Regardless of its root, this is not a government or private crisis, it is an American crisis. We must not, for instance, judge the success of the American Recovery Act bonds or P3s solely on their ability to reduce the cost of raising capital for government projects. These Reinvestment Bonds aimed to preserve and create jobs and to channel capital to solve long-term needs.

When FDR announced the fifth wave of War Bonds during the Second World War on June 12, 1944, he made clear: "There is a direct connection between the bonds you have bought and the stream of men and equipment now rushing over the English Channel for the liberation of Europe." He went on: "There is a direct connection between your Bonds and every part of this global war today."[10] Likewise, the public interest must be in the driver's seat of our bond-driven recovery and reinvestment today.

The tail must not wag the dog. One of the main problems with the international approach to P3s has been a recurring inability to define compelling public purposes and then to tailor project structure to achieve them. Instead, attention has been mainly paid to catalyzing investment at the front end. Rarely have we asked whether projects have advanced the public interest. Too often, we point to successful projects that have, for instance, undermined human rights and environmental concerns. Frequently, marquee projects universally promoted as international models have been riddled with financial problems. At the same time, even projects with little endogenous financial value have been great societal successes. As a result, we must be wary of arguments presenting P3s as inherently profitable. Similarly, P3s need not be profitable to justify their use.

At the same time, our subsidy structure must be attuned to promoting the underlying public value system justifying the project itself rather than private profitability. If a project stumbles, for instance, a public commitment might be best devoted to saving a project rather than its investors.

Thus, although Presidents Obama and Roosevelt share a common approach toward infrastructure as a foundational right with both present value and as essential to producing public goods and promoting equal opportunity, they differ in their approaches. While Roosevelt created a network of quasi-public corporations to pursue public works, Obama favors supplementing quasi-public projects with complementary ones premised on partnerships among government, banks, and private firms. Regardless of which approach one prefers, each raises fundamentally different questions of accountability.

The prevailing approach in America today toward transparency, publicity, and accountability is tailored to making the FDR approach promote the public interest. It is ill-suited to the Obama approach to reinvestment through P3s. In fact, the Obama P3 approach is more amenable to the strategies devised by the Progressive Movement in the early twentieth century, by Supreme Court Justice Louis Brandeis, philosophy professor Morris R. Cohen, and economist Robert L. Hale to put the public interest in control over our economy. This theme was first set out in Chapter 5, and we will return to it throughout the remainder of the book.

In other words, the basic legal foundation of the New Deal state – the Sherman Anti-Trust Act, the Glass-Steagall Act, the National Labor Relations Act, and other staples – could not be more relevant today. Each is essential for envisaging an accountable Obama-style recovery. At the same time, these agencies and laws need to be revisited and adapted. Importantly, despite attacks on government over the last thirty years, the state remains much more powerful today than in the nineteenth and early twentieth centuries. As a result, from the perspective of a private investment bank today like Goldman Sachs, a government partner in a project carries more weight in the marketplace.

The government is simply bigger and stronger than it was in the days of the Money Trust. For this reason, we next turn to how government uses P3s to get things done internationally and how they came to play such an important role within foreign policy.

7

P3s and Foreign Affairs

I. Bringing P3s Home

Over the last twenty-five years, throughout the world, governments have shifted away from the quasi-public system toward a P3 one. The United States is a latecomer to this movement. For this reason, we have an opportunity to learn constructive lessons from the international experience. In addition, because many of the same investment banks, law firms, insurers, and construction companies involved in international projects are turning their attention increasingly toward the American market, lessons are transferrable. For example, we have yet to incorporate basic lessons from international experience about which types of P3 contracts are highly correlated with renegotiations and cancellations and conversely those agreements that have proved more durable. And through our own participation in international and American public banks as well as our diverse agencies within P3s overseas, we have ourselves developed a public institutional capacity in this area. As well, U.S. public interest groups have been on the forefront of driving transparent P3 projects for decades, and thus they possess constructive experience with contracts and regulatory agencies.

Because of the widespread use of P3s internationally, both commonalities and divergences exist in experience with them across regions, countries, and sectors. For this reason, generalizations are difficult. At the same time, this chapter provides a rough overview of how P3s came to be the dominant way of carrying out infrastructure and energy projects throughout the world. We then turn to how governments use companies to accomplish policy goals in this area in order to demonstrate the use and misuse of subsidies.

The United States has played an active role through our membership within international banks, public investment banks, and executive agencies in promoting P3s abroad. Moreover, we have provided subsidies to our banks, insurance firms, and infrastructure companies helping to drive the shift around the world away from the Roosevelt quasi-public system and toward P3s. This shift has largely been catalyzed by international infrastructure banks. Thus, while the United States is, of course, exceptional in many respects, looking at how this shift was effectuated is instructive.

In fact, members of Congress like Representative Nancy Pelosi have been central figures in promoting progressive P3s internationally. Also, key figures such as Lawrence Summers, Timothy Geithner, and David Lipton have played roles in promoting P3s internationally. For instance, after the East Asian currency crisis, together they played a role in advancing P3s as a response to the regional crisis, termed the "Swat Team from Washington" by *Business Week*.[1]

II. The Third World Debt Crisis Restructuring

The P3 model was reintroduced in the 1970s in response to the so-called Third World Debt Crisis. As we shall see, this story is not simply about how things were done abroad. As the discussion in the Introduction made clear, our U.S. domestic economy is intimately linked with Africa, Asia, and Latin America. Nowhere is this connection clearer than in the story of the introduction of P3s abroad. As we shall see, P3s laid the foundations for the world factory system, which resulted in both greater trade, globalization, and economic growth as well as in the structural unemployment and disenfranchisements of large numbers of our own citizens.

This section focuses specifically on the role that infrastructure has played following decolonization, as newly independent states first pursued a Tennessee Valley Authority–styled New Deal approach focusing on self-sufficiency and energy independence. This approach was termed *import substitution*. It then explains how the so-called Third World Debt Crisis was a catalyst for a major restructuring of the postcolonial economies. The self-sufficiency model was abandoned not only by local officials but also at the impetus of the United States and its allies. It was replaced with an economic model that was again outward oriented as the colonial system had been, focusing less on self-sufficiency and instead on export-led growth. This increased integration was premised on the idea that countries that trade together and invest within one another's economies are more likely to settle disputes peacefully. From the perspective of many developing countries, another aim was to leapfrog development stages and increase competitiveness by building infrastructure capacity for greater manufacturing and a high-technology economy. The countries of East and South East Asia were most successful on this front.

To make this shift possible, the United States and its allies made massive investments in a basic global infrastructure, laying the telecommunications lines and water pipes, building the power plants, constructing roads, and putting in place an interoperable global container port system. We used P3s to lay the global public infrastructure that was a precondition to the creation of the world factory system. Before we laid this public infrastructure, it was not possible to outsource manufacturing away from the United States. Literally no workable phone lines existed to make call centers possible or to allow the global integration of the monetary system. Thus, arguments for globalization premised on theories of comparative advantage are specious. They ignore the massive public investments that were a prerequisite to the global economy as we know it today.

Again, as Vice President Al Gore rightly said in 1998, as countries in the region were in the throes of a P3-driven financial crisis: "After all, we are the nations that, together, created an economic miracle for Asia and the whole Asian-Pacific region."[2] At the same time, as P3 water and electricity projects went under right and left and as the so-called economic miracle showed fractures, the United States and others disclaimed responsibility. The regional crisis deepened when road and electricity usage decreased, making payments to P3 investors less forthcoming.

III. From Quasi-Public to P3s

In the wake of decolonization, newly independent states around the world embarked on an ambitious nation-building exercise. For centuries, colonial powers had oriented the economies of overseas holdings outward. For instance, valuable mineral resources were controlled by foreign companies. Railroads were laid to move minerals from mines to ports to fuel an inequitable international economy. The preeminent colonial administrator and an overseer of decolonization, Baron Frederick John Dealtry Lugard stated candidly: "Let it be admitted at the outset that European brains, capital, and energy have not been, and never will be, expended in developing the resources of Africa from motives of pure philanthropy." Moreover, he went on to explain how infrastructure and industry had, to his mind, been bequeathed to the colonized:

> By railways and roads, by reclamation of swamps and irrigation of deserts, and by a system of fair trade and competition, we have added to the prosperity and wealth of these lands. We have put an end to the awful misery of these lands, and checked famine and disease. We have put an end to the awful misery of the slave-trade and inter-tribal war, to human sacrifice and the ordeals of the witch-doctor. Where these things survive they are severely suppressed. We are endeavoring to teach the native races to conduct their own affairs with justice and humanity, and to educate them alike in letters and in industry.[3]

This meant that the colonial government's job was "to protect the interest of the merchants and others who are engaged in the development of its commercial and mineral resources."[4] That was the representation. The reality was quite different. J. S. Furnivall argues that the concern for "world welfare" was, in large part, driven by a pragmatic need to paint commercial self-interest "with the warm glow of humanitarianism."[5] Wolfgang J. Mommsen elaborates: "Colonial expansion and imperialism were justified at home above all else by the argument that colonial rule brought civilization, justice and Christian codes of conduct to still underdeveloped regions of the world."[6] As a result of this colonial order, which extracted more from the public interest than it contributed, with national independence new governments sought to reorient economies inward to promote self-sufficiency, equity, and growth.

To do so, officials embraced the New Deal state model, setting up networks of Tennessee Valley Authority–styled public corporations to build roads, rails, water systems, and other basic infrastructure that was a prerequisite to domestic development. In addition, plans were put in place to decrease reliance on foreign goods and expertise. Moreover, many newly independent states also had to address a persistent carryover from colonialism. As a condition to recognizing many new states, previous colonial powers demanded the maintenance of control over oil, gas, and mineral wealth by their companies. This persistent foreign control over natural resources is perhaps unsurprising given the fact that Baron Lugard and likeminded others oversaw decolonization. This managed transition away from colonialism is reflected in the main United Nations Declaration on the matter adopted in 1960. It was entitled the "Declaration on *Granting* of Independence to Colonial Countries and Peoples"[7] (emphasis added). Thus, national independence was *granted* rather than *recognized*. Nonetheless, new governments began to set forth plans for redressing the economic dependence that resulted. Their aims were not very different from our own efforts today to reduce dependence on foreign-controlled supplies of energy or our Buy American efforts.

Faced with a legacy of economic dependence, newly independent states were in a hurry to take political independence and translate it into genuine self-sufficiency. To jumpstart growth, nascent government institutions took control over economic decision-making away from colonial governments. Elected officials conceived economic plans to lay the foundation for self-sufficiency and growth. Government was to "take an active, indeed decisive, role" in economic decisions.[8] It would make investment decisions and create incentives and regulations so as to ensure that domestic and foreign companies advanced public interest aims. Realizing that goals could not be achieved overnight, five- to ten-year plans were put in place.

This overseas version of the New Deal was not qualitatively different from our own approach in the 1930s and then within the postwar boom. The main difference between our own approach and that of the new states was one of presentation. Gunnar Myrdal explained: "Although some Western countries play down what economic planning they have, and try to convince themselves that theirs is a 'free economy,' the South Asian countries tend to play it up, and pretend that their planning amounts to much more than it does." In a hurry, newly independent states were "accepting an idea even before they were able to translate it into reality."[9] At the same time, while planning in the United States was ad hoc, in newly independent states, efforts were made to move swiftly and sweepingly. It was a time of hope and goodwill.

For this reason, new states were "in a hurry." They had to put "the modern infrastructure" in place "in order to mobilize popular support for planning and development." An overriding urgency was widely felt. For this reason, it was not acceptable to "wait for an infrastructure to emerge spontaneously from below." In fact, the main purpose of the new state was to lay this infrastructure that was a precondition to self-sufficiency. The hope of postcolonial governments was itself pinned on the ability to create this foundation. Myrdal explained how, "if a modern infrastructure cannot be created by state intervention," then "there is scant hope of any development at all." As a result, "[t]he sense of urgency is logical." Many feared that the gains of national independence would be overwhelmed by material conditions and seemingly intractable problems carried over from colonialism if this infrastructure policy did not succeed. As a result, the international consensus was that "no choice" existed "but to create the institutional infrastructure by government policy," which would itself lay a foundation for growth.[10]

The stated aim of the United States was to reinforce and advance this agenda, although the Cold War and other geopolitical concerns often clouded, redirected, and undermined those intentions. After hundreds of years in which foreign investments took out more than they contributed, newly independent states were keen to ensure that goodwill and capital were used to lay a sound economic foundation. The United States was a main supporter of this active government role in the economy, even if we did not always admit it.

Myrdal, who was awarded the Nobel Prize for Economics in 1974 for his role in advancing the efforts of these newly independent states to achieve genuine independence, explained how "both private businesses and governments in the West" had great interest in activist governments in these states. If governments abroad set out plans in which U.S. commercial "special projects are fitted," then that would make it "more likely that they will not fail." For this reason, laissez-fairists could contradict "their ideological preferences at home." In fact, the commitment to this approach meant that "[w]here planning" lagged, the United States and its allies sent "experts to help formulate a plan." The drive was so strong that "intergovernmental organizations, governments, private foundations, and universities" were mobilized and "supplied personnel for planning."[11] Infrastructure banks thus played a central role in promoting these Tennessee-style plans.

We carried out our efforts through a series of agencies and international organizations. With our allies, we had established the World Bank in 1944. The purpose of the World Bank was to do for the newly independent countries what the Marshall Plan had done for Europe. That is, the World Bank would create a foundation for growth by lending money and providing expertise to the Tennessee Valley Authority institutions in newly independent states. Dams, roads, railway lines, and water pipes were constructed.

In practice, the World Bank and other infrastructure banks often favored the commercial concerns of fully industrialized companies and Cold War–driven geopolitics over equitable development. As a result, a vibrant international public interest movement emerged. These groups succeeded in driving large-scale reforms to the infrastructure banks, putting in safeguards against displacing communities without adequate compensation, protecting indigenous rights, providing avenues for redress against environmental and social damages, and increasing accountability – much as our New Deal state aimed to ensure that the public interest rather than the Money Trust and robber barons drove investment decisions.

Of course, just like within the United States, the overseas New Deal system did not itself ensure broad-based equal opportunity. W. E. B. Du Bois made a point about the U.S. New Deal situation that was equally applicable abroad, in varying degrees: "In the Tennessee Valley beneath the Norris Dam, where do the Negroes come in?"[12] Likewise, in *Of Mice and Men*, John Steinbeck's character Crooks explained how the American Dream remained illusory in 1937 for many who escaped the Dust Bowl, bound for California:

> I seen hundreds of men come by on the road an' on the ranches, with their bindles on their back an' that same damn thing in their heads. Hundreds of them. They come, an' they quit an' go on; an' every damn one of 'em's got a

> little piece of land in his head. An' never a God damn one of 'em ever gets it. Just like heaven. Every'body wants a little piece of lan'. I read plenty of books out here. Nobody never gets to heaven, and nobody gets no land. It's just in their head. They're all the time talkin' about it, but it's jus' in their head.[13]

Even in the postwar period, the American Dream remained for many, as Langston Hughes explained, *deferred*.[14] Thus, even after Eisenhower's much-celebrated public works road project and the ascendancy of the welfare state, Dr. Martin Luther King Jr. would reiterate Du Bois's point in the midst of the Civil Rights Movement, saying: "The economic highway to power has few entry lanes for Negroes."[15] We must thus be mindful of the inequalities that inhered under the New Deal and import-substitution models. Nonetheless, this reality should be a reminder to take the public interest more seriously.

As these import-substitution efforts got off the ground, governments also began revisiting the persistent colonial legacy of foreign control over oil, gas, and mineral wealth that had carried on into national independence. While national independence successfully asserted the political independence of previously colonized individuals and communities, frequently a condition was placed on international recognition of new states to accept that foreign multinationals maintain control over natural resources. As a result, existing contracts that often bordered on the unconscionable were kept in place. These contracts were referred to as the unequal treaty system.

For instance, it was not unusual for a contract to run for decades and give a foreign company control over resources in large parts of a country. At times, foreign companies controlled all natural resources within a country, including undiscovered oil wells. For this reason, decisions over natural resources mainly benefited overseas firms. Also, companies made decisions about extraction and price that advanced their own interests with little attention to the host country's concerns. It was these types of unequal bargains that undermined self-sufficiency that newly independent states sought to rebalance.

As the market value of these resources increased in the postwar boom without newly independent nations sharing the benefits, governments began to argue for revisiting these unequal contracts. This movement gathered steam and was actively opposed by fully industrialized countries and their extractive firms. Something serious was at stake. Fully industrialized countries depended on these overseas sources of energy and minerals to fuel their own economies and to maintain influence. For instance, the wealth of former colonial powers such as Great Britain was heavily dependent on maintaining postcolonial control over natural resources within its previously colonized countries. These countries were not only dependent on foreign oil, but they had grown used to controlling supply, volume, and price.

However, with commodity prices at their height, the time was ripe for the revisiting of these unequal colonial bargains, and thus a round of renegotiations was touched off. New states banded together to pool resources in the impending efforts to renegotiate. They called their coalition the New International Economic Order. It was very unpopular among previous colonial powers and their oil, gas, and mineral firms. When it became clear that these countries meant business and that they were simply exercising a well-trodden right to control their natural heritage that fully industrialized countries had long advanced for themselves, the renegotiations got under way.

Despite fiery rhetoric and exclamations of moral affronts to the sanctity of contract, many companies made a cost-benefit analysis and decided to renegotiate on mutually agreeable terms, sharing the upside benefits of the resources. Commodity prices were high, and many companies had been enjoying the lion's share of them. So these renegotiations simply meant reaching a mutually beneficial price point. Other companies, either too unpopular to stay or else wanting out, turned to the governments and asked for the present and future value of their investment. The New International Economic Order coalition countered with an offer of present value. This was called the fight over the Hull formula. A number of investor-state arbitrations behind closed doors resulted in a private justice system, with erratic results and no clear consensus about valuation emerging. However, when the dust settled, a dramatic shift had occurred in the control over oil, gas, and mineral wealth.

Then the so-called Third World Debt Crisis hit. Commodity prices fell through the basement; the previously colonized countries found themselves heavily indebted, rather than flush with cash. For many countries, the hopes of a steady equitable revenue stream from their newfound control over natural resources dried up.

It was then that this period of import substitution and domestic self-sufficiency became fully derailed. A series of conditioned bailouts followed, laying the groundwork for not only the dismantling of the national independence New Deal states, but also reorienting economies outward and away from the self-sufficiency model – what became known as export-led growth. Infrastructure banks played a central role. At the same time, however unequal the bargaining power was within these bailouts and renegotiations, many countries created opportunities to rebalance economic power through decades of strategic investment.

When UK Prime Minister Margaret Thatcher and U.S. President Ronald Reagan took charge in the late 1970s and early 1980s, the allies embarked on a systematic dismantling of New Deal states both at home and abroad. Reagan began a decades-long divestment from the domestic economy and a concentration of wealth and privilege among a narrower set of firms and individuals. Privatization moved this agenda forward with the selling off of state assets and properties and the ceding of management control away from the public and toward private firms. After almost thirty years of this Reagan Revolution, we are now left with many of the costs of this movement's excesses and distorted incentives: failed levies, fallen bridges, and a cumulative *D* on our infrastructure report card issued by the American Society of Civil Engineers. However, that is getting several decades ahead of our story. Nonetheless, prominent members of the Democratic Party were critiquing the Reagan Revolution along these lines in the late 1980s.

That said, the basic idea was to divest from our own economy and social state and to promote governments abroad that catered to the needs of our investment banks and large firms. For this reason, in the opening remarks to F.A. Hayek's *The Road to Serfdom*, Milton Friedman praised states like Egypt, Malaysia, and Singapore, with which the U.S. government partnered to offer massive subsidies to American firms. In the same breath, Friedman bemoaned the persistence of state intervention in the economy within the United States, specifically the persistence of President Lyndon Johnson's Great Society programs. Friedman sympathized with President Ronald Reagan's frustrations with an inability to dismantle fully the New Deal state. He had stern words for President George Bush Sr. for promoting the market-distorting Clean Air Act and the Americans with Disabilities Act.[16] In other words, Friedman set out the underpinnings of this post–Third World Crisis approach to the appropriate role of government in the economy: state intervention was desirable when it lured American companies abroad through massive market-distorting subsidies that made outsourcing commercially viable and profitable, but the New Deal's constraints on Gilded Age excess and the basic social contract that emerged from the ashes of the Great Depression were to be dismantled.

Accordingly, in response to the Third World Debt Crisis, the United States and its allies began dismantling not only our own New Deal state, but also the Tennessee Valley system that had arisen abroad in the wake of decolonization. The aim was to replace their Tennessee companies with our own private firms.

This international effort took aim at the import-substitution model. Whereas after independence, governments had pursued strategies to develop internal economies of their own, we argued for a departure. While the goal under import substitution had been to reduce reliance on imports by fostering local production capacity and to discourage dominance by foreign firms that would undermine this attempt at self-sufficiency, the new model took a different approach. The idea was to gear domestic industrial capacity toward meeting the needs of foreign companies. The purpose was to transfer technology away from these companies and into local partners. Although the successes and shortcomings of technology-transfer-premised strategies is a hotly debated topic, China is an example of a country that successfully pursued this approach.

To effectuate this shift, we redirected the international infrastructure banks. These banks shifted away from promoting the Tennessee model and toward advancing public-private partnerships. Rather than facilitate Tennessee authorities, the banks would instead offer subsidies to our companies to create an infrastructure overseas. At the same time, our infrastructure companies and government divested from America's economy. An infrastructure bank–driven effort in turn began to lay the basic foundation of the world factory system that would eventually promote the outsourcing of substantial parts of the U.S. economy. In other words, these overseas investments undermined our own manufacturing base. The argument at home, made by successive presidents and prominent economists across the political spectrum, was that we would compensate for the loss of these jobs by retraining our own workers to fill better-paying and more durable jobs. In practice, our national competitiveness was eroded over time by building state-of-the-art infrastructure abroad for our manufacturing firms while we divested from our own.

Before export-led growth happened in full force in the 1980s and 1990s, a colonial world free port system was in place connecting the global economy in a threadlike web. This system was used basically to ship goods around the world. It had little manufacturing capacity and was not sufficiently linked up as a global network. Few countries had even functioning industrial parks, with South Korea and Ireland being exceptions.

We then used our infrastructure banks and public-private partnerships to transform the colonial free port system into our own world factory system. When the Third World Debt Crisis hit, the infrastructure banks actively funded:

(1) telecommunications lines around the world (making it possible to outsource call centers, to have corporate decision-making spread over secure networks, to facilitate global banking communications);
(2) systematically retrofitted ports around the world to make them interoperable (the container port system was put in place, which made the shipping system possible);
(3) power plants (to make factories run and keep them going as demands increased);
(4) water systems (to, for instance, make the outsourcing of chip manufacturing, which is highly dependent on large flows of water, possible);
(5) financial infrastructure (stock markets were created so that risk could be placed overseas and tax liabilities shifted across multiple jurisdictions); and
(6) transportation (so that manufactured goods could get to ports and flown out of countries).

So, the job of infrastructure banks was to create this infrastructure, transforming a world free port system into a manufacturing one, which is a precondition to the corporate decisions to outsource. It was done systematically, very methodically, and at great public expense. Countless projects and infrastructure bank reports were produced during this pre–world factory system period to advance this restructuring.

For instance, the World Bank explained the need to adapt the colonial free port system into the global manufacturing one. It detailed how "merchandise may be moved in and out" of ports, "stored in warehouses for varying periods and repackaged as needed." However, upgrading ports into factory zones means "provid[ing] building[s] and services for manufacturing." Instead of simply moving goods in and out of a port, a factory zone involves the "transformation of imported raw materials into finished products." Importantly, unlike import substitution, which gears this manufacturing capacity in a newly independent state toward a self-sufficient domestic market, a factory zone is more integrated into the global economy than the domestic one. It is "a specialized industrial zone estate located physically and/or administratively outside the customs barrier, oriented toward export production." The idea is to have the infrastructure banks create the infrastructure "facilities [to] serve as a showcase to attract investors and a convenience for their getting established."[17] In other words, through the infrastructure banks, the United States and its allies built the public infrastructure of outsourcing, and, in turn, fully industrialized countries shed jobs.

As indicated, these zones in the new states were geared toward serving mainly overseas interests. Some were even literally fenced. Guards patrolled their borders. Customs officials studiously charted the flow of goods in and out of the zones. The boundaries were so sharply drawn that factory zones were considered a country within a country. Some commentators even focused on their militaristic aspects, highlighting the fact that zones may be surrounded by barbed-wire fences, "a new form of foreign settlement adapted to the new situation."[18] When I visited a zone in Malaysia that had attracted world-class high-tech firms from Silicon Valley and Seattle, the front door to the zone headquarters was guarded by the military.

Although the colonial heritage of these zones is difficult to miss, the factory zones represent a major retrofit. Zones now aimed to act as segments of multichained manufacturing systems. For this reason, infrastructure banks had to make massive investments. In addition to factory buildings, the infrastructure might include communications lines, electricity, transportation, and waste disposal. Often, as in the case of the electronics industry, outsourcing is only appealing if large-scale investment in power and water infrastructure happens. Also, various secondary services were required such as banks, hospitals, restaurants, and shipping agents.

To create these zones, the infrastructure banks wrote "how-to" reports and books. In fact, a series of institutions such as the United Nations Industrial Development Organization (UNIDO) were created to lead the charge. UNIDO was formed in 1967 and offered assistance in setting up these factory zones. It issued reports, funded feasibility studies, and along with infrastructure banks spearheaded promotional events, dispatching experts around the world. Moreover, UNIDO put out a how-to book for countries wishing to use public-private partnerships to create the infrastructure of zones.[19] The UNIDO book, and others like it, detail the extensive role that the new states were expected to play in order to ensure that overseas investors were guaranteed profits and could offload risks. The United Nations Center on Transnational Corporations offered technical assistance through its Advisory and Information Services Division. UNIDO established the World Free Zone Association to help countries package their zones effectively, producing how-to reports that detailed the best practices in attracting firms.

The idea then was to underwrite these factory zones around the world. Once they had been prepared, a two-step process was detailed. First, the zones must "fill up the vacant space as rapidly as possible." While the international infrastructure banks provided large-scale up-front capital to build this infrastructure, they typically did so through public-private partnerships. This meant subsidizing U.S. firms to build roads, but then making newly independent states responsible for paying off these investments. In other words, the idea is "to recoup the large infrastructure costs" put out by ensuring that "the facilities [were] already in place (water supply, electricity, telephones, access roads, etc.) and the factory buildings already constructed" so that "investors can get their manufacturing operations off the ground in record time" and thus "occupy the territory very rapidly." For this to work, foreign companies must become aware of this outsourcing opportunity. The U.S. government thus offers a range of databases and educational events and opportunities. The idea is then that "the word gets out very quickly in the international community concerned."[20]

Once word gets out, the next stage is where "the real take-off occurs." In other words, the United States and its allies built these zones to cater to their own firms' needs. As a result, "[b]ecause of these sociological links," a wave of outsourcing will happen. The possibility of "'occupying the territory' within a very short term" will be overwhelming.

Importantly, getting this system off the ground depended not only on building this public infrastructure of outsourcing. The U.S. government also had to engage in massive law reform. The Glass-Steagall Act was not revoked to pave the way for a subprime mortgage crisis. The real opportunity that it opened up was financing productive activity overseas. The passage of Securities Regulation Rule 144A lowered the reporting requirement for what are now our TARP banks, so that they could engage in risky P3 investments without letting their shareholders know. Given the fact that many of these investments abroad were backed by the Full Faith and Credit of the United States of America meant that, in practice, Rule 144A increased our public liability. This liability became real when these P3 projects drove the East Asian economies under in the late 1990s, and countries scrambled to rescue essential infrastructure with state pension funds.

In exchange for bailouts, governments were told to downsize their public-sector work force. Moreover, the bailout money was tied to the introduction of another wave of P3 projects. Just as with the post–Third World Debt Crisis P3s, we provided our own public subsidies to the TARP banks and AIG to sweeten the opportunity. We expected the East Asian countries to do the same.

However, this bailout had additional costs. In order to consume the productive capacity being created in East Asia, we had to maintain consumptive power at home. This was a particular challenge as we moved away from a manufacturing economy and toward a service-based one. The solution resulted in the financing of unsustainable levels of personal debt. Our government, banks, and insurance firms promoted a domestic economic model premised on consumption rather than production. We offered the opportunity of home ownership through Trojan Horse subprime mortgages.

We took out debt to drive to work as gasoline prices escalated. Gas tank money went off to the Middle East and then was largely recycled back into the United States. When Dubai ports sought to invest in our strategic Northeastern ports with that recycled gasoline money, we said no. It was against our national security. However, at the same time, our banks welcomed those recycled petro-dollars into their own coffers, as Dubai's investment fund turned around and purchased a 4.9 percent equity stake in Citi for $7.5 billion. In turn, the banks offered us extended lines of consumer debt with that money from the Middle East. Finally, it all fell apart, as we had become increasingly dependent on the logic of an unsustainable transnational public-private-partnership–based economy.

We are now at a crossroads. The international shift away from the quasi-public system and toward the P3 model produced many demonstrable successes overseas. A visit to our Rust Belt makes clear that benefits and burdens were unevenly distributed. In promoting a mix of quasi-public and P3 projects within America, we must be mindful to learn lessons from how certain groups abroad successfully leveraged the projects to produce growth and opportunity. We must also learn from the serious costs both at home and abroad in order to promote a durable New Deal. Successful P3s depend on an ability to use companies effectively to drive reinvestment in America. We turn next to how this role of firms has worked abroad.

8 Companies as Policy Organs

I. Uses and Abuses of Companies

The Introduction made the point that the members of Congress and others aim to model the Obama Bank on the European Investment Bank (EIB). Likewise, Secretary of Energy Steven Chu had, prior to his appointment, advocated the creation of a clean energy bank based on the United States Export-Import Bank (Ex-Im Bank) and the Overseas Private Investment Corporation (OPIC). Each is a public investment bank. While the EIB is a bank formed by several governments, both the Ex-Im Bank and OPIC are U.S. banks. Most countries are members of intergovernmental banks. Every fully industrialized country has its own public investment bank, as do a good number of emerging market countries. The most prominent public investment bank is the World Bank, which was created by the Allied Powers to promote development. Moreover, as we shall see in this chapter, the United States also promotes overseas projects through a range of additional domestic agencies that double as foreign affairs institutions.

Proponents of basing the Obama Bank on these infrastructure banks do not seek to mimic their institutional design in its entirety. Instead, the appeal of these banks is essentially threefold. First, these banks are vehicles for promoting a range of public purposes. Second, banks also engage in cross-infrastructure sector planning, coordinating energy, transportation, and water policies, for instance. This planning typically aims to integrate regions comprising several sovereign territories. Third, although banks have historically pursued projects through a range of vehicles, within the United States, politicians, bankers, and private firms are interested in how the infrastructure banks pursue projects through public-private partnerships (P3s) or leveraging.

Importantly, public investment banks are, without exception, not static institutions. Each has evolved over time. For example, after the Second World War and into the 1980s, the World Bank financed government-carried-out projects rather than partnerships. In the late 1980s, as a part of the larger trend toward P3s, the World Bank reoriented its lending and institutional structure. It created the Multilateral Investment Guarantee Agency (MIGA), which offered insurance to P3s. Also, another of its constituent organizations, the International Finance Corporation (IFC), which has devoted itself to promoting private-sector participation in development since being created in 1956, took on greater prominence. Similar banks that had long devoted themselves to partnerships began to play a greater role in the 1980s and 1990s. Others reoriented their lending programs away from supporting government projects and toward P3s.

This chapter does not provide a formalistic survey of the various banks, their commonalities and differences, and their history and present practice. Instead it focuses on how government banks and agencies use *companies* as policy organs to carry out infrastructure and energy projects overseas. How to create carrots for companies to advance public purposes within P3s is at the core of our concerns.

One of the main purposes of this chapter is to explain how P3 projects internationally have not simply sprouted up on local soil. The United States and its allies devoted substantial public resources to ensuring the profitability of P3 investments. The international experience has been premised upon free market statism, a transnational public-private partnership. For this reason, when we talk about the success of China in building a state-of-the-art infrastructure, we must recognize the role of American corporate subsidies in building projects. Also, as we advocate for a World Bank or European Investment Bank for America or as we create an Export-Import Bank or Overseas Private Investment Corporation for our domestic market, it is sensible to familiarize ourselves further with how these institutions function. They are dynamic institutions with a rich mixed history. As well, the successes of the projects that they support often depend on reinforcing institutions and policies.

II. Doing Things with Companies

Our government uses companies to carry out foreign policy goals. Companies may deliver aid overseas or combat terrorism. At times, a goal may simply be to promote the competitiveness of American firms. Wide-ranging public agencies, including the Department of Agriculture, the Department of Commerce, the Department of Defense, the Ex-Im Bank, OPIC, and the Small Business Administration, call upon companies to do specific tasks. Many sectors of the economy are implicated, from agriculture to high technology and from energy to textiles.

To entice companies, agencies wield a range of carrots. Subsidies take far-ranging forms, and their intensity varies. Support takes on at least eight forms:

(1) advice (expert, policy consultation, security assistance, etc.);
(2) education;
(3) feasibility studies;
(4) financing (grants, guarantees, loans, insurance, etc.);

(5) information and analysis (commentaries, databases, directories, guides, libraries, market profiles, publications, etc.);
(6) legal assistance (compliance, dispute settlement, enforcement, legislative advocacy, etc.);
(7) promotional activities (events, facilitating overseas contacts, high-level advocacy, making markets accessible, missions, opportunity identification, video conferencing, etc.); and
(8) training.[1]

At times, government agencies charge companies for services.

The colonial Levant Company charter of 1600 indicated that company merchants could "place in the top of their ships and other vessels the arms of England in a red cross and white."[2] Certainly, most companies no longer travel waving the flags of their states of incorporation.[3] Nonetheless, today the U.S. government and many of its powerful allies use corporations as foreign policy organs.[4]

Perhaps the highest-profile case in recent memory is the use of companies to reconstruct postwar Iraq.[5] The U.S. General Accounting Office concisely stated the private corporation–oriented approach toward Iraq: "The United States has relied heavily on private-sector contractors to provide the goods and services needed to support both the military and reconstruction effort in Iraq."[6] The controversy that has arisen therefrom relates mainly to the use of private military companies[7] and to the tendering process of two sets of U.S. government reconstruction contracts.[8] It extends to the execution of the reconstruction contracts generally.[9] Our concern here will be with the two sets of reconstruction contracts.[10]

The first was a no-bid award to Kellogg, Brown & Root, a subsidiary of Halliburton, which was the company that Vice President Dick Cheney headed before stepping down to run for vice president.[11] The second contract involved an award to Bechtel, which was invited with seven others to put in bids for non–oil-based reconstruction projects.[12] The Halliburton contract was an indefinite-delivery–indefinite-quantity (IDIQ) contract. These umbrella contracts consolidate multiple orders into a single tender. This only compounds corruption risks in the procurement process.[13] The Bechtel contract at issue is a cost-plus-fixed-fee arrangement.[14] Such contracts are criticized because they do not include an incentive to keep costs down. The U.S. government's Federal Acquisition Regulation makes the point: "This contract type permits contracting for efforts that might otherwise present too great a risk to contractors, but it provides the contractor only a minimum incentive to control costs."[15] The Center for Public Integrity has charted the extensive circulation of officials from the prime contractors to the administration and the numerous campaign contributions.[16] These connections only further reinforce claims that the interests of government officials and these companies are difficult to disentangle.[17]

Furthermore, the U.S. government used Bechtel to fight the counterinsurgency. The second wave of the contracts between USAID and Bechtel inserted an extensive subcontracting regime whereby Bechtel was to award the bulk of its contracts to Iraqi companies and laborers. The logic of this subcontracting regime was that a labor clause mandating local workers within the Bechtel contract would be used to convince Iraqis to join forces with the United States; in other words, these Iraqis would become U.S. workers rather than possible recruits for the insurgency. Importantly, the Iraq reconstruction effort should be understood as an aspect of a military strategy, rather than as a civilian postwar reconstruction effort. When viewed from this perspective, the accountability inquiry takes on a different inflection.

Less high-profile is the extensive use of government loans and insurance policies to subsidize corporate nationals overseas.[18] For example, the U.S. government offers war insurance and reinsurance for commercial marine vehicles. It allows the government to insure vessels carrying out “the interest[s] of the national defense or the national economy.”[19] Ships must be owned by U.S. nationals and be engaged “in essential water transportation or in the fishing trade or industry, except watercraft used exclusively in or for sport fishing.”[20] In 2001, President Bush reinforced this coverage so as to address the attacks of September 11th and how they might impact on commercial vessels in the Middle East. The Presidential Memo on Marine War Risk Insurance Coverage provides:

> Approve the provision by the Secretary of Transportation of insurance or reinsurance of vessels (including cargoes and crew) entering the Middle East region against loss or damage by war risks . . . for purposes of responding to the recent terrorist attacks, whenever, after consultation with the Department of State, it appears to the Secretary of Transportation that such insurance adequate for the needs of the waterborne commerce of the United States cannot be obtained on reasonable terms and conditions from companies authorized to do an insurance business in a State of the United States. . . . I hereby delegate to the Secretary of Transportation, in consultation with the Secretary of State, the authority vested in me . . . , to approve the provision of insurance or reinsurance for these purposes.[21]

Similarly, in response to terrorist threats, the government has provided terrorism risk insurance to its corporate nationals at home[22] and abroad in the case of air travel.[23] In an effort to ensure that government contractors are properly insured, in situations like Iraq reconstruction, the government requires contractors to carry Defense Base Act insurance.[24] This requirement extends to subcontractors, American or otherwise, in Iraq.[25]

Many other U.S. agencies and programs use businesses to conduct foreign policy.[26] These include the Department of

Agriculture (Commodity Credit Corporation,[27] Foreign Agricultural Service[28]), the Department of Commerce (Trade Information Center, Manufacturing and Services Unit, U.S. Commercial Service, BuyUSA Program), the Department of Defense (Defense Security Cooperation Agency's Foreign Military Sales program), the Department of Health and Human Services (Office of International Affairs), the Department of State (Foreign Military Financing Program, Trade Policy and Programs Division, Direct Commercial Sales Program), the Domestic International Sales Corporation,[29] the Patent and Trademark Office, the Securities and Exchange Commission (Rule 144A),[30] the Small Business Administration, the United States Agency for International Development (Commodity Import Programs[31]), and the U.S. Trade and Development Agency. For example, the U.S. Department of Commerce organizes trade missions with select participants from government and the private sector to promote business interests abroad.[32]

Furthermore, the U.S. government may take retaliatory measures against countries that expropriate the property of its corporate nationals.[33] With regard to intergovernmental organizations, the government may respond to expropriations in the following way:

> The President shall instruct the United States Executive Directors of each multilateral development bank and international financial institution to vote against any loan or other utilization of the funds of such bank or institution for

> the benefit of any country to which assistance is prohibited under subsection (a) of this section, unless such assistance is directed specifically to programs which serve the basic human needs of the citizens of that country.[34]

Such a public response to expropriations of private property has been controversial and has its roots in expropriations of U.S. corporate property in Cuba[35] and Latin America.[36]

III. Government Banks

Many U.S. corporate subsidy programs occur in the context of the recent wave of P3s in developing countries and transition societies discussed in the previous chapters. It is important to note, however, that the transnational network of institutions that subsidize these private corporate nationals of fully industrialized countries predates the late 1970s.[37] Government insurance programs are an important example.[38] In fact, the origins of the insurance programs in the postwar period are traceable to the Marshall Plan.[39] It provided insurance for U.S. companies operating under its auspices. This insurance initially covered the risk of dollar incontrovertibility.[40] The President's Committee for Financing Foreign Trade, chaired by Winthrop Aldrich of Chase Bank, came up with the idea for this insurance.[41] With time, this corporate subsidy program was transferred to the Agency for International Development (AID) under its Office of Private Resources, where it expanded such programs considerably. In 1959, these programs shifted their mission solely to offering inducements for U.S. corporations doing business in developing countries.[42]

In 1971, these AID programs were transferred to the newly created OPIC,[43] with strong support from the private sector.[44] OPIC is under the direction of the secretary of state and "mobilize[s] and facilitate[s] the participation of United States private capital and skills in the economic and social development of less developed countries and areas, and countries in transition from nonmarket to market economies." Specifically, it "conduct[s] financing, insurance, and reinsurance operations." OPIC may also participate in the "identification, assessment, surveying and promotion of private investment."[45] It aims to have "positive trade benefits for the United States."[46] OPIC is a public corporation; however, its board is made up of both public and private officials.[47] Eight of the fifteen directors come from outside the government. Of these "[a]t least two" must "be experienced in small business, one in organized labor, and one in cooperatives."[48] This requirement is reminiscent of the Defense Department programs discussed in the Chapter 3. Much is made of the fact that OPIC operates on a self-sustaining basis. However, this should not obscure the fact that its guarantees are "backed by the full faith and credit of the United States."[49]

At its inception, the idea of OPIC was subject to controversy relevant to our concerns. It was an effort to remake foreign assistance so as "to reflect new priorities and new directions – primarily the increased use of private enterprise in development."[50] For example, in a House of Representatives report on the legislation proposing OPIC, congressmen John C. Culver, Benjamin S. Rosenthal, Edward R. Roybal, and Jonathan B. Bingham argued that "U.S. investment has come to be viewed too often as a form of economic colonialism which extracts more than it contributes." For this reason, "[b]efore the U.S. Government enters the business of supporting the export of American capital, it should assure itself that each project is both commercially feasible and beneficial to the long-range development goals of the country." They worried that OPIC would undermine foreign aid objectives, instead of "be[ing] guided by business motives." These "interests of U.S. business" they argued, "are not necessarily congruent with the needs of the developing countries or with U.S. interest." They worried that "[a]dditional problems will arise through an increased identification of the U.S. Government with business interests." As a result, they argued, "[f]oreigners, suspicious that U.S. motives in the developing world are solely to support private American business, may well see vindication of their views in the activities of a separate corporation largely run by business." American private enterprise, they underscored, might ultimately not benefit from the "public image implications" and "additional stigma of being subsidized by the U.S. Government and of having come at its behest."[51] Representatives H. R. Gross, Edward J. Derwinski, and J. Herbert Burke tied the OPIC subsidies to a broader approach: "Over the years foreign aid has been used to help industry, the farmers, and labor as well as to subsidize professors who are otherwise ungainfully employed. So maybe we should not be too surprised that OPIC wants to cut in some bankers and businessmen on this round for a piece of the foreign aid pie."[52] Members of the Senate Committee on Foreign Relations argued "that the free enterprise system was subverted when the Government, in effect, underwrote foreign investment risks."[53]

OPIC is required to abide by environmental and worker rights standards and also by social development objectives in the projects that it finances. It does so through its Office of Investment Policy, which reviews projects[54] and works with the U.S. Department of State's Bureau of Human Rights and Labor.[55] The country in which the supported project is located must at least be "taking steps to adopt and implement laws that extend internationally recognized worker rights."[56] This requirement can be waived in situations the president determines are "in the national economic interests of the United States."[57] With regard to worker rights, contracts generally include the following clause:

> The investor agrees not to take actions to prevent employees of the foreign enterprise from lawfully exercising their right of association and their right to organize and bargain collectively. The investor further agrees to observe applicable laws relating to a minimum age for employment of children, acceptable conditions of work with respect to minimum wages, hours of work, and occupational health

> and safety, and not to use forced labor. The investor is not responsible under this paragraph for the actions of a foreign government.[58]

OPIC also holds public hearings to decide whether projects should continue to be supported[59] and to give an opportunity for interested members of the public to be heard.[60] OPIC hears complaints about projects through its Office of Accountability, which is geared toward problem-solving and compliance review.[61]

A public interest–oriented evaluation of the evolution and current practice of OPIC not only would require pronouncements of institutional purpose but also would need to scrutinize real-world practice. Such an evaluation has not been undertaken. At the same time, OPIC's social commitments have been the subject of intense and ongoing criticism from nongovernmental organizations. This criticism echoes earlier congressional concerns. However, it now goes further, focusing not just on the advisability of corporate subsidies generally, but also on encompassing the human rights and environmental practices of OPIC-subsidized projects.

Another government organization important in promoting the interests of U.S. businesses abroad in the P3 context and beyond is the U.S. Ex-Im Bank, which fosters the international competitive advantage of U.S. firms vis-à-vis foreign corporate nationals. The Ex-Im Bank aims to "aid in financing and to facilitate exports of goods and services, imports, and the exchange of commodities and services" abroad and "to contribute to the employment of United States workers." To do so, it has the powers of "authorizing loans, guarantees, insurance, and credits."[62] Among other things, the Ex-Im Bank aims to promote the interests of small U.S. businesses.[63] At least one of the president's five appointees to the Board of Directors must be "from among the small business community and shall represent the interests of small business"[64] and at least three members from this community must sit on the Advisory Committee.[65] Similarly, OPIC offers special treatment to small businesses.[66]

The Ex-Im Bank also predates the recent wave of P3s. It dates back to 1934, with the Roosevelt administration's Depression-era efforts to encourage ties with the Soviet Union and to address the failure of the banking sector to finance exports.[67] It is the result of the merger of two banks: one directed at Soviet trade and the other at Cuba. The bank quickly broadened its scope.[68] Then-President Franklin D. Roosevelt underlined its function "to aid in financing and to facilitate exports and imports and the exchange of commodities between the United States and other Nations or the agencies or nationals thereof."[69] William H. Becker and William M. McClenahan, Jr., tell us that "[o]rganized American exporter and banker groups applauded the founding of [the bank]."[70] Many countries have similar banks, some of which predate the Ex-Im Bank, such as banks in Germany, Great Britain, France, Italy, and Japan.[71] These banks both compete with one another and coordinate their subsidies for multinational consortium-based commercial endeavors.[72] Although coordination is an increasing reality, it is important not to lose sight of the fact that the background norm is competition based. The Ex-Im Bank coordinates its activities also with private banks.[73]

Many export credit agencies belong to the International Union of Credit and Investment Insurers, the Berne Union, which dates back to 1934 and includes both governments and companies.[74] The Organization for Economic Co-Operation and Development also has a division devoted to the work of national export credit agencies.[75] Export credit agencies are allowed some freedom under the World Trade Organization regime[76] and have been subject to their own informal "gentlemen's agreement" since 1978.[77] At times, their activities have come under scrutiny from nongovernmental organizations, many of whom have formulated the Jakarta Declaration for Reform of Official Export Credit and Investment Insurance Agencies.[78]

IV. Intergovernmental Banks

The United States does not act solely through national agencies. More broadly, through intergovernmental organizations, the government uses companies to carry out foreign policy goals. This happens in many ways. For instance, regional and international development banks offer subsidies to corporations. Likewise, the International Monetary Fund (IMF), the Bretton Woods Institution charged with overseeing the international financial order, through its conditionalities, advances policies that promote the entrance of such companies into developing country markets. Also, U.S. government representatives to multilateral development banks are, for example, to report potential procurement opportunities to the secretary of the treasury, secretary of state, and secretary of commerce so as to encourage U.S. companies to take advantage of these international inducements.[79] The U.S. government joins these organizations in part to promote the interests of their corporate nationals, as do other governments.

In 1988 the World Bank Group established MIGA to insure P3 investments. The idea for such an agency can be traced back several decades;[80] however, governments were skeptical about whether the interests that they advanced through domestic insurance agencies like OPIC would be preserved through the introduction of such an intergovernmental organization.[81] For example, they feared competition between their own agencies and MIGA.[82] Its aim is "to encourage the flow of investments for productive purposes among member countries, and in particular to develop member countries." To do so, it offers the following inducements for companies:

(a) issue guarantees, including coinsurance and reinsurance, against non-commercial risks in respect of investments in a member country which flow from other member countries;

(b) carry out appropriate complementary activities to promote the flow of investments to and among developing member countries; and
(c) exercise such other incidental powers as shall be necessary or desirable in the furtherance of its objective.[83]

MIGA insures against a host of risks, including currency transfer, expropriation and similar measures, breach of contract, and war and civil disturbance.[84]

The United States sought to influence the early activities of MIGA so as to conform to a series of commerce-related and human rights–related goals. Because MIGA is essentially an organization devoted to subsidizing corporate activity, these goals should be understood as shaping the nature of the interface among governmental and intergovernmental action and the promotion of U.S. corporate enterprise. Specifically, the United States sought to discourage the issuing of guarantees on proposed investments that would

(1) be in any country which has not taken or is not taking steps to afford internationally recognized workers' rights to workers in that country;
(2) be subject to trade-distorting performance requirements imposed by the host state that are likely to result in a significant net reduction in –
 (A) employment in the United States or other member countries or
 (B) other trade benefits likely to accrue to the United States or other member countries from the investment or

(3) increase a country's productive capacity in an industry already facing worldwide capacity for the same, similar or competing product, and cause substantial injury to producers in another member country.[85]

MIGA is an institution established to shift international assistance toward the privatization model and coincides with a move away from financing state-based projects within the World Bank.

The IFC is another World Bank Group institution devoted to promoting corporate activity in developing countries through which the United States uses corporations as foreign policy organs. It was established in 1956. The IFC's overall aim "is to further economic development by encouraging the growth of productive private enterprise in member countries, particularly in the less developed areas."[86] It does so by working with private companies in a number of ways:

(i) in association with private investors, assist in financing the establishment, improvement and expansion of productive private enterprises which would contribute to the development of its member countries by making investments, without guarantee of repayment by the member government concerned, in cases where sufficient private capital is not available on reasonable terms;

(ii) seek to bring together investment opportunities, domestic and foreign private capital, and experienced management; and

(iii) seek to stimulate, and to help create conditions conducive to, the flow of private capital, domestic and foreign, into productive investment in member countries[87]

Importantly, unlike other World Bank Group institutions, MIGA and the IFC directly aim to promote private investment in developing countries.

At times, U.S. government involvement in overseas commercial activity through intergovernmental organizations has been tied to environmental and human rights conditions – the result of effective environmental and human rights campaigning. For example, MIGA and the IFC must incorporate such conditions into their subsidy practices. The IFC has guidelines in this regard that have become the industry standard. Claims against IFC and MIGA projects may be brought to the compliance advisor ombudsman within the World Bank Group.[88]

More broadly, "[t]he United States Government, in connection with its voice and vote . . . shall advance the cause of human rights."[89] This requirement covers U.S. participation in several intergovernmental institutions: the AfDB, ADB, European Bank for Reconstruction and Development, IDB, World Bank institutions, and IMF.[90] The secretary of the treasury is responsible for reporting on all loans considered by the international financial institutions "to the Chairman and ranking minority member of the Committee on Banking, Finance and Urban Affairs of the House of Representatives, or the designees of such Chairman and ranking minority member, and the Chairman and ranking minority member of the Committee on Foreign Relations of the Senate."[91]

Furthermore, the Pelosi Amendment of the International Development Finance Act 1989 aims to tie U.S. involvement in projects through multilateral development banks to respect for the "environment, public health, and the status of indigenous peoples in developing countries."[92] The Pelosi Amendment addresses the failure of multilateral banks "in some cases to provide adequate safeguards for the environment, public health, natural resources, and indigenous peoples."[93] The safeguards have an economic rationale; "sustainable resource use and consultation with affected communities" should be used "where costs could be reduced."[94] Importantly for our purposes, the Pelosi Amendment was amended in 1997 to make clear that it applied to loans made by the international banks to private companies,[95] clarifying also that International Finance Corporation–financed private projects would be included.[96]

These regulations dictating the nature and form of U.S. government involvement in overseas private commercial activity must be judged not only by their pronouncement. They derive their meaning ultimately from social practice. Studies of such practices are few. Furthermore, in at least one instance, the spirit of the Pelosi Amendment has been undermined in a project financed by the Inter-American Development Bank. That project, the Camisea natural gas pipeline in Peru, was funded by the bank despite human rights and environmental objections. These objections had initially been voiced in the context of an application for loans within the U.S. Export-Import Bank, which denied funding. Most commentators attributed the declination to environmental problems with the project. At the same time, Philip Merrill, the chairman of the Ex-Im Bank, simply referenced "situation specific" concerns, making clear that the bank still is "interest[ed] in financing U.S. exports for energy projects throughout the world."[97] Despite the inability to garner support from the Ex-Im Bank, when the project sought financing through the IDB, such concerns resulted in an abstention by the U.S. board member to the bank, rather than in a U.S. veto, which would have been in line with the Ex-Im Bank's denial and perhaps the spirit of the Pelosi Amendment.[98] Nonetheless, it is important to stress again that our knowledge of the use of corporations as foreign policy organs is limited. Assessments are at this point mainly impressionistic. Furthermore, the fact that governments and companies collaborate with one another should not itself be sole grounds for condemning the resultant public-private enterprise.

V. Conclusion

When Congresswoman DeLauro announced the infrastructure bank legislation on May 20, 2009, she declared that the bank would be modeled after the EIB. Advocacy for the EIB as a model also emerged out of the Commission on Public

Infrastructure at the Center for Strategic and International Studies, which was co-chaired by Rohatyn and then-Senator Warren Rudman.[99] This commission played a driving role in creating the Dodd-Hagel bank legislation.

Perhaps the most important lessons concerning the EIB are to be learned from how to balance region-wide policies with national development concerns. The EIB seeks to advance both of these through its TEN-Ts program, which seeks to create a Europe-wide transportation infrastructure encompassing roads, bridges, airports, waterways, and rail projects. Much has been accomplished by the EIB at the regional level. Emulating successes with rail are important and essential, albeit with the recognition that in practice the EIB has shown a bias toward roads, sometimes to its own consternation.

At the same time, it is also essential to learn from some of the difficulties that the EIB has encountered in advancing the TEN-Ts program. For example, because the EIB gives more weight to regional goals than to national development ones, this has meant that important regional projects were unworkable because the national goal was not sufficiently thought through. As a result, national politicians could not justify expenditures on certain key regional projects. One can certainly imagine that this will be a predictable issue in many states; certainly, difficulties convincing citizens and legislators that the payoff of pursuing P3s is sufficient have frustrated many project planners, including government and private-sector champions.

The most important aspect of public banks is their ability to define a coherent thought-through public policy. This planning function is essential for our own infrastructure bank. Of course, our experience with using companies to accomplish goals within a P3 project is mixed. Success has also depended not only on isolated infrastructure bank policies. Transnational P3s result from law and policies in many countries. Deal structures depend on tax laws abroad and often major regulatory overhauls at home. In fact, reforms to public finance law can have greater influence over a nascent P3 market's growth than the creation of an infrastructure bank. We next turn to a discussion of P3 transparency, specifically how to address the fact that even successful projects must not only benefit from convergences of interests but also must contend with serious conflicts. To do so, we draw not only on international experience with P3s, but also on our domestic one.

9 Transparency

I. "Electric Light the Most Efficient Policeman"

A central theme of this book has been how policy-makers promote infrastructure banks and P3s as an effective way to advance public values. In doing so, they point to the banks as exemplars of forward-looking planning that make effective use of companies to accomplish goals. Increasingly, these international banks and P3s are presented as inherently progressive institutions. For instance, at a 2007 Roundtable with then–Treasury Secretary Henry Paulson, California Governor Arnold Schwarzenegger set out the basic argument that we are as likely to hear from former Vermont Governor Howard Dean or Pennsylvania Governor Ed Rendell as from former Florida Governor Jeb Bush or former Speaker of the House Newt Gingrich:

> As we have seen in Europe very successful public-private partnerships, we have seen it in British Columbia and in Vancouver, where they have wonderful public-private partnerships, or P3s as I call it, where trade is happy, the trade unions are happy, the private sector is happy, the politicians are happy, the people are happy. So, it's a win/win situation. That's what we want to do also in California.[1]

These unqualified bipartisan endorsements of the international infrastructure banks and P3s as win-win propositions not only paint in primary colors, but they also distort the picture. Moreover, they impede grounded discussions of how to model an accountable institution and projects.

The accountability problems are aggravated by the fact that we are getting off on the wrong foot with them in two ways. The first wave of U.S. P3 deals since the 1980s was mainly tax-shelter schemes, a series of Sale-in, Lease-out arrangements and tax-depreciation road contracts. This class of P3s has accountability problems built into its DNA and is prone to degrading public assets rather than cultivating them.

Because we invest in P3s as groups and also, like mortgage debt, slice, dice, and recombine their debt, the cost of a bad investment can be high. Infrastructure funds that hold large numbers of P3 projects may permit arrangers and certain investors to opportunistically enter and exit. This investment structure can destabilize funds or even drain equity out of them. Moreover, P3 projects have relied on credit ratings from Moody's or Standard & Poors and on underwriting from insurers like AIG, much like mortgage-backed assets. Furthermore, at times, governments have both implicitly and explicitly guaranteed investments.

In other words, a decision made in Manhattan to pursue a tax-sheltered P3 will likely impact on Bakersfield, and vice versa. The second problem with our recent bullish foray back into P3s through the American Recovery and Reinvestment Act (ARRA) is that we have made them essentially exempt from accountability. The approach to P3 accountability is out of sync with Obama's basic axioms as set out in the book's Introduction.

As discussed in previous chapters, ARRA has two parts: cash payments (in Division A) and tax incentives (in Division B). Discussions of the stimulus mainly reference the Division A shovel-ready projects and treat Division B as comprising tax breaks. However, Division B is full of tax-incentive-driven P3 bonds, not simply tax cuts. But the law and the president's memorandum promoting accountability and limiting permissible lobbying for stimulus projects only provide oversight of the direct grants in Division A. No meaningful federal oversight exists over the projects under ARRA's P3 tax incentives. The Presidential Memorandum flatly states in Section 4: "(b) This memorandum does not apply to tax-related provisions in Division B of the Recovery Act."[2] These are accountability-exempt P3 bond issues.

Division B authorizes generous new tax credits and tax-exempt borrowing. It will have a major impact on the Treasury, influencing spending priorities, and will set the stage for the next wave of our recovery. Monitoring is essential. Federal oversight should leave considerable discretion to state and local governments. However, the scale of the tax subsidies counsels against a hands-off approach. Oversight is especially necessary under the provisions that encourage P3s.

The law repeals the Alternative Minimum Tax for private-activity bonds issued between 2004 and 2010. The first beneficiaries are P3s arranged over the last five years. The first question here is: What is the public interest justifying a retroactive subsidy to P3 projects initiated under the previous administration? In other words, what were the Bush administration's public interest purposes driving P3s during that period, and on what grounds are we deciding to reinforce them? Similarly, who are the individual and corporate beneficiaries of these government-subsidized ARRA bond proceeds?

The second class of projects implicated by the retroactivity provision are those that the economic crisis put on hold. Division B has already started to reactivate these projects. For example, shortly after ARRA's passage, the Port of Oakland announced a $700 million P3 port development deal, and Florida made public a $1.8 billion Interstate-595 road partnership. The law also authorizes $15 billion of tax-exempt bonds to encourage investment in distressed areas and in high-speed rail.

Simply putting these projects under the existing law's oversight is not the answer. Accountability for P3s requires vigilant monitoring of private firms as well as governments. Furthermore, the time frame is wrong. Tax subsidies facilitate long-term, large-scale P3 investments, rather than the short-term projects envisaged by the law's direct grants. The accountability provisions sunset in September 2012, but most P3s will not have fully started by then. Federal action is necessary to ensure accountability in the form of either a second Presidential Memorandum to govern Division B or the extension of an infrastructure or clean energy bank's jurisdiction over them.

Without public accountability, P3s are prone to abuse as discussed at various points throughout this book. Accountability and oversight must extend to P3 bond provisions in ARRA as well as to the infrastructure and energy bank–supported projects. Both international and domestic experience with P3s demands a specific type of accountability.

This chapter proposes an approach to accountability with American roots. It is the concept of transparency put forward by Justice Louis Brandeis. President Barack Obama draws from Justice Brandeis in devising his own approach to transparency when he argues that sunlight is the best disinfectant. However, when it comes to P3s, other aspects of Brandeis's approach become important; specifically, transparency must also incorporate the "electric light [of] the most efficient policeman"[3] making clear the interests at stake. Moreover, transparency must not only be reported on a Web site, it must also be publicized more broadly.

Furthermore, the approach to P3 accountability must be tailored to how projects are actually structured. P3s raise particular challenges. For example, the oversight board created to monitor ARRA is not attuned to monitoring P3s. First, it will wrap up before many of the bond-oriented projects are fully under way. The average Build America Bond runs for twenty to thirty years. Also, the oversight board does not bring banks, firms, subcontractors, ratings agencies, insurers, and other vital participants adequately under its jurisdiction.

The current law requires a state or local official to sign off on spending projects. This is not enough. The law should make subsidies conditional on oversight of subcontracting and transparent accounting by private partners and service providers. Also, as we transition away from an ARRA regime, it is essential to have in place a public investment bank. This bank must not only be forward-looking in its investments. ARRA and related projects should be brought under the orbit of the bank so as to promote both accountability and coordinated planning decisions.

As argued in the Introduction, this book proposes a mega-bank that brings all infrastructure and energy projects that are driven by federal subsidy under its jurisdiction. A mega-bank would address the balkanization of planning and accountability. Coordination and centralization of authority are necessary when it comes to accountability. Bringing projects within the bank's jurisdiction will combat a tendency within P3s to cherry-pick investment-grade projects and thus balkanize planning and prevent the ability of the government to use profitable projects to cross-subsidize non–commercially viable valuable and essential social equity–producing projects. The importance of retaining this rent-control aspect of the state, wherein the revenue-generating projects cross-subsidize essential but unprofitable ones, is particularly important when it comes to P3s. For instance, when a government transfers a profitable project like parking meters into a partnership one, it weakens its own portfolio of state-owned assets. As a result, a government's credit rating and ability to raise general obligation debt may suffer.

In addition, as this chapter makes clear, our infrastructure bank must address the fact that P3s are moored not only in government policy, but also in the same network of finance – insurers, rating agencies, TARP banks – that contributed to our crisis. This book's Introduction argues that one of the main purposes of recapitalizing the TARP banks and rescuing AIG was to use them as instruments to promote the public interest through their participation in P3 projects. This reinvestment strategy must be predicated on a realistic assessment of the risks inherent in this approach. Accountability depends on addressing such risks, not glossing over them as win-win partnerships.

Accountability throughout a project's life cycle is essential; this includes the planning stage. Projects suitable for P3s often have broad national impact. In fact, the purpose of the infrastructure and energy bank P3s is to promote national and regional goals. Those who benefit from projects are typically eager to move forward. But the federal government must mandate public participation to be sure that those with a financial interest in the outcome do not dominate decision-making. This possibility is aggravated by how the infrastructure and energy banks are presently being envisaged.

Transparency attached to federally subsidized state and local borrowing is a novel concept. Under current practice, the government provides tax subsidies but does not approve individual bond issues. If a project goes wrong, the federal authorities may prosecute individuals for fraud and corruption, but the Treasury does not seek to recover the value of misspent tax benefits. The pairing of accountable grants and accountability-exempt bonds in the stimulus law highlights this asymmetry. All projects that benefit from the stimulus ought to be transparent and accountable, whatever the subsidy. To make transparency backward-looking embraces a concept of forensic accountability that is not suited to progressive public interest–minded planning.

Not only must ARRA's scope be expanded and its institutional approach to accountability be transformed to address the special issues raised by P3s, but the philosophical underpinnings of the emerging approach to accountability must be revisited. It is not appropriate to P3s. Chapter 4 set out the concept of free market statism that underpins our approach to reinvestment. Accountability under this approach depends on a clear articulation of the public interest, which must in turn drive not only government but also private-sector decisions. Our status quo approach to P3s and reinvestment focuses mainly on holding the government partner to account, albeit in limited ways.

President Obama aims to bring accountability to our recovery mainly by promoting a concept of transparency that he attributes to the turn-of-the-century Supreme Court Justice Brandeis. The idea is to make the work of government visible: "We will launch a sweeping effort to root out waste, inefficiency, and unnecessary spending in our government, and every American will be able to see how and where we spend taxpayer dollars by going to a new website called recovery.gov." Obama credits Brandeis with setting forth this approach to transparency: "I firmly believe what Justice Louis Brandeis once said, that sunlight is the best disinfectant." This concept of transparency, according to Obama, "is not only the surest way to achieve results, but also to earn back the trust in government without which we cannot deliver the changes the American people sent us here to make."[4] While Obama's long-standing commitment to transparency in government advances accountability aims, it misses another central point that Brandeis was making, tailored specifically to P3s.

The intention here is not a sophomoric reminder to our president to read more closely. Instead, something significant is at stake with how we conjure Brandeis on transparency. When Justice Brandeis crafted his concept of transparency in the midst of the Gilded Age, he was speaking to P3-related issues. It is important to stress that this parentage of Obama's concept of accountability is rooted specifically in an attempt to address the systematic undermining of the public interest by nineteenth- and early-twentieth-century P3s. That is, Brandeis's disinfectant remarks were aimed directly at the need for transparency when it came to P3 railroads and other public works sectors. Moreover, Brandeis's prescriptions in turn formed a foundation of our New Deal regulatory state. The New Deal itself grew up in part as a way of asserting public interest–based control over a toxic P3 system. Brandeis did not direct his transparency prescription simply at making government more accountable. He set his sights on the undue influence of P3 financiers on our public interest.

Brandeis was condemning the concentration of public-private power within America that the P3 railroads reinforced. He quoted President Woodrow Wilson at length to make clear what was at stake when discussing transparency:

> President Wilson has said wisely:
>
> "No country can afford to have its prosperity originated by a small controlling class. The treasury of America does

> not lie in the brains of a small body of men now in control of the great enterprises. . . . It depends upon the inventions of unknown men, upon the originations of unknown men, upon the ambitions of unknown men. Every country is renewed out of the ranks of the unknown, not out of the ranks of the already famous and powerful in control."[5]

In other words, the purpose of transparent accounting of the interlacing of private and public control over our society and institutions was to combat the oligarchizing of our democratic society. Equal opportunity and national economic health was at stake. Furthermore, as with Bernini's sculptural depiction of David, Brandeis argues for a concept of accountability in which the line between spectator and participants is eroded. Transparency is an instrument in ongoing struggles over who controls the public interest. And, as with Bernini, Brandeis is clear: the battle is underway and Goliath is not yet slain.

For this reason, when P3s are introduced today to move infrastructure decision-making away from the earmark system and toward projects being made on the merits, it is imperative not to lump together a deeply flawed earmark system with a rich American tradition of participatory accountable public interest–oriented planning. Thus far, certain P3 advocates have done just that. The idea is to recreate a private procurement system with its own accountability rules.

It is not just a case of throwing the baby out with the bathwater. Instead, some P3 planners set their sights on the corruption and inefficiencies associated, to their mind, with not only the earmark system but equally with environmental and labor regulation and equity-oriented development. All are at times viewed as inefficiencies of the present system. Under this approach, participatory planning is reformulated as a financial risk to the interest of planners, a risk that must be mitigated at the least possible cost to the project's commercial interests. The international model that we are redirecting on our domestic economy sees aspects of the public interest as risks to be mitigated. By reformulating public interest concerns as risks to project profitability, financial institutions in effect domesticate the common good.

In 1913, in the midst of the Gilded Age, Justice Brandeis wrote *Other People's Money: and How the Bankers Use It.* Brandeis was writing about early efforts to regulate bankers who had concentrated power over large swaths of the American economy. Brandeis thought that these financial oligarchs were subverting the public interest through their control over the supply of money. One of Brandeis's main targets was the nineteenth- and early-twentieth-century P3 railroad financers; he used the example of JP Morgan's control over the New York, Westchester, and Boston railroads, as well as the New Haven line, Portland Terminal Company, and the Maine Railroads. They were, according to Brandeis, extracting excessive profits for personal gain from basic social infrastructure.

Brandeis set his sights specifically on the bond issues for these projects, presaging ARRA Division B bond projects.

Brandeis argued for P3 bond accountability. In other words, Brandeis's disinfectant point was explicitly tailored to P3 bond issues, the most nontransparent aspect of today's recovery.

These Gilded Age P3 bankers were charging excessive service fees to arrange deals. Brandeis argued that the only rationale for service fees in the context of the P3 railroads was if the bankers were shouldering risks proportionate to their fee structure: "A large part of these underwriting commissions is taken by the great banking houses, not for their services in selling bonds, nor in assuming risks, but for securing others to sell bonds and incur risks."[6] However, the bankers' involvement, Brandeis argued, aggravated risks rather than lessened them. As a result, bankers were using their monopolistic control over the flow of money to extract tolls from those who wanted access to it.

In this context, Justice Brandeis strongly urged making the interests and strategies of these oligarchic bankers transparent. Brandeis made the point that "[p]ublicity is justly commended as a remedy for social and industrial diseases." Brandeis continued: "Sunlight is said to be the best of disinfectants; electric light the most efficient policeman."[7] Brandeis then went on to underscore the importance of publicity. He did not believe that publication of neutral data was the aim. Sunlight itself would not necessarily reveal the interests behind the data. Moreover, understanding the interests behind P3 deals was a precondition to assessing whether they should go forward in the first place; Brandeis firmly embraced forward-looking rather than forensic accountability.

Brandeis explained the danger of the partnership structure of P3s and related financial schemes involving banking oligarchs. In doing so, he spoke using the metaphor of "[t]he battlefield," which had to be "surveyed and charted." The idea was to identify the "hostile forces" and ensure that they were "located, counted and appraised." This was what Brandeis had in mind as "a necessary first step – and a long one – toward relief." For Brandeis, this interest-based concept of transparency would, in turn, be "[t]hat potent force" in the "impending struggle" and thus "be utilized in many ways as a continuous remedial measure."[8] In speaking about accountability in the language of interests and struggle, Brandeis was conjuring the most influential legal theorist within New Deal thought: the nineteenth-century German law professor Rudolph von Jhering, whose refrain that social change was not an abstraction pervaded the law reviews at the time. Instead, change was interest-based, an earthly struggle, "a struggle, a struggle of nations, of the state power, of classes of individuals."[9] The fact that Brandeis was tailoring his vision of disinfectant accountability to P3s makes his approach particularly relevant for our purposes.

With regard, then, to the P3 railroad bonds, Brandeis pointed to known excesses by JP Morgan in its issues. However, he also made the point that the commissions being charged were largely nontransparent: "The aggregate commissions or profits so taken by leading banking houses can only be conjectured, as the full amount of their transactions has not been disclosed, and the rate of commission or profit varies very widely."[10] Today's service fees on P3 bonds, when they do occasionally become public, are likewise disproportionate to the services on offer. Moreover, efforts by financial institutions to structure P3s so as to make them amenable to large service fees have recently come under attack.

Christopher J. Ailman, the Chief Investment Officer of the State of California's Teachers' Retirement System, recently critiqued this practice: "We never felt that the 2-and-20 fee is appropriate for what we want to do with infrastructure." Here, Ailman was referring to a fee system whereby a 2 percent service charge is tolled for financial management and 20 percent on performance. Essentially, like the tax-haven-driven P3 deals, this approach sets up an incentive to engage in short-term investment strategies. Ailman went on: "Infrastructure should be a 10- to 20-year investment." The fee-driven approach or general partnership model, "where you make money and get out," is not appropriate.[11]

Moreover, the fee structure creates an incentive within the finance community to create a bubble. For instance, when the P3 market first heated up in the United States after the Iraq War, as Carlyle Group, Babcock & Brown, and Goldman Sachs created funds to invest in projects, a mini-bubble was created. Kathryn Leaf Wilmes, who is a principal at Pantheon Ventures Inc., explained how: "There was a bit of a bubble with some groups overpaying and overlevering assets."[12] This drove a market exuberance in which false projecting of the future value of the market drove pricing structures. When fee structures are tied to a percentage of asset valuation, it can create an incentive to cultivate an asset bubble. Brandeis made a point still applicable not only to P3s but also to our subprime mortgage crisis: "It is to extractions such as these that the wealth of the investment banker is in large part due."[13] Our financial crisis is a cost of these extractions.

We are now exempting the service providers and financiers of P3 projects from almost every accountability oversight. However, Justice Brandeis urged Gilded Age P3 railroad accountability by "compel[ling] bankers when issuing securities to make public commissions or profits they are receiving." Such a prescription could be readily carried out with recovery.gov. The use of the Web as a disinfectant and an instrument of publicity could be pursued in tandem with Brandeis's horse-and-buggy solution: "Let every circular letter, prospectus or advertisement of a bond or stock show clearly what the banker received for his middleman-services, and what the bonds and stocks net the issuing corporation." Such publicity, according to Brandeis, was also an indication of the safety of a P3 investment, a measure of banker confidence in the infrastructure project. Furthermore, "[i]f the bankers' compensation is reasonable, considering the skill and risk involved, there can be no objection to making it known."[14] The same goes, I would argue, for every service provider involved in a P3 project. Furthermore, disclosure must extend to all facets of P3s, including insurance policies underwritten by AIG and others as well as the basis of ratings issued by Moody's and Standard & Poors.

In fact, public interest organizations such as United States Public Interest Research Group (PIRG) have been on the forefront of promoting greater disclosure and a meaningful accounting of P3 projects. Dr. Phineas Baxandall, Senior Analyst for Tax and Budget Policy at U.S. PIRG, explains the approach: "Our position is that private uses of public funds and public assets should receive at least as high level of scrutiny than if functions were purely public. Our presumption is that everything should be open record and publicly disclosed." In line with Justice Brandeis's approach to disinfecting Gilded Age P3s through sunlight, Baxandall underscores: "A key thing has been not to exempt 'proprietary' information, or to make strict conditions and time limits for what can be called proprietary so it isn't just a way for companies to shield documents from public scrutiny."[15] Like Brandeis's sunlight-as-a-disinfectant approach, the PIRG concept of accountability is attuned to the interests standing behind the deals. Furthermore, PIRG consistently argues that the availability of this information is a precondition for evaluating whether deals should move forward – a cornerstone of Brandeis's concept of transparency.

Federal efforts at advancing transparency are limited. As the U.S. PIRG example underscores, meaningful accountability is largely driven by public interest groups. It must be forward-looking not forensic. P3 planners typically oppose efforts at deliberative participatory decision-making. Thus, P3 accountability is largely a forensic exercise. The astronomical service fees charged for the ill-considered Chicago Skyway airport P3 deal, which ultimately did not go forward, netted the following fees for service providers:

Legal Services	
Mayer Brown	$2,107,299
Pugh Jones	$462,482
Katten Muchin	$100,000
Sanchez & Daniels	$43,000
Financial Advisors	
Goldman Sachs	$8,400,000
Loop Capital Markets	$300,000
Cabrera Capital Markets	$300,000
Gardner Rich	$252,080
Professional Services	
David D. Orr	$1,580
Causey Demgen & Moore	$4,950
JP Morgan Institutional Trust	$6,600
TOTAL	**$11,977,992**[16]

What seem to be excessive fees here might be indicative of the shortcomings of the deal itself. However, these fees were not disclosed until after the deal fell through and are thus an example of forensic accountability. Significantly, the publication of the fees resulted initially not only from a commitment to good governance by P3 planners. Instead, public interest groups successfully drove the Aldermen to push for their publication.

At worst, P3s reinforce a preexisting tendency within free market statist approaches to allow the tail to wag the dog. In the case of P3s, this approach means ceding public policy-making over our reinvestment to not only the Treasury Department, but also to TARP banks, AIG, sovereign wealth funds, and credit ratings agencies. As this chapter describes, these private institutions are the main protagonists of P3s and thus the target of efforts to hold projects accountable. Treating partnerships as win-win propositions comes across as inappropriately naive, even if, one hopes, it masks tough behind-the-scenes bargaining.

Brandeis himself was not concerned with accountability as an abstraction or generalized concept; instead the aim was to address a concentration of shared power between bankers and a set of politicians. Like his cohorts, Brandeis aimed to put the public interest back in the driver's seat.

The series of substandard P3 deals into which state and city governments have entered over the last twenty years with strong federal government encouragement is a case in point. At this point, however, it is worth noting that many cities, states, and federal agencies do not presently have the requisite expertise and institutional capacity to evaluate P3 arrangements, let alone champion their use.

International infrastructure banks have not always been progressive accountable institutions. Moreover, many of the common good–promoting aspects of these banks have resulted from concerted efforts by public interest organizations. The leadership of the international infrastructure banks and the drivers of P3s have often resisted accountability. So, although Governor Rendell rightly promotes the leveraging aspect of banks, it is important to address the broader experience to ensure that we learn lessons from both the good and shortcomings. Rendell and others would be best served by a deeper canvassing of experience.

Infrastructure banks have evolved into more accountable institutions as a result of public interest group efforts. At the same time, standard practice for international banks throughout much of their lives has been to: bypass citizen participation in basic planning decisions, not take the negative environmental or social impact of projects seriously, displace communities without adequate compensation, and offer no redress for local communities negatively impacted by projects. Local communities around the world have fought hard to make banks live up to their lofty ideals.

Over the last twenty-five years, large numbers of campaigns have been mounted in different countries, sectors, and specific projects. It is widely considered one of the most mature and successful areas of public interest advocacy, particularly in the extractive and infrastructure P3 sectors. A number of widely read books and papers have detailed successes from the creation of the World Commission on Dams, to the infrastructure bank safeguard policies extending now to private banks and companies, to the numerous tribunals within the World Bank and regional development banks devoted to providing a forum for project-affected communities, to the Alien Tort Claims Act litigation in U.S. federal courts with mirror litigation now not only in fully industrialized countries but also increasingly in developing ones such as Ecuador. As a sign of the prolific public interest group successes, the practice field has far outpaced our knowledge about how it operates.

Public interest successes have focused on both internal and external governance. Advances in internal governance policies include increased transparency, accountability, and democracy/participation. Also, infrastructure banks have reformed policies toward gender of staff, board reform, complaint response system, and disclosure of payments to governments. External advances have been made to projects, debt relief, and structural adjustment. Projects encompass extractive industries (oil, gas, mining), power, dams, and transportation. Public interest groups have campaigned successfully for policies increasing the respect of projects for concerns such as displacement, environment, human rights, participation, indigenous rights, dispute resolution, and information disclosure.

Efforts have resulted in many substantial changes to the governance of infrastructure banks and specific P3 projects.

At times, prominent members of Congress, such as Speaker of the House Nancy Pelosi, have championed these efforts, making clear to investors and international infrastructure bank leadership that the United States will not tolerate the use of P3s to evade public accountability. Our infrastructure bank must incorporate these governance advances.

Moreover, while the European Bank has successfully promoted integrated transportation networks in many ways, it has not excelled where good governance has been concerned. The international experience with P3s offers a warning against such an approach. In most parts of the world, P3s were introduced in conjunction with diminished project accountability. In many situations, leaving public accountability mechanisms at the door was a condition placed on flowing capital into infrastructure projects through P3 vehicles. As a result, control over project policies moved to investment banks, insurance firms, and ratings agencies.

The European Bank's planning decisions in Central and Eastern Europe have been mixed. For the most part, beyond a thin watchdog function, citizen input is relegated to decisions to pay tolls for roads. This exclusion of citizens from the early stages of projects means that infrastructures start off with a serious democratic deficit. Moreover, participatory planning is a basic non-negotiable American value not universally shared around the world or always across the Atlantic.

Instead, the European Bank adheres strongly to what anthropologists call the "fire-fighting" approach to P3s; that is, don't worry about causing a mess now, we'll clean up later. This approach to the U.S. infrastructure market is already too prevalent among private investors. It places participatory planning and sustainability in opposition to private commercial interests.

For example, KPMG and the *Economist* Intelligence Unit recently issued a report: "The Changing Face of Infrastructure: Frontline Views from Private Infrastructure Providers." This survey of private-sector executives working on P3s (28 percent U.S.-based) advanced the position that: "Political, social, environmental gridlock is suffocating the infrastructure deal flow pipeline."[17] In fact, another study surveying the P3 market by the leading law firm Freshfields Bruckhaus Deringer related: "The most striking finding is that the US has by far the highest proportion of projects – 62.1 per cent, or $106.5bn – still stuck in the pre-approval stage."[18] Forty-seven percent of those surveyed in the KPMG study took the position that "sustainability concerns"[19] were getting in the way of their aims and thus impeding projects from moving out of the planning stage.

When we talk about approaches to infrastructure that pit commercial expediency against sustainability, it is always worth keeping the levies of New Orleans, the I-35 bridge in Minnesota, and our drinking water in mind. Recklessness, as a public policy choice, has serious human costs.

This position, which makes democracy and sustainability oppositional to investment decisions, was reinforced recently by an editorial in an industry journal, *Infrastructure Investor*. It explained how local pension funds should hire professional managers to "provide political cover." It explained how "public pension funds are already subject to distracting political influences." These democratic demands by the principals of pension funds must be undermined by the managers, according to *Infrastructure Investor*. The best way to do this is by hiring a fiduciary, or professional manager, "to defray these influences." While the idea of investing in local projects that directly benefit pension fund principals "makes for great politics," according to the journal, "it glosses over the fact that the seller requires a high price and the buyer a low one." When principals make claims on their agents, it is good policy to hire "a professional asset manager." That way, when decisions are made to subvert the interests of pension fund principals, the professional "manager can be accused of driving a hard bargain." It is all the better to "withstand political demands that local pension money be concentrated on local projects." In fact, subverting the directives of principals should be done "unapologetically."[20]

Rather than view citizens as partners within P3s, the European Bank sees their participation as costs to be mitigated. For instance, at a government-industry meeting in Paris shortly after the terrorist attacks of 2001, I sat in a workshop run by the European official who devised their cost-benefit approach to community participation. He drew a cost curve for a classroom of investment bankers and lawyers that started as a flat line and slowly and mildly sloped upward. He went on to explain how the European Bank–driven P3 projects only incur citizen costs as projects mature. If citizens start to complain effectively, then the cost curve of the project will gradually go up. In other words, the idea is that the European Bank is to rush ahead full steam without any accountability or citizen participation. Then, if citizens mount effective campaigns to have their concerns heard after projects have been steamrolled through, the European Bank will respond in the most cost-effective way to minimize the impact of those concerns on the P3 project. The least-expensive way of minimizing the impact of community concerns on project profitability will be pursued, even if it means sidelining citizens rather than addressing their underlying concerns about project equity.

For decades, citizens have agitated effectively, transforming infrastructure bank institutions dramatically. The Obama Bank must canvass these banks from the perspective of citizens impacted by projects, rather than simply from the perspective of service providers and financiers who have benefited from them. Thus far, the discussions of the infrastructure and clean energy banks make no mention of these citizen-driven efforts. In fact, hard-fought accountability gains have been largely excised from the discussion. This oversight is reflected in the intense wave of P3 contracts in the United States since the Iraq War.

II. Summary

This chapter described the central role that public interest groups have played in driving more accountable equitable infrastructure banks and P3 projects. The aim was four-fold. First, accountability is a prerequisite to an equitable durable reinvestment strategy. For this reason, basic accountability policies must be adapted from the international experience and built into our own institutions and projects. Within international infrastructure banks and P3s, participation of public interest groups has driven progressively accountable durable projects.

Second, in the nineteenth and early twentieth centuries, America and the rest of the world experimented with unaccountable P3 railroad projects. As a result of the serious social, labor, and financial disasters, accountability devices were put in place across the nation. We are now engaged in a systematic law reform effort in America that overturns many of these accountability safeguards. If this wave of law reform is done hastily and without deliberation it may be tantamount to having repealed the Glass-Steagall Act. Moreover, our first wave of P3 projects has been moored in many of the financial innovations that drove the growth and then demise of our mortgage market.

Third, the presentation of P3 accountability in the U.S. context as a nonissue because of the win-win nature of the approach is a naive projection of joviality on what must be hard-nosed bargaining. The United States is gaining an international reputation among financiers as the jurisdiction of choice, where the sweetest deals are on offer. It is not only viewed as the least risky place for capital, but it also is evolving into a market in which the government underwrites private risk.

Moreover, the win-win approach ignores a serious difficult accountability issue lying at the heart of the P3 approach. As the next chapter explains, P3s are not bilateral arrangements between the government and a private firm. Instead, P3s bring together TARP banks, AIG, Moody's, and sovereign wealth funds. Projects are highly leveraged and can be backed by the full faith and credit of the United States. Moreover, it is likely that a sizable percentage of P3s will go under or seriously stumble. As a result, we may find ourselves with toxic P3 assets sliced and diced throughout the international financial order. This risk is palpable. In addition, many American pension funds are increasingly tied up in P3 projects. If we are to go down this leveraged route for drinking water, transportation, and winter heating, we must assess and mitigate risks effectively.

Fourth, a basic injustice is done when we treat international infrastructure banks and P3 projects as models of accountability when in fact they have at times undermined many of our most cherished national values. The U.S. government has often been at the forefront of reforming these international institutions when confronted with the reality of the severe environmental damage caused as well as the undermining of indigenous rights perpetrated throughout

introduction of P3s into infrastructure sectors through technical assistance, tied aid, and loans and insurance policies. Host governments were often receptive because they faced substantial infrastructure needs and possessed limited financial liquidity. Many countries had large budget deficits that made tax-payer or sovereign loan–financed infrastructures not practicable.[1] Here, project finance provided access to international pools of capital through off-balance-sheet financing, which made projects possible. Through project financing, lenders relied on revenue generated from user charges of projects rather than on government payments.

On the normative level, fully industrialized and developing countries together argued that P3s were driven in large part by the inefficiencies of public infrastructure companies. In countries transitioning away from communism, these arguments took on particular salience. Some made the case that P3s mitigated corruption risks.[2] At the same time, P3 projects have often been criticized for alleged corruption in the tendering stage.[3]

Projects are carried out predominantly through specific contractual techniques. Regulations are also important, but they play a secondary role. In fact, contracts are sometimes viewed as *de facto* regulatory regimes. Significantly, contractual-based projects also often involve executive-based power.

Projects are generally governed by an overarching concessionary agreement. However, for a large project, a cluster of more than forty contracts may formalize arrangements among the numerous actors involved. The company formed to carry out the project is itself the product of a series of contracts.[4] Furthermore, infrastructures, regardless of sector, touch upon wide-ranging legal subject areas from labor, to construction, to intellectual property, to finance, to licensing. As a result, a single overarching concessionary contract tells only one part of the legal picture. In addition, the institutions charged with carrying out the agreements and regulating the infrastructure project give meaning to the nature of agreements and how they operate in practice.

This chapter highlights key areas of infrastructure law. It does so with an eye toward not only international norms and best practices, but also specifically with a concern to how legal instruments can serve the interests of the United States. To do so, it provides: (1) an overview of the legal context; (2) a discussion of model laws; (3) guidance on subsidy decisions; (4) a discussion of select aid-enhanced projects; and (5) a series of recommendations.

II. Overview of Legal Context

Major projects throughout the world are generally carried out through concessionary contracts, meaning that the government cedes a mix of ownership and control over a public activity to a private-sector entity. This agreement formalizes relationships among a range of parties over the project life cycle from contract award, construction, and operation, to maintenance. Concessionary contracts include a range of types. However, legal treatise writers have not spent time systematically evaluating whether certain types are inherently better suited than others to specific sectors, projects, and circumstances. Thus, little guidance exists for the United States as it seeks broadly applicable appropriate contract choices. In fact, one lesson of contract choice is that it is of secondary importance. In other words, contracts do not serve their intended purpose of holding projects together across the board, regardless of type. The next chapter, in fact, argues that contract clauses may be more significant.

Nonetheless, this section provides guidance drawn from available evaluations. In doing so, it avoids making claims about general correlations between concession type and sector, mainly because of the absence of systematic reliable data.

One study of independent power projects (IPPs) in developing countries and contract types presents project failure and success as determined by host country involved rather than contract type. Eric Woodhouse argues that power projects have been successful in Thailand, the Philippines, and Mexico. In contrast, he argues that experience in China, Argentina, and India has been less rosy. He hypothesizes:

> Across our country sample, the most important factors appear to be: (1) some kind of constraint on government behavior stemming from domestic institutions, (2) more developed *domestic* legal framework for private investment, and (3) some factors that sustain the government's financial

> viability (either relatively less severe economic crisis, a financially viable electricity sector, or project factors that reduce government exposure to currency and other economic risk).[5]

However, in conclusion, Woodhouse remains largely critical of contract as a means for effectively mitigating risks. Certainly, contracts do not eliminate risk. Thus, the management of risk is ultimately subject to a variety of extralegal factors.

It is nonetheless suggested that flexibility and local content are important factors in maintaining projects in the power sector. Woodhouse argues:

> However, legal outcomes (contract stability) are not an effective way of evaluating country or project performance. We make this argument for two reasons. First, almost all IPP contracts are altered in some way, and these alterations do not preclude a positive outcome for the project as a whole. Second, government commitment to refrain from arbitrary or opportunistic expropriation should not be measured by raw legal outcomes, but by the overall ability of the government to manage IPP commitments credibly.[6]

For our purposes, it is important to highlight that many cities and states do not always possess the local financial and government capacity to make projects strongly local in content.[7]

Countries such as Malaysia have had success in doing so because of an ability to grow local capital markets and a state pension fund capable of keeping projects going in time of crisis. For example, Malaysia used conservative projects to help launch local capital markets. It also bailed out projects during the East Asian currency crisis through strategic use of its state pension fund. Thailand, China, and India have also demonstrated an ability to infuse projects with local content.

The main distinguishing feature among concessionary contracts is a differential mix of ownership and control over the project life cycle. On one end of the spectrum, the lease grants a private company control over an infrastructure for a fixed term. On the other end of the spectrum, the government cedes both ownership and control over an infrastructure project through a Build-Operate-Own arrangement. Many intermediary contractual forms exist between these two extremes. Variegation in the ownership-control configuration over the project life cycle is the main difference among contractual forms. The next chapter explains how Iran has used a series of service contracts to mimic a P3 arrangement.

The most discussed contractual arrangement is the Build-Operate-Transfer (BOT) agreement, with its use in Malaysia's North-South Expressway being the first East Asian project and the Channel Tunnel connecting the United Kingdom and France the most talked about fully industrialized one. Both projects have faced difficulty recouping sunk costs through user charges.[8] In the North-South

Expressway example, serious pressure was placed on the project as a result of protests among users and pressure from parliament.

However, since most project finance deals rely on users to pay down projects, the difficulties engendered are by no means unique to BOT arrangements. In times of economic downturn, projects fail, because the user base has reduced financial capacity. For this reason, the East Asian crisis resulted in failed projects throughout the region. Both the post 9/11 crisis and the present downturn also have resulted in problems with generating user fees. Governments that turned to international financial institutions such as the World Bank for relief showed themselves less capable of localizing projects effectively.

Ensuring project profitability may also depend on government subsidies when poor communities are the anticipated users. It is important to note that relying on poor people to pay down investments has its own set of difficulties. These problems will no doubt be increasingly prevalent in Millennium Development Goal P3 projects unless these infrastructure investments quickly produce multiplying effects. Both the World Bank and United States advocate P3s to build infrastructures for the urban poor.

As the name suggests, under the BOT arrangement the project company builds the project, operating it long enough to recoup costs and garner an agreed profit, before transferring the infrastructure back to the government. The appeal of this arrangement is that the government only involves the private sector for a limited term. BOTs were first used in Turkey within the power sector, facilitated through the passage of a specific law.[9] Preference for the BOT form may have more to do with its popularity and buzz among lawyers and its promotion by international financial institutions than by it necessarily being the optimal arrangement to allocate control.

Effective government support for BOT projects is often a prerequisite to their success, as with China's experience.[10] The United Nations Industrial Development Organization (UNIDO) makes clear in its instructional book that government must play an active role in BOT projects. In the Philippines, the private-sector participants in the power sector, which had pursued BOT contracts, became the subject of intense domestic distrust and anger.[11] Another variation of this arrangement, the Build-Own-Operate-Transfer agreement was used by Oman to pursue its Al Manah independent power project. This contractual form was chosen because it provided access to foreign capital and mitigated completion risk effectively.[12]

One rationale for contract types that transfer ownership to the private sector is that they may encourage companies to take a long-term interest in projects. In addition, ownership might be ceded in situations in which a government does not want to be involved in a project because of inefficiencies in state-owned enterprises.

The concessionary contract is meant to restructure what commentators refer to as the obsolescing bargain developed by Vernon. Eric J. Woodhouse explains:

> Much of the literature on managing risk for long-term investment has viewed these risks through the lens of the "obsolescing bargain." This seminal model posits that negotiating leverage in a large private infrastructure project shifts during the project life cycle. Initially, the government needs private investors and thus offers attractive terms. Once operational, the investors require a long amortization period to attain their expected return while the host government has already secured what it needs; the original bargain has become obsolete. Theory predicts that the host will force a change in terms – either by outright nationalization or by squeezing revenue streams as far as possible. As the incidence of wholesale expropriation declined, subsequent development of the original obsolescing bargain hypothesis primed analysts to be wary of subtler attacks on project value, so-called "creeping expropriation."[13]

Of course, not all projects create valuable underlying infrastructure assets as presumed by this model. Nonetheless, an important task of the contract is to establish a set of durable relationships that take into account the tendencies of actors to behave strategically and in a self-interested way over a project's life cycle.

The task of an attorney is to advance the strategic interests of his or her client. Successful advocacy depends not only on knowledge of client needs, but also on an understanding of customary practice and the interests pursued by other parties to an agreement. For this reason, effective legal counsel is a precondition to successful negotiation. The overarching concession might be justified based on its ability to hold the project together over time. As a result, lawyering geared toward facilitating deals rather than shepherding a project from conception to completion may be inefficient.

Throughout the life cycle of any project, participants seek to enter and exit a project for a fixed purpose. For this reason, the contract must be viewed as a nexus of interests, rather than as a neatly ordered system whereby the contract form itself determines how all of the actors fit together and relate to one another. As discussed later, this need to hold projects together and the difficulty of law in serving this function in practice raise distinct challenges for countries experimenting with new regulatory and contractual approaches to projects. For example, project debt might be sold by an investment bank, shifting the ownership/control arrangement dramatically and possibly undermining incentives built into the project.

The main treatises on infrastructure project law are descriptive, providing a menu of concessionary types. This menu comprises a mix of acronyms differentiated from one another in how the ownership/control configuration evolves through the project life cycle, for example, BLO, BLT, BOO, BOOT, BTO, DOT, ROL, ROO, and ROT.[14] These treatises offer little guidance to project participants for choosing among the menu of contractual options. Rather than hypothesize why such advice is not forthcoming, this section offers reflections for U.S. government officials on how to approach contract choices.

The overarching concessionary contract is put in practice through a cluster of secondary contracts. This cluster coordinates the range of actors involved in a project. Tamara Lothian and Katherina Pistor argue that the viability of projects depends on effective coordination of the parties that are subsidiary to the concessionary agreement but nonetheless contractually conjoined. These parties include not only the host government, but also local investors, lawyers, and community organizations.[15] This task may be particularly difficult for a small local government in situations in which the foreign bank or company has better access to legal counsel and in which interests may diverge over time. The experience of projects across sectors and contract types makes clear that all parties must aim not only to have infrastructures be built and maintained; parties must also prepare for the possibility of renegotiation and failure.

Coordination is also an important issue domestically. For example, "a private telecommunications provider in Zimbabwe in the 1990s had a license awarded to them by the Supreme Court, but were simultaneously branded as an illegal operation by a presidential decree. Huge delays resulted as this issue was being sorted out."[16] In Malaysia, P3s were subject to interbranch controversy. Ultimately, executive dominance at the expense of the judiciary's power dissuaded project renegotiations as a result of domestic discontent. For example, the North-South Expressway faced opposition from the parliament.[17] In Bolivia, the government was unable to keep its promises to Bechtel and ultimately turned into an antagonistic party.

In addition, successful projects are often tied to executive branch coordination of an infrastructure portfolio. If infrastructure projects are justified in part on their ability to catalyze larger societal economic development strategies, such as the Marshall Plan and the New Deal, then having the infrastructures within the portfolio coordinated is important for many reasons. These will be discussed later. However, for present purposes, it should be noted that governments should devise an infrastructure plan, detailing the rationale not only for individual infrastructures, but also thinking through how each project will be coordinated. This includes not only ensuring multiplying effects and density of networks, but also making sure that each project contributes concretely to overall development strategies.

As we shall see, Malaysia put in practice this coordination through its Multimedia Super Corridor plan in a highly effective way, resultant in part from the inclusion of infrastructure projects in an overall development plan. Likewise, Singapore's economic success has depended on careful infrastructure policy. Similarly, Japan's technopolis program has worked because of infrastructure planning. The infrastructure bank concept in the United States is premised on a recognition of the need for planning.

The Wild West mentality produced in situations of liquidity and appetite for P3s must be tempered. The shift away from quasi-publics and toward P3-based ones must not be an excuse to forego careful planning. Gunnar Myrdal's work on the rationale for infrastructure projects within state economic plans is equally relevant for P3s. Myrdal stressed the importance of a coordinated plan to use capital effectively to finance particularly large infrastructure needs in emerging economies.

We also see examples of successful planning in infrastructure projects tied to extractive endeavors. For example, this coordination harks back to colonial-period efforts to bring metals to ports. In many African countries, the Chinese government facilitates the coordination of infrastructure and extractives projects through package deals to governments. The extent to which host governments can use these extractive and infrastructure packages to deliver on larger coordinated infrastructure efforts that directly contribute to diversified local economies is a difficult but important coordination task. Great controversy currently exists over promises by the Chinese government to contribute to such government plans in Africa, both in writing and in practice.

At the international level, coordination is also significant. Coordination between the donor community and local governments is necessary to ensure that projects are sustainable. For example, USAID has provided assistance to many Egyptian water projects to build capacity. Likewise, donors may help to finance feasibility studies for countries considering P3s. The same goes within the United States, as we see with the efforts to coordinate the building of a high-speed railway not only across states but also even challenges within California itself.

For an ambitious multicountry infrastructure, coordination requires tremendous political and commercial will. For example, the Fiber Optic Cable Link Around the Globe (FLAG) required tremendous intergovernmental coordination with the private company carrying out the project. To link up more than twenty jurisdictions, FLAG had to touch down physically in many countries. This required a license from each jurisdiction. Importantly, executive branches often have discretion over these grants. Licenses thus raise concrete political risks. The U.S. Export-Import Bank provided political risk insurance to the project. One risk was that a government would grant and then revoke a license. In the FLAG case, this risk was concrete, as one jurisdiction – under customary practice – granted a license based on not responding to faxed requests. In projects like FLAG and other transnational infrastructures, it is important for governments to assess their domestic benefits from cessation of licensing and linking up more broadly.

For example, the call center network has been made possible by these transnational information infrastructure projects. Similarly, the construction of airports through P3s has also been essential to making export-led growth possible. Likewise, the European expansion into Central and

Eastern Europe brings with it financing for integration projects in power and transportation. Importantly, in situations such as these, it may be that interests diverge or are at least prioritized differently by parties. For example, the EU prioritizes integration over national development in its infrastructure investments.[18]

Differences in priorities still affect African countries, because the legacy of colonialism was an infrastructure that pointed toward metropolitan power rather than toward African neighbors. Similarly, for many years, transnational cables financed by fully industrialized countries put in place differential pricing structures that disadvantaged developing countries. Within the United States, the cross-state infrastructure networks are not even throughout the country. Moreover, states with sparse populations are likely to have the ability to generate less toll revenue for a road project. For this reason, P3 projects will be more prevalent in denser population areas barring compensating subsidies.

Similarly, constituencies within countries may be differentially affected by these integrationist projects, from laborers in Western Europe to U.S. unions that face increased competition as a result of infrastructure build. Other issues include the tying of infrastructure assistance to particular technologies that create a path dependency that may last for decades. Fully industrialized countries such as the United States are facing this issue in Florida with the introduction of European tunnel technologies for the Miami Tunnel P3 project.

Intergovernmental coordination is also achieved through the participation of host state export credit agencies. The examples of effective use of political risk insurance packages to sweeten deals and lessen risks for project participants abound. Moreover, this coordination can take on new dimensions when multiple export credit agencies participate in projects together and also in cases in which MIGA also contributes. It is widely thought that the use of foreign government agencies in projects not only sweetens financial terms, but also provides informal government assistance in resolving disputes. For example, MIGA is viewed by some practitioners as bringing with it an implicit promise that the World Bank will smooth over difficulties and facilitate negotiations to lessen risks of project disruptions and failures. Thus, the presumed model of ECA competition coexists with coordination.

Along these lines, the participation of a federal infrastructure bank in a project may lessen the risk of project failure or renegotiation. The bank's guarantee structure might result in this lessening. As well, infrastructure bank officials may be effective informal arbitrators of disputes.

Also, secondary contracts are important internationally. For example, within the reconstruction of postwar Iraqi projects, a large network of subcontracting agreements were seen as essential for facilitating local support for projects. Here, the second wave of Bechtel contracts was carried out through subcontracting agreements comprising more than

80 percent of the overarching contract.[19] In contrast, the reconstruction of infrastructure in New Orleans was only minimally conditioned on such local labor input requirements.

In addition, after 9/11 with the drying up of capital markets internationally, attorneys well-versed in Islamic finance law and legal techniques were able to tap a more liquid source of capital. For projects throughout the Middle East, knowledge of Islamic finance techniques and the contractual devices that accompany them are prerequisites for attorneys.

As well, China's Three Gorges Dam with its massive scale and large numbers of investment bankers, companies, and government entities involved means that the project can only be usefully understood through a massive number of contracts with a weblike arrangement. As projects revise and renegotiate at times, new contractual and regulatory instruments enter the scene.

One of the main purposes of an infrastructure contract is, based on an assessment of risks, to allocate the responsibility for mitigating risks onto the shoulder of the party best able efficiently to mitigate them. Risks are far-ranging and include:

Political Risks: political support risks, taxation risks, expropriation/nationalization risks, forced buy-out risks, cancellation of concession risks, import/export restrictions, failure to obtain or renew approvals, delays in approvals, conflicting authorities, public-sector monopolies, bidding risks

Country Commercial Risks: currency inconvertibility risks, foreign exchange risks, devaluation risks, inflation risks, interest rate risks, financial closure risks

Country Legal Risks: changes in laws and regulations, law enforcement risks, delays in calculating compensation, judgment enforceability risks, transparency risks, stabilization risks, arbitration award enforceability risk, inappropriate legal structures for project finance, legal challenges to project awards, changes to contracts and approvals

Development Risks: bidding risks, planning delay risks, approval risks, transnational risks, resistance/protests by interest groups (unions, civil society, etc.), failure to complete supporting infrastructure, unforeseen delays (archeological, environmental, etc.)

Construction/Completion Risks: delay risk, cost-overrun risks, re-performance risk, completion risk, *force majeure* risk, loss or damage to work, liability risk, failure to meet performance specifications, default by contractors or equity holders, strikes, demonstrations, war, sabotage

Operating Risks: associated infrastructure risks, technical risks, demand risk (volume and price), cost escalation risks, management risks, *force majeure* risk, loss or damage to project facilities, liability risk, supply risks, payment risk[20]

Risks are assigned to the project company, insurers (public, private, foreign, and international), contractors, host government, and investors.[21] No systematic study has broken down the relationship between contract type, risk definition and allocation, and impact on a project.

Regulatory risks are often a concern of foreign investors. The Stanford Global Projects Legal Counsels' backgrounder makes the following argument:

> Government regulations with regard to price, entry into the industry, quality of service and so on can affect the success of a private infrastructure project. Private investors may be subjected to detailed industry regulation that may hamper profitability. If host authorities can control price settings, volume or the service that is provided, this could potentially constitute a large risk to the private investors. Unclear rules regarding property rights and lack of regulation can also lead to problems. Unclear land titles for instance could lead to a situation wherein the rights to the land are contested after the private investor has embarked on the project. Addressed more broadly, as governments have moved from owning and operating infrastructure utilities to regulating private sector utilities providing such service, they have attempted to create new "independent" regulators as part of the project's legislative framework. However, the creation of such new regulatory institutions has been quite slow, and as a result, private sector infrastructure suffered from the "immaturity" of the regulatory regimes to which they have been subjected.[22]

For foreign investors, however, regulatory risks are not altogether straightforward. At times, a government might benefit from a discretionary executive power.

In modeling a regulatory agency, Luis Andres, Jose Luis Guasch, and Stephane Straub set forth a number of criteria for measuring autonomy. These include:

> Decision-making autonomy measures the likelihood that regulatory decisions are based on technical as opposed to political criteria. This dimension has three aspects. The first aspect is independence of appointment, which measures the extent to which the appointment process avoids a purely political appointee without adequate technical knowledge of the sector. The second aspect is duration of appointment, which indicates whether a regulator can be reappointed and hence might be less likely to act independently and issue professionally and technically based decisions. The third aspect is collegiality of decisions, which measures the relative difficulty of regulatory capture, thought to be lower when multiple regulators act jointly within a board structure.[23]

Related regulatory risk may result from regime change. Renegotiations may be part of a larger change in government. For example, the Dabhol plant in India was threatened when a new government came into power that was decidedly less friendly to the investors.

The tendering stage also involves a number of risks. Although discussions about tendering risks typically center around corruption and transparency issues, other important risks exist. For example, if a project involves highly technical work, then a government must sufficiently specify technical aspects of the project in the tender. Otherwise, multiple companies might bid on a project assuming different technical approaches, making the project bids difficult to weigh against one another. For example, a Central American highway project rehabilitation failed because bids did not specify road type and surface. As a result, the highest court ordered a re-bid.[24] At the same time, one purpose of a competitive bid is to encourage multiple competing technical solutions. Importantly, competitive bidding has also been tied to greater incidence of renegotiations.[25]

While the responsibility for mitigating specific risks may be shouldered by certain parties, insurance schemes are also put in place as a backstop in the event that a payout is required as compensation for the failure to effectively mitigate a risk. In other words, a contract might place the onus for mitigating a political expropriation risk rightly on the host state government's shoulders. Similarly, the host government might be contractually responsible for shouldering the risk of nonenforceability of an international arbitration award. However, if the host state fails to mitigate these risks, then the ability of another party, such as the investment bank financing the project, might be directly and substantially affected. As a result, an insurer might provide a payout according to the terms of its agreement with the bank. At the same time, the realization that risk mitigation, project success, and insurance are intertwined creates an incentive among project participants to work together to mitigate risks.

International law firms are generally responsible for allocating risks through contract. Countries and companies draw from the same pool of law firms. Lawyers are mainly affiliated with elite firms in the United States (New York and Washington, DC) and the United Kingdom. The practice area is referred to as global project finance or P3. John Flood argues that the small number of firms and the market dominance of U.S. and UK lawyers are tied to the dominance of investment bankers from these jurisdictions in financing infrastructure projects globally.[26] He argues that the networks linking bankers and firms result from common university affiliations and historical linkages between banking institutions and law firms dating back to the post–World War II Marshall Plan. Flood made this observation in 2002. Since then, the financing patterns of infrastructure projects have changed dramatically, moving increasingly toward sovereign wealth funds and hedge funds. However, an impressionistic review of major deals suggests that the law firms have maintained the strength of their position.

Although law firms are obviously significant conditioners of contract choice, it is also worth noting that legal and accountancy decisions may be primarily determined by banks and companies. That is, service providers might be brought in to formalize deals and to provide paper.

From the perspective of small jurisdictions within the Untied States, the overarching purpose of an infrastructure contract is to produce high-quality and affordable infrastructure. These cities have greater needs and less capital and technological expertise than wealthier parts of the country. Governments must thus choose contractual forms tailored to this particular set of circumstances.

A number of rules of thumb might be set out regarding how to think about the cessation of control to private firms.

First, governments must assess their overall infrastructure portfolio. This involves both prioritizing projects from a development perspective and determining which projects are likely to be profitable and which more speculative. One of the risks of P3 is that it may reduce the ability of government to cross-subsidize projects. As a result, governments must think carefully about how to make strategic use of their infrastructure portfolio.

A main reason for using private firms to carry out greenfield (new-build) projects is the private willingness to shoulder risk. Because of budgetary constraints, a private firm might be better able to attract finances to pursue a risky project. For this reason, in return for the risk-taking, the private firm captures upside profits from a successful project. This scenario is one in which a government will cede greater control. In contrast, for a less-risky project, one would expect the government to capture the upside benefit in greater proportion. It is this risk/return ratio that should govern government decisions in the first instance, rather than the advancing of subsidies to lessen risks.

Because a government's infrastructure portfolio may be diverse in terms of profit potential, it must think about how to cede and maintain control across projects. This militates against adopting P3s on an ad hoc basis. Of course, riskiness is one of many factors.

If a main purpose of a project is to produce an infrastructure asset that will be under the control ultimately of the government, then control over the construction phase must be carefully managed. A government that cedes too much control over construction and maintenance may: (1) not end up with the requisite expertise to service the asset when it returns to government hands; (2) not be able to monitor the construction phase sufficiently to ensure that the asset is durable and will be turned over to the government in workable shape; and (3) not be capable of effectively monitoring the project company and thus to mitigate the risk that the private actor may overextract value from the project through accountancy techniques.

In addition, governments should view the ownership/control decision over time. The reality of infrastructure projects is that they are often subject to renegotiation, regardless of the contractual and regulatory structure in place. It may in fact be that a main power that the government wields is the ability to trigger renegotiation. Although one would not want to advocate the forward-looking strategic consideration of renegotiation options, at the same time, renegotiation may be useful to think about as a defensive posture to combat opportunistic behavior on the part of private actors. Such opportunism may take many forms through strategic exit strategies that undermine project durability.

Projects face both common and diverse sets of issues throughout their life cycles. Decisions over how to approach and handle such issues are mediated through contractual terms and related through regulatory decision-making. Like overarching contract choices, these problem-solving decisions are not easily amenable to generalization. That is, parties often have diverging interests and contracts are, as a result, the product of bargaining. Nonetheless, for cities and states new to the P3 infrastructure game, a number of observations might be made to guide decision-making and choices over contract clauses and terms.

This section aims to present a number of legal areas of particular importance, highlighting the policy issues at stake and the pros and cons associated with choices with a specific eye to the needs of many cities and states at the early stages of seeking P3 private involvement in infrastructures. These areas include: (A) long-term issues, (B) government coordination, (C) financing decisions, (D) expertise, (E) technology transfer, (F) guarantees, (G) regulation, (H) participation, and (I) dispute resolution. Each is discussed in turn.

Major projects often have a long life cycle, sometimes between twenty and forty years. As a result, project profitability will likely fluctuate over this life cycle. The contracting parties recognize this reality, and each will seek terms to offload the attendant financial risks. As a result, upholding the sanctity of the concessionary contract over the life of a project as interests diverge may be a substantial challenge.

Lawyers disagree sharply over how best to mitigate these risks for their clients. One school of thought, often associated with U.S. lawyers, argues that contracts that stipulate how such risks will be allocated among the parties in exceedingly specific terms are optimal. After the rash of renegotiations following the East Asian currency crisis, this genre of contract was criticized. However, an example of a project success through this type of contractual approach is the Shajiao C plant in China: "the joint venture agreement provided a means for a corporatized state entity to compensate the foreign investor for adverse regulatory changes."[27] Many of the midwestern deals, with their lengthy contracts, fit within this genre.

Others argue that flexible contracts are better suited to mitigating such risks, arguing that fixed terms are not enforceable as a practical matter given government's discretionary power to renegotiate terms. However, before flexible contracts are viable, governments might first need to establish a track record demonstrating a capacity and willingness to support projects over their life cycles.[28]

The long-term success of a project may depend less on the costs of conflict resolution or antagonistic renegotiations than on careful amicable negotiations among project participants. Here, the twinned flexibility of contracts and local regulatory agency decision-making are important in maintaining productive projects over time.[29]

Infrastructure projects are a component of a larger economic development strategy.[30] For example, the Mexican Maquiladora system, Malaysian high-technology national growth strategy, call centers in India, Qatar's Education City, and extractive industry projects around the globe all require infrastructure as a precondition to their viability and success. Recognizing the need to build synergies into such economic development strategies, Malaysia offered companies that invested in large-scale infrastructure projects preferential treatment to tender on subsequent government projects. Mexico's Panama-Puebla Plan makes infrastructure projects the cornerstone of its regional strategy, hoping to jump-start the long-neglected Chiapas region through such initial infrastructure investments. Like the Panama-Puebla Plan, transportation infrastructure projects extending the reach of the European Union (TEN-Ts), fiber-optic cables linking countries around the world (FLAG), the transportation linkages between South Africa and Mozambique (Maputo Corridor), and infrastructures crisscrossing the African continent (Lighting Africa) also aim to integrate countries economically and politically.

As a result, governments should seriously consider integrating infrastructure decision-making within government. Infrastructure projects within a single country often involve multiple government actors:

> The design and implementation of concessions require the coordination of several government actors. Sectoral ministries will usually be responsible for developing overall sectoral policy, finance ministries will usually have a close interest in the public revenue liability implications of particular projects, and environmental ministries or authorities may have an interest in projects, as may ministries of justice, competition authorities, and others. Some coordination will also be necessary between actors at central, provincial, and municipal governments regarding, for example, necessary approvals or the granting of guarantees.[31]

Effective contracts may depend on efficient coordination within government. For example, in the Philippines, government regulation of the power sector involves the coordination of multiple agencies.[32]

For this reason, the establishment of a powerful government authority does not mean wiping the institutional and regulatory slates clean. However, inefficiencies associated with legacy must be addressed so that agencies can work together and coordinate interests. Here, divergent and conflicting interests at the regional and local levels and in relation to national programs must be sorted out. Cohering wide-ranging policy interests is essential not only for national economic development. It is also necessary to send a unified signal to external investors. This external signal indicates to investors that the government is likely to support long-term projects and is devoted to cutting through any existing red tape associated with operating in the country.

If governments do not have a realistic element of command and control, then it is likely to reinforce the fact that many projects do not mature past the Memorandum of Understanding stage.[33]

The coordination of government, private, and intergovernmental organizations can be effectively carried out through a well-functioning contract. The most exhaustive reflection on the effectiveness of contracts in coordination has occurred at low points in the market. For this reason, discussions often are preoccupied with contractual failures. We see this in the thematic preoccupation of Stanford University's first two meetings of general counsels who have carried out major projects. However, one example of a project considered to be effective in coordinating actors is Laiban B in China:

> This paradigm has indeed been successfully deployed. The political and legal risks were mainly borne by the government, the construction, operating, and technical finance risk were mainly borne by the consortium in charge of the project, and the force majeure risks were shared between the government and the consortium.[34]

At the same time, the focus on contract failure in the face of large numbers of renegotiations may distort our impression of the empirical record.

Malaysia has been successful in coordinating its projects. In the 1980s and 1990s, the country pursued a large number of greenfield projects. Many of these projects were a precursor to the creation of a high-tech-based economy, organized around the Multimedia Super Corridor (MSC). The MSC was a 15-by-40-kilometer strip of land, a large-scale science park through which the country sought to leapfrog to fully industrialized nation status through the creation of a knowledge-intensive society.

Malaysia's MSC infrastructure strategy involved a number of specific projects that were built within this strip of land: the North-South Expressway, a toll road; the Kuala Lumpur International Airport; a telecommunications backbone; power plants; and several others. Coordination was central.

First, the projects themselves were part of a large development strategy. Thus, they were not freestanding. The road reinforced the airport, for instance. Also, the telecommunications infrastructure's success depended on robust power generation. The projects were thus not pursued on an ad hoc basis even though they involve wide-ranging actors and were pursued over time.

Second, the government pursued the infrastructure in order to make its MSC strategy successful. To do so, it sought to coordinate the private infrastructure concessionaires with the larger development objective. It thus offered significant perks to companies that invested in both infrastructure and, at the same time, non-infrastructure-based aspects of the MSC. For instance, a company that invested in infrastructure was given preferential treatment in subsequent tenders for the MSC.

Overall, government guarantees are an essential element of any P3. However, when putting in place a guarantee, a government must ask: (1) what is the purpose of the guarantee; (2) is the guarantee necessary to achieve that purpose; (3) is the guarantee appropriately crafted so as to achieve the purpose; and (4) can the guarantee be more narrow and still achieve its objective? Once a guarantee is in place, a government must regularly revisit how it functions in practice. As a project evolves, a guarantee may shift in the role that it plays. A guarantee may either cease to serve its intended purpose or undermine its original justification. Also, as discussed throughout this chapter, guarantees may have a distorting effect in both design and practice.

Cities and states in financial crisis may be particularly needy when it comes to financing infrastructures. P3 techniques everywhere, most notably project finance, are themselves geared toward attracting private capital to finance much-needed infrastructure. At the same time, it is important to choose contractual terms suited to both lessening risks inherent in financial dependence and maximizing benefits should economic growth occur.

These governments are particularly prone to pricing and exchange rate fluctuations. Internationally, even projects in countries like Brazil have faced financial difficulties due to shifts in exchange rates. For this reason, governments should hedge against fluctuation risk by sourcing some capital domestically. To do so may require parallel strategies, as discussed. That is, infrastructure projects for cities and states in financial crisis are necessarily part of larger development strategies. They should be used to promote economic goals such as efficient resource extraction or export-led growth or densification of urban economies.

Part of this larger development strategy should be an effort to grow or mature local sources of capital. Examples here are domestic stock markets, indigenous banks, and pension funds. In Latin America, the need for local sourcing strategies through capital markets and pension funds has been underscored. The World Bank and Inter-American Development Bank have both advocated municipal bonds as a means for financing infrastructures.[35] Because of the reliable revenue stream associated with well-functioning infrastructures, select projects can contribute to the strength and resilience of local markets.

These local sources of capital are also often strategically important for rescuing infrastructure projects in times of crisis. Leading project finance lawyers argue that domestic sourcing makes renegotiations more efficient:

> Some observers have commented that projects largely financed by domestic financial institutions (such as Thailand and Malaysia) were more likely to come to a reasonably quick negotiated settlement with the project sponsors because of such financiers' vested interest in the local economy and their susceptibility to pressure from the host government.[36]

For this reason, contracts should include provisions that allow for local purchases of projects during downturns on acceptable terms. For example, during the East Asian currency crisis, Malaysia used its pension plan to rescue distressed infrastructure projects. In Thailand, the government shouldered the costs of several important power projects during the currency crisis, an investment that paid off as the projects have subsequently thrived.[37] Accounting for this possibility is important, because foreign firms will likewise seek parachute provisions for such circumstances. Because infrastructure projects may have a several-decade life cycle and because many cities and states may face turbulence or growing pains during such a period, it is important to account for such a scenario contractually.

Many cities and states face particularly high information costs in relation to infrastructure projects. This is particularly true in infrastructure sectors with high levels of specialism such as telecommunications. Contract negotiations must account for this information differential both at the outset and in order to ensure that terms are relatively enforceable. Governments must accrue expertise in order to negotiate, monitor, and judge success.

Two high-profile examples of inefficiencies attached to failure to staff projects with local engineers with the requisite expertise are Iraq and Afghanistan. The infrastructure reconstruction in both countries relies on local engineers to succeed. However, for understandable reasons, experienced engineers have emigrated from the countries. As a result, the reconstruction efforts, which are often P3 projects, have stumbled. The U.S. government and the aid community recognize this. Tree of Life, a New York–based public interest group, has been established to provide this expertise. Likewise, a U.S. government–financed effort has sought to train Afghani engineers within American educational institutions to build capacity. Similarly, efforts have been made to train local engineers in the context of private-sector participation in the power sector. In addition, Egyptian wastewater projects explicitly recognize the importance of trained engineers to ensure effective tendering in the cities of Aswan, Mansoura, and Nuweiba. Nongovernmental efforts by groups such as Engineers Without Borders also devote themselves to assistance, as do reconstruction efforts generally through armed forces engineers. There is a growing literature on the organizational culture of projects, focusing on the need for an intercultural makeup, inclusive of expatriates, to ensure functioning projects.[38]

The insight of the need to localize projects is a truism of many public interest group campaigns involved in infrastructure, including Friends of the Earth, and is shared by project planners who incorporate multi-stakeholder processes in project decision-making.

At the early stage of an infrastructure project, cities and states must make a range of decisions that require a high degree of expertise. For example, decisions about whether to structure a sector based on competition or monopoly may not be readily evident. Moreover, certain aspects of a sector may be more amenable to competition but other segments better served by monopoly.

It may be that decisions over whether to structure a sector on a competitive model versus on a monopoly may be complex. On the one hand, competition may lead to technological innovation. It may also result in greater economic efficiency. On the other hand, Theodore Moran has argued that a monopoly may be more amenable to effective regulatory oversight because of the transparency and efficiency that comes from monitoring a single actor.[39]

A city or state may not have the indigenous expertise to make these decisions. An aspiring corporate entrant into the city may make the case for a certain market structure that favors its interests.[40] This risk may be mitigated in several ways. First, an inexperienced city may introduce competition into the tendering process so that aspiring entrants must make the case for market structure. Such a solution might itself produce greater knowledge about the pros and cons of certain market structure decisions.[41] Regardless, a city without internal expertise is best suited by carefully contracting it in. At the same time, the government must be mindful of the fact that a certain amount of advice is necessary in order to sort through expert knowledge.

When P3s occur in infrastructure sectors, an earlier generation of local firms may resist restructuring, as with the telecommunications sector in Zimbabwe.[42] Furthermore, a country may divide an infrastructure into several parts at the impetus of foreign investors who see such an internal division of labor as mitigating against the obsolescence bargain risk.[43]

In the Philippines, the Electric Power Industry Reform Act of 2001 divides the power sector into generation, transmission, distribution, and supply.[44] In 1996, Abu Dhabi issued Decision No. 1, restructuring its power and water sectors. In doing so, the government created a new regulatory authority. The aim was to introduce P3s by dividing the sector into parts. It introduced new rules for existing projects and a plan for increasing capacity.[45] Through subsequent government action, the sector is now divided into several parts with varying degrees of P3 and competition.[46]

Experts are also necessary to ensure that an infrastructure is appropriately regulated and monitored. Regulatory systems must be informed by expertise even in areas such as pricing. Also, even in fully industrialized countries, monitoring has become a significant challenge. For example, in the United States, Paul Verkuil argues in a book-length study that expertise has migrated into the private sector over time because of higher salaries. As a result, the capacity of government to monitor the performance of projects has been seriously curtailed. He advocates the creation of a corps of public interest–minded government officials with the expertise to oversee projects.[47]

Many cities face substantial problems along these lines. In the first instance, government officials should consider creating positions devoted to oversight that offer competitive salaries. Another option is to contract in such expertise, making sure that personnel are independent auditors.

In Taiwan, the Public Construction Commission has played an important role in ensuring that projects are properly procured. It oversees tenders and awards. It also is responsible for undertaking project feasibility and development with the private sector. In this regard, the Commission serves a role in facilitating private participation in the country through contracting in as appropriate, joint initiatives, or supporting private standalones. Significantly, Taiwan has often maintained public control over the engineering aspect of projects.

An example of such a project was the mass rail transit system in Taipei in the late 1980s. This project was spearheaded by a consortium of foreign firms including Parsons Brinckerhoff and Bechtel, which designed and engineered the project. The government, however, was responsible for building the project and continues to expand its weblike infrastructure. Aspects have been carried out by joint local and international groups. To build local capacity to engineer and construct the projects, international assistance was brought in. This internationally coordinated effort has involved local, U.S., Japanese, and European firms.

In Micronesia, the government and others have recognized the need to build local capacity to ensure properly functioning projects. President Mariny Mori established the FSM Program Management Unit to carry out the Compact Infrastructure Development Program. It moved the unit into the executive branch to ensure closer oversight and coordination with the program's purpose. The unit will have a citizen from Micronesia at the helm "to facilitate coordination with state governments and stakeholders"[48] and will comprise twenty-four staff members including engineers and inspectors. The decision to have closely held local managerial control resulted with a disatisfaction by the country and others with the use of a firm in Hawaii, leading ultimately to the suspension of infrastructure aid by the U.S. government. A minimum of twenty-five percent of contracting work must go to local firms.

Given the compelling premise on which these initiatives are based, it is important for the federal government to consider earmarking money for the building of local capacity across the country. Efforts might include circulating engineers through universities and government offices. It might also include financing local educational programs.

One purpose of introducing P3s to build infrastructures is to initiate or mature the process of technological transfer to local firms and entrepreneurs.[49] This purpose is particularly important in contractual schemes like the BOT arrangement, whereby the local government will eventually take control of a project. Under the BOT arrangement, the concessionaire builds the project and operates it long enough to recoup costs and garner an agreed-upon profit. Then the infrastructure transfers back to the government. If the government and its indigenous firms do not possess the requisite technological expertise to operate and maintain the project, then the government will likely have to extend its contractual relationship with the foreign firm. This extension would result in lost revenue for the host government. Governments should transfer technology through contractual mechanisms such as corporate partnership and subcontracting agreements.

At the same time, the government must take care not to build inefficiencies into the infrastructure construction and operation by facilitating rent-seeking behavior by local firms. Thus, in other words, technology transfer should not be a pretext for the inclusion of inefficient local control.

The regulation of infrastructure projects serves multiple purposes, from consumer pricing, to environmental impact, to decisions over maintaining monopolies or competition-based sector models, to means for dispute resolution. Certain cities may face a challenge akin to countries that have a legacy of renegotiations and expropriations; that is, they must use regulations to assuage investors that the country is turning the page from a *perceived* history of poor economic management, political risks, uneven demand, and regulatory uncertainty.[50]

For cities and states with limited track records as sites for P3 investment, the existence of a coherent and convincing set of regulations might usefully send a signal of safety and friendliness to investors. Importantly, small cities often cannot realistically promise the same set of safeguards that a more economically and institutionally built-up country might.

For this reason, as discussed later, provisions such as recourse to dispute resolution must be carefully thought out. Most likely, it is not productive to investors to require disputes to be heard, in the first instance, within local courts prior to having a route to international arbitration tribunals made open. At the same time, if cities allow for disputes to be heard directly within international tribunals, to make such regulatory provisions effective, they must be (1) contractualized and (2) carefully worked out with the insurers of projects who may as a matter of course require the exhaustion of local remedies prior to a payout.

Small cities must be mindful of the fact that regulatory systems are neither a panacea nor entirely convincing in their appearance of actual enforceability. For example, as with extractives projects, contracts may supersede regulations as a practical matter. Regardless, contractual and regulatory systems are intertwined,[51] as postcontract regulations can *de facto* renegotiate the terms of an agreement. As well, if regulations are put in place to indicate the long-term security of an infrastructure project in relation to the government, then the *de facto* ability of governments to change regulatory systems over time may undermine any regulatory system's appearance of functionality, but particularly one in a low-income city.

Cities and states should be aware of alternative mitigation devices pursued by other parties to the agreement. Also, they must give due consideration to how to propose and negotiate (in a way that advances interests) alternative security and stability devices.

As will be discussed later, many parties to an infrastructure project have exit strategies. For example, a banker may plan to enter a project, extract a benefit, and then exit. As a result, a government may in effect be the lender of last resort. For this reason, governments must think carefully about ensuring that a project is secure and stable. They must do so in a way that accounts for this opportunistic behavior. Governments possess certain powers to lock in participants. Although it is advisable to exercise these powers carefully and judiciously, it may be necessary to use exchange rate controls strategically to mitigate risks. It may also be necessary to stipulate that a percentage of projects should be financed within domestic capital markets.

Governments must also think about projects on a short- and medium-term basis. That is, if a project were to fail and not deliver the quality underlying infrastructure asset sought, then what could the government do to ensure that it benefits nonetheless? One example here might be technology transfer. Another example might be demand that a project company contribute to a local development financial pool or build local institutions such as schools and hospitals as a condition for entry. Such conditions are increasingly demanded by African countries as a precondition to Chinese company involvement. The cons of such measures are, of course, that in a buyers' market, it is difficult for a government to determine terms.

As will be discussed in the later section on subsidies, most governments have a hand in consumer-pricing decisions, with the interest of promoting the public interest generally and also at times a specific set of low-income consumers. The use of regulations to set prices may squeeze the profits of companies reducing incentives to improve services.[52] That is, if too many gains derived from improving services are extracted by the government through regulation, then it might not make economic sense for private firms to upgrade infrastructures.[53]

Government guarantees for P3 projects are increasingly important as companies demand assurance that user-fee-based contractual schemes will generate reliable returns. The thirst for guarantees is evidenced by the progressive move toward limited recourse financing. At one extreme, guarantees may take the form of direct loans or grants. These guarantees are geared to situations in which projects are not viewed as commercially viable. Moving along the spectrum, governments might guarantee an agreed level of return on a project regardless of usage on an annual basis. A related guarantee tailors itself to specific consumption in which minimum usage levels are provided. Other guarantees are in practice risk-mitigation devices, from guarantees by the government to shoulder currency devaluations or compensate for change of law or to extend the term of a concession if profit has not been recouped within the agreed-upon time period. Guarantees of all kinds are a reality of P3 projects.[54]

In cash-strapped cities and states, with their relatively risky operating environments, governments generally must often offer guarantees. More important than the type of guarantee on offer is a reasoned evaluation of the degree of the guarantee. For example, what is an appropriate minimum return to guarantee? Should a government guarantee against the failure of a public corporate partner to fulfill obligations to the investor, and in what fashion?

The rule of thumb must be that the host government provides only the level of guarantees necessary to assuage investors. However, as with many areas of privatized projects, such an assessment may depend not only on a body of evidence that is unavailable but also on the judgment of experts that are not available.

Increasingly, the norm across infrastructure sectors internationally is that project-affected persons should participate in decision-making. However, even among fully industrialized countries, the degree and type of participation remain a subject of debate. For example, the European Union in its TEN-T programs, which are integrating newly acceded countries into the Western European infrastructures (ports, roads, rails), advocates incorporating project-affected communities during the postplanning stages. On the one hand, increased participation at earlier stages may lead to prolonged decision-making and even aborted projects. On the other hand, early buy-ins by project-affected groups may mitigate the risks of later-stage instabilities, disruptive politicized price renegotiations, and abandoned projects. Thus, arguments about inefficiencies are raised in both scenarios. No empirical work has been conducted to sort out the real-world meaning of this policy divide. Furthermore, provisions related to participation are not readily available, and thus no solid empirical basis exists for making contract-based claims for participation-related assertions.

Countries in practice have generally done poor jobs in achieving participatory infrastructure projects. Instead, attention has been paid to allowing for a degree of participation as a means for mitigating project problems. In other words, if project participants successfully make demands on a project, then participation will be broadened. This broadening may occur through participatory community planning meetings or revising contracts to make toll payments more affordable because of legal cases mounted (Hungary M5) or because of protests (Bolivia and Bechtel).

Participation has been particularly foreclosed or inadequately addressed within dispute-resolution arenas. The arenas with substantive power are often closed to civil society actors. For example, ICSID did not allow Bolivian civil society groups and international public interest groups even to file an amicus brief. Moreover, the various ombudsmen that have been established within international organizations like the World Bank and regional development banks serve an advisory role.

Efforts within P3s have been made in the context of the Equator Principle banks to broaden participation. At the same time, no uniformity exists in Equator Principle application, as banks decide how to implement them on a bank-specific basis. Moreover, banks customarily assign Equator responsibility only to the lead bank. Furthermore, no study has been conducted looking at how the Equator Principles function in practice. Thus, it is not possible to realistically assess their success or failure. Instead, efforts to do so are to be viewed as normative.

With regard to dispute resolution, concessionary contracts typically stipulate choice of forum and choice of law. It is important for governments to take into consideration the pros and cons of these two determinations. At the same time, no empirical evidence exists in this area related to frequency of certain types of stipulations within these clauses. Furthermore, arguments concerning what investors demand in relation to domestic or international dispute-resolution options, the enforcement of these provisions, or their effects on decision-making does not exist. For this reason, arguments made in this area must be viewed as largely prescriptive. As with many other areas, an absence of reliable systematic empirical evidence means that generalizations or conclusions are not verifiable at present.

Fully industrialized country investors commonly seek to have disputes governed by the law of their own home states. Barry Metzger, former General Counsel of the Asian Development Bank, sets out the argument for choice of law:

> To the maximum extent possible, such contracts are governed by foreign law rather than the law of the host country. In choosing the laws of well established, developed country jurisdictions (such as New York, England or France) it is believed that the parties (and, in particular, foreign investors and foreign financiers) will benefit from greater clarity and certainty in the interpretation of their contracts, given the large body of jurisprudential precedent and scholarly commentary, and the greater commercial and financial sophistication of judges and arbitrators in such countries. Most often the project documentation, involving contracts with host governments and its agencies, will be governed by the laws of the host jurisdiction. Foreign laws will more often govern the financing documents and some of the contractual arrangements among the project sponsors.[55]

Moreover, Metzger goes on to make the choice of forum case:

> In the event of a dispute, such a dispute is to be taken, if possible, to a foreign court or arbitral tribunal rather than to the courts of the host country. This is intended to access the greater commercial and financial sophistication of courts and arbitral tribunals in major international centers, as noted above, but it is also intended to avoid often corrupt courts in many emerging market host

> countries to avoid bias against foreign investors and foreign financiers. The expectation is that a judgment or arbitral award will be obtained and then enforced against the defendant's assets outside the host country or enforced in the host country, often pursuant to international convention or bilateral agreements for the enforcement of foreign judgments and arbitral awards.[56]

When making sense of the arbitration record, it is important to realize that a small percentage of disputes find their way to the tribunals.

Among practitioners, there is a sense that arbitration is not a satisfying dispute-resolution process. It is inconsistent and time-consuming. Decisions also must be enforceable, which is not a foregone conclusion. Also, some practitioners express dissatisfaction with the quality of judgments. Furthermore, recourse to arbitration may be viewed as arising out of an ultimate failure of a project, an irretrievable one. That is, if a troubled project cannot be renegotiated and ends up in a tribunal, then a decision to resolve a project through arbitration may simply be a signal of failure.[57]

This stated ambivalence about arbitration among practitioners reinforces an interview conducted with a leading insurance provider. This insurer related how decisions regarding whether to pursue arbitration are largely driven by the insurers. For example, whether the insurer requires the project company to exhaust local remedies to garner a payout is important.

In addition, to address these inadequacies of the arbitration market, Arbitral Award Default (AAD) coverage has arisen within the insurance industry. AAD covers against inability to achieve timely judgment enforcement. This coverage varies according to insurance provider. At the same time, a number of features are associated with it: (1) a judgment must be secured against a national or subnational governmental entity; (2) the award cannot be from a domestic tribunal, it must issue from an international one; (3) all rights of appeal must be exhausted – it must be "final and binding"; (4) the award must be nationally enforceable; (5) "reasonable efforts" must be made to enforce the judgment; and (6) investor stake in the enterprise limits award amount. Many aspects of AAD coverage are not fixed, and they may depend not only on the insurer but also on the insured and the specific project.

A second type of coverage is Denial of Justice (DOJ) coverage. It may be purchased in conjunction with AAD coverage. However, DOJ coverage is more difficult to secure. DOJ coverage insures against an unwillingness of the host country to cooperate with arbitration. It may involve the country's undermining efforts or outright thwarting of the practical avenue toward arbitration. It may also cover situations in which any decision to pursue arbitration is ill-advised because of, for instance, hazards.

However, this coverage raises a number of practical problems: (1) which party is ultimately responsible for making the arbitration process function; (2) a distinction might exist between undermining a process and an expected and encouraged adversarial behavior that is not sharply delimited; (3) if a case is brought against a private entity in a tribunal and the host government influences judicial decision-making, can a sovereign-based claim be made; (4) under the policies some continuity of sovereign action is typically required, and sovereigns may intervene in material ways but not on an ongoing basis; (5) should the insurance policy also cover situations in which tribunals are not functioning because of local conflict; (6) given that these dispute-resolution procedures can drag on for long periods, what is a reasonable time span before a claim can be made on the insurance policy; and (7) as with AAD coverage, the appropriate means for calculating payouts may not be altogether evident. These and other practical difficulties are why DOJ coverage is not prevalent.[58]

The choice of forum relates mainly to whether disputes will be heard in national courts or international arbitration tribunals. It may be that access to an international tribunal is only open once available national courts have been exhausted. This need to exhaust local remedies may be reinforced by insurance policies that make the use of national courts a precondition for payouts. Requirements to access local courts are assumed to run against the interests of foreign companies, which express concerns about the possibility of an unbiased resolution of conflict in countries in which executive branches may wield a modicum of control over the judiciary.

From the perspective of government officials, the choice of forum decision is not absolutely clear. On the one hand, if the domestic courts of such countries are familiar and either objective or friendly to national interests, then it seems that a local court choice of law provision would be optimal. However, if a main purpose of a concessionary contract is to attract foreign capital and technological expertise into the domestic infrastructure sector, then a choice of law provision that stipulates a local court as the decision-making arena may send a contrary signal, dissuading investment. Ultimately, it might be sensible for cities and states to stipulate that disputes will be heard in domestic courts in the first instance, with a right of appeal to international tribunals. Such an arrangement would allow the host government to demonstrate fair treatment.

A choice of law provision raises a slightly different set of questions and attendant challenges for many governments. A concessionary contract might stipulate the national law that will govern a dispute regardless of forum. No hard and fast rules exist setting forth the "best" law for any country or sector or project. Instead, government officials must make a fact-specific decision on which nation's law would be optimal. Such a decision must be based on judgment and prediction rather than entirely knowable information. As a result, governments must retain expert legal counsel to make this determination. Such counsel must have knowledge of wide-ranging jurisdictions, the project at issue, and the interests of the host government. For example, if one chooses UK law to govern a project, it might be that such law favors the TNC's intellectual property rights but disfavors its contractual standing.

III. Model Laws

A number of international organizations have produced model laws or guidelines for P3 infrastructure projects. Like the lawyer treatises setting out the contractual menu for projects, these model laws are mainly useful for their coverage rather than for the explicit direction that they offer to governments. At the same time, since these efforts are geared explicitly to governments seeking foreign involvement in their infrastructure sectors, they indicate to governments what regulatory and institutional measures must be in place to signal friendliness to foreign capital and capacity to deliver on promises.

This section discusses several initiatives: (A) the United Nations Commission on International Trade Law (UNCITRAL) Legislative Guide and Model Legislative Provisions; (B) the United Nations Economic Commission for Europe (UNECE) guidebook; (C) the Organization for Cooperation and Development (OECD) Principles for Private Sector Participation in Infrastructure; and (D) the United Nations Industrial Development Organization (UNIDO) BOT Guidelines. In doing so, it does not provide an exhaustive overview of these initiatives. Instead, the aim is two-fold: first, to introduce the initiative, and second to discuss its relevance to cities and states.

The UNCITRAL Legislative Guide and Model Legislative Provisions provide governments with the building blocks that foreign investors expect when making infrastructure decisions.[59] One main accomplishment is to advance the case for governments adopting coherent coordinated infrastructure rules that are transparent.[60] They are premised on the argument set out earlier that governments benefit from a coordinated infrastructure environment both legally and institutionally.

In line with this spirit, UNCITRAL provides a framework that accommodates diverse existing practices, rather than prescribing certain conduct. Importantly, Catherine Pedamon has argued that the UNCITRAL project is consensus-based and meant to apply to wide-ranging circumstances internationally. Thus, it focuses less on prescriptions and more on options.

For instance, UNCITRAL details what a transparent competitive tendering process would entail.[61] However, it is careful to allow for the practice of unsolicited proposals for projects to exist in parallel to this more rule-bound competitive option.[62] Similarly, UNCITRAL indicates that projects should be governed by national law, while at the same time reinforcing the legitimacy of deviating from such a practice.[63] UNCITRAL here simply reinforces the legitimacy of the present array of practices. For this reason, governments should look to the UNCITRAL materials for an indication of what practices currently exist, a brief rationale for them, and a fleshing out of the best-practice procedural and institutional environment conducive to investment.

With regard to the concession contract, UNCITRAL once again provides boilerplate guidance. It lists procedures and clauses.[64] It does not tailor its advice to the needs of specific countries. For this reason, the clauses set forth in the UNCITRAL material must be viewed within the context of the guidance set out in the previous section. For example, many of the concessionary provisions rely on government expertise to make them effective.

The United Nations Economic Commission for Europe in 2007 published the *Guidebook on Promoting Good Governance in Public-Private Partnerships*. This guidebook is mainly directed at mid- and high-income countries, so its overviews and prescriptions are thus tailored to a particular set of concerns. For this reason, the relevance of the guidebook's prescriptions for weaker governments is not stated. Nonetheless, many of the prescriptions can be easily applied to those contexts.

Overall, the guidebook provides a fairly descriptive presentation of existing practice at a high level of generality. To the extent that it provides concrete prescriptions, it advocates a set of principles to guide partnerships that are not easily distinguishable from the Washington Consensus, the World Bank safeguard policies and their counterparts within regional development banks, and the

Equator Principles. Regarding governments with weaker bargaining power, the guidebook does little to sort out the underlying challenge of whether good governance leads to more efficient projects in the short term. The discussion earlier in this book addressing participation, expertise, long-term contractual issues, and other matters addresses a similar set of concerns as the guidebook, but in much more detail.

The OECD Principles for Private Sector Participation in Infrastructure differs little from the UNECE guidebook in its prescriptions. Both aim to internalize both efficiency and good governance interests into projects. The level of generality in both documents makes their advice useful at the level of aspiration; however, the difficult trade-offs do not receive detailed attention. Such trade-offs, as discussed earlier, are more pronounced in regions facing crisis. The OECD principles do prescribe subsidies that, as indicated in this book, are by no means straightforward in their policy advisability.

In contrast to the general discussions of projects in the UNECE and OECD documents, UNIDO in 1996 published a very detailed how-to guidebook, BOT Guidelines, for governments pursuing BOT infrastructures. Although the discussion is narrower than the other documents and UNCITRAL materials in its focus on one type of concession, it has the advantage of presenting nuts and bolts. UNIDO sets out the proactive role that governments must play throughout the project life cycle in detail. It includes discussions of principles and sample project documents. While on its own the

Guidelines does not offer definitive advice, UNIDO does provide an initiation into project decision-making that is helpful for novices in government who aim to get up to speed. It is a useful primer for government officials seeking to understand how specialists think about P3 projects.

IV. Subsidy Decisions

Even with a series of guarantees, infrastructure projects may not be commercially viable or profitable without subsidies. Carl S. Bjerre argues that governments are under an affirmative duty to internalize the demands of project-affected people into infrastructure contracts. He draws on the work of Nobel Prize–winning economist Armatya Sen to make this point.[65] Stephen Wallenstein disagrees, seeing infrastructure projects as no different from shopping malls in the duties that they confer on project participants.[66] Generally, among commentators, the Wallenstein position is a minority one; however, sharp disagreement exists over which party is best situated to ensure that public interest considerations are internalized into projects. Rather than focusing only on social risk mitigation, projects should be designed to produce public goods with policies put in place to achieve this goal.

This section deals with subsidies, one type of legal means for pursuing the public interest through a redistributive device. It does not address the range of other regulatory, contractual, and dispute-resolution-oriented means for internalizing project-affected communities into decision-making processes and for redressing alleged grievances.[67]

Subsidies may be provided by the host government, the home government of the corporation, or by a public bank. Although subsidies play a role in most major infrastructure projects, commentators are sharply critical of their legitimacy and effectiveness. Here, we discuss a number of common host state government subsidies with an eye to their advantages and drawbacks. We then turn briefly to the range of home state and public bank subsidies, providing advice on how cities and states might approach this maze of foreign subsidies. It also discusses renegotiations.

Commentators view subsidies with suspicion despite a friendliness toward them by governments. On the one hand, subsidies can sweeten the deal for companies, making an otherwise unattractive investment that promotes the public good into one that is commercially appealing. They also may involve making macroeconomic decisions that increase the consumer base. On the other hand, critics note that subsidies may reduce the incentives of private companies to make infrastructure projects efficient and profitable.[68] They may also offload costs of a project on to the government while concentrating the benefits accrued in the hands of the firm.

However, when economies experience downturns, as happened in Argentina and East Asia, governments that do not effectively address diminished user appetite for infrastructure payments face failed projects.[69] In Hungary, the P3 M5 highway faced trouble when users decided that the cost of tolls was too high and they decided instead to travel on a substandard nontoll parallel road. In Bolivia, Bechtel's water concession involved charging rates to users that were prohibitively expensive, resulting in wide-scale protests and eventually ICSID arbitration and a failed contract. As well, in Tanzania, one project faced protracted arbitration, resulting in the state utility regulator paying out fifty percent of its revenue to keep the project afloat.[70]

Controversies over tolls in fully industrialized countries also pose a significant risk. Examples include:

> Portugal's Vasco da Gama bridge was built and operated by an international consortium under the assumption that a toll of US$2 would be levied on commuters. However, violent commuter revolts and a lack of activity on the bridge indicated that the tariff was too high. As a result, government subsidies were used in order to promote traffic on the toll bridge, thereby leading to a situation where the taxpayers and not the users, were paying the bills. As another example, the Dulles Greenway in Virginia was one of the first private toll roads in the United States. The initial traffic flow predictions were extremely optimistic and the actual traffic volume fell short by over a third. This led to the toll prices being reduced by nearly 40% in order to attract more customers. In late 1997, this reduction in revenue led to a major and unavoidable refinancing and debt restructuring of the project.[71]

Appetite for tolls may depend on how such obligations are introduced.

At the extreme, critics of subsidy schemes argue that poor people, the main target of subsidies, do not ultimately benefit from the buttressing of user spending power. They argue that the main obstacle to poor people is the availability of infrastructures, rather than competitive cost structures. For this reason, critics advocate that money earmarked for subsidies should instead be allocated to increasing access to infrastructures through additional build and increased grid connectivity.[72] Of course, such strong arguments must be tested in fact and prescriptions attuned to multiple infrastructure sectors and various low-income groups within a country. Nonetheless, governments implementing cross-income subsidy schemes should be mindful of these arguments, because it may be that such subsidies ultimately target wealthy consumers in practice.

Host governments can choose from a number of subsidies. Regardless of the subsidy employed, a number of criteria should be applied to determine its appropriateness and success. First, governments should ensure that subsidies benefit the target class.[73] Second, the subsidy must make the infrastructure service affordable to the user. Third, it must not distort use. Fourth, the subsidy must not create inefficiencies in service provision. Fifth, it must not undermine competition.[74] Sixth, the subsidy itself must be transparent and amenable to measurement in financial terms.[75] Seventh, the transaction costs of implementing the subsidy should be minimized. And eighth, the external costs to the economy writ large from the subsidy should be minimized.[76]

Government subsidies may be financed from a range of sources and take several forms. One infrastructure project or sector may be cross-subsidized from another. A second subsidy involves governments ensuring revenue streams for companies. Examples are "take-or-pay" or "take-and-pay" clauses. Each involves making up any difference between user demand and agreed company revenue streams. This subsidy is generally funded through the tax base of the government. A third subsidy involves providing consumers with financial support that can, in turn, be used to finance infrastructure use.[77]

The take-or-pay clause is perhaps the most popular subsidy scheme. Although it is widely used, experts regularly discount its effectiveness almost without exception. Many view it as putting in place a disincentive for companies to produce profitable quality infrastructure goods for consumers. As well, during the East Asian currency crisis, governments reneged on their take-or-pay obligations.[78]

A range of subsidies exist from external actors, including national export credit agencies and international financial institutions. Subsidies include loans, insurance, feasibility studies, expert advice, and direct grants. They are often tied to the involvement of specific firms.

A large-scale project may be financed through subsidies from multiple export credit agencies and international financial institutions like the World Bank's International

Finance Corporation or Multilateral Investment Guarantee Agency. Regional development banks might also be involved.

The maze of subsidy programs is complex. Export agency and other public financial institution subsidies often represent not only deal sweeteners, but also privileged access to private firms. At the same time, it is essential for governments to conduct due diligence about the range of subsidies available, the opportunities they bring, and the conditions on lending.

UNCTAD has commissioned an internal study that provides guidance and analysis of this maze, which is one of the most important yet nontransparent areas of the international infrastructure project field.

Renegotiations form a significant part of developing country experience with privatized infrastructure projects. During the 1990s, almost half of projects faced some renegotiation in sectors other than telecommunications. At the same time, evidence exists that renegotiations do not necessarily correlate with investor dissatisfaction. Not enough information is available, however, to reach a conclusion on this front. The cause of renegotiations may not be tied to P3 *per se* but instead to the overheated markets of the 1990s. At times, as discussed at other points in this book, renegotiations were tied to user unwillingness to pay tolls or currency fluctuations.

The Stanford Global Projects group has produced a body of literature on renegotiations in the infrastructure sector.

The overall conclusion of the group is that present legal approaches have largely failed to hold projects together. They noted that the contractual and regulatory underpinning of projects has rarely been maintained throughout a project life cycle. The contract has not been successful in helping projects to sustain political challenges, currency shifts, and public protests. The contracts have not been workable vehicles for allocating risks and responsibilities. The guarantees that contracts have built in have not resulted in durable projects. And, as discussed earlier, the pursuit of arbitration-based avenues to achieve redress has been viewed as inadequate and only as a device for sorting out failed projects.

Although the Stanford group underscores contract failure, it places blame also on many extralegal factors. However, the take-home lesson of the legal studies of renegotiation is that contract is not an effective device for gluing a project together over its life cycle. The Stanford group goes on to advocate for various mixed forms of public-private participation and increased governance. At the same time, it is not altogether clear that these models are qualitatively different from the status quo situation.

It might instead be more useful to expect less from the regulatory and contractual schemes. Among interdisciplinary legal scholars and many lawyers and judges, it has long been understood that law cannot itself solve problems or hold together relationships. Instead, the context in which law operates is typically viewed as most important.

Countless studies of how law works reinforce this point. Thus, it should not be surprising that attempts to dot the *i*s and cross the *t*s do not mitigate risks on their own.[79]

The regulatory and contractual aspects of contracts might then be better understood as the story of the life, death, and revision of contracts, and the formulation and amendment of regulation. More important than the contract life cycle are the project life cycle and the quality of the underlying infrastructure asset. For this reason, governments should not view contracts and regulatory structures as unrevisable constants in the infrastructure sector. Instead, they should plan for realistic amendments and perhaps inevitable cancellations. Thus, an argument exists for adopting a more realistic, more modest, lest hubristic view toward the legal aspects of P3s. Such a sober assessment might be important for a government to extract its own value from the P3 by understanding and thus controlling the process more effectively. That is, if other parties plan based on the possibility of regulatory and contractual failure and behave strategically accordingly, so too should governments.

An argument can also be made that more open, participatory tendering processes may make projects more durable. For example, although rule-bound projects are important for ensuring buy-in over a project's life cycle, it is equally if not more important to include participants in the planning stage. Civil society actors may be more likely to shoulder toll increases, for instance, if citizens are part of the decision-making surrounding toll pricing. For example, the M5 tollway in Hungary and other EU extension projects have had difficulty at the toll payment stage. The cause of this difficulty may be that the EU has decided not to allow for robust civil society participation in the early stages of its projects. Instead it advocates a fire-fighting approach whereby the project sponsors only cost in project inefficiencies when opponents successfully make their claims heard.[80]

One important take-away lesson from renegotiations is the need to rebalance incentives over the life of a project. Also, nontransparent or corruption-prone tendering may create a legacy of unsustainable bargains. Moreover, although commentators regularly warn against subsidies that create a disincentive on the part of firms to produce efficient infrastructures, it may be that the absence of subsidies means projects for which consumers are asked to shoulder unworkable costs.

A significant finding from a Stanford Roundtable on renegotiations bringing together general counsels from financial institutions and leading lawyers suggested an overall dissatisfaction with arbitration tribunals in managing renegotiation risk in an effective manner. Likewise, local courts were viewed similarly. Furthermore, not enough is known about whether public international insurers contribute to efficient renegotiations. Inevitably, a question remains as to whether rigid or flexible contracts play any role in renegotiation outcomes. Regardless, agreements that tie in multiple parties and are structured so as to produce consensual mutually productive results may lessen the collective pain of inevitable renegotiations.[81]

This chapter has discussed a number of contractual and regulatory issues, guidelines and model laws, and specific international programs within the infrastructure sector. An effort has been made to present many of the principles underlying these efforts with an eye specifically toward their applicability to cities and states seeking P3-based involvement in infrastructures. We next turn to how newly independent states used contracts and P3s in order to turn the page on colonial-period unequal treaties.

11

Emancipation

I. Introduction

In the previous chapters, we looked at institutions such as infrastructure banks and policy instruments like partnerships that aim to promote durable equitable growth. In foreign affairs, public-private partnerships (P3s) emerged as a response to the excesses of colonial-era concessionary agreements, often referred to as the unequal treaty system. This chapter focuses on the need to see partnerships themselves as diverse. The aim is also to focus on some of the difficulties countries have faced in using P3s to promote development and to remedy power imbalances. Despite sector-based differences, the next two chapters show how P3 contracts function similarly across infrastructure, oil, and metal minerals – the common contractual task of recouping up-front investments through incremental fees attached to extracting crude oil or road user tolls.

During colonialism, most contracts or treaties entered into between colonial enterprises and local societies dictated terms that are repugnant to modern sensibilities. Colonial companies often claimed open-ended rights to natural resources. At times, agreements ran without a stipulated end. A contract might have claimed a right to all resources, discovered or not, throughout the entire country. Moreover, the value of extracted oil, gas, or minerals was largely claimed by the overseas power on its own, and it rarely shared these resources. Thus, partnership agreements arose out of an effort to revisit these agreements, often extinguishing them and creating new contracts, in order to redress imbalance. What emerged were public-private partnerships.

Over time, partnerships too have been subject to recurring criticism. Critics have increasingly claimed that a partnership in the context of gross power imbalances might in fact be simply a unilateral command. This claim, made often in times of elevated commodity prices, has driven many renegotiations in the last several years. Regardless of the normative inflection of partnerships, in practice, it is more important to look at how control over projects is actually shared in order to assess whether they advance or impede the public interest. This chapter looks at the transition from the colonial concession to the partnership agreement in an effort to highlight the importance of contracts for allocating benefits and burdens.

The bulk of these partnerships have been formed through the international infrastructure bank programs. This chapter looks at key regulatory and contractual issues mainly in the energy sector, but the issues are broadly applicable across P3 sectors. To do so, it provides an overview of contract types and then a discussion of several high-profile recurring issues. In discussing contract types, the chapter first provides a brief historical backdrop. It then turns to the major types: (1) modern concession; (2) production-sharing agreement; (3) joint venture; and (4) service contract, including risk service contracts, pure service contracts, and the technical assistance contract.[1] Both the history of traditional concessions and the enumerated present-day contract types are applicable to the oil and gas sectors and also to metal mineral extraction. For this reason, they will be discussed together.

II. History of Contracts

Historically, the principal contractual form in the extractive industry was the concession. A concession essentially grants a private company the exclusive right to explore, produce, and market natural resources. This contractual form has survived to this day; however, it pervades the United States in a vastly different form. Nevertheless, our understanding of the modern concession and other contractual forms for exploiting natural resources may be understood as a reaction against some of the excesses of the traditional concession. For this reason, it is useful to recount some of the basic features of traditional concessions, which sound repugnant to modern ears.

Importantly, the financial bargain struck between the host government and the foreign company was highly uneven, at times teetering on the verge of the unconscionable. Companies paid small sums to the host government for the rights to its natural resources. Typically, the compensation was not tied to the value of the resource itself. It was, however, tied to the volume produced. For example, the Oil Concession of 1934 between the State of Kuwait and the Kuwait Oil Company Limited, a Great Britain firm, states,

> (d) For the purpose of this Agreement and to define the exact product to which the Royalty stated above refers, it is agreed that the Royalty is payable on each English ton of 2,40 lb. of net crude petroleum won and saved by the Company from within the State of Kuwait – that is after deducting water, sand and other foreign substances and the oil required for the customary operations of the Company's installations in the Sheikh's territories.[2]

Because companies determined the volume of production, this meant that the interests of governments and companies could and often did diverge. That is, it was not always in the interest of companies to exploit resources fully.[3]

In addition, the scope of the traditional concession was broad, particularly with respect to duration and geography. For example, a foreign company could be granted rights from forty to seventy-five years. The Kuwait contract was to run for seventy-five years.[4] At times, the company secured rights over large tracts of land. This control could extend to the entire country.[5] The broad remit meant that the interests of companies in exploiting resources were not always congruent with those of the host government. For instance, a company might not always have a financial interest in comprehensive exploration. Thus, potential sources of revenue for the host government might not be identified and pursued. And because the contract granted exclusive rights to the foreign company for the period of the concession, the government could not seek a different and thirstier company. Exploration was contractually tied up. At times, certain parameters for exploration were set. This was the case in the Kuwait contract, which stated,

> (a) Within nine months from the date of signature of this Agreement the Company shall commence geological exploration.
>
> (b) The Company shall drill for petroleum to the following total aggregate depths and within the following periods of time at such and so many places as the Company may decide:

- 4,000 feet prior to the 4th anniversary of the date of signature of this Agreement.
- 12,000 feet prior to the 10th anniversary of the date of signature of this Agreement.
- 30,000 feet prior to the 20th anniversary of the date of signature of this Agreement.[6]

Importantly, these parameters allowed the company great freedom in determining the nature, scope, and extent of exploration.

These aspects of the concession agreement did not survive decolonization, the New International Economic Order, and the creation of OPEC. Expropriations and renegotiations as well as newly formed contracts saw to this. Importantly, as we move toward the present-day partnership-based contractual models, there is a concerted effort to rebalance specific contracts to remove many of these outmoded features.

III. Contract Types and Regulatory Models

Today, extraction contracts are premised on transnational public-private partnerships.[7] A transnational group of governments and companies generally shares control over the financing, exploration, production, and marketing of natural resources in varying degrees. For example, a foreign government may involve itself in a project through an export credit agency that advances loans to a project company; this is also the case, for example, in the Baku-Tbilisi-Ceyhan project. Through the involvement of export credit agencies, foreign governments may influence project decision-making. This influence may be amplified in situations in which several export credit agencies are involved in a single project and coordinate their activities. At times, intergovernmental banks may also be involved in a project. For example, the Inter-American Development Bank is involved in the Camisea project. Likewise, the International Financial Corporation is involved in the Baku-Tbilisi-Ceyhan and Chad Cameroon pipelines. The involvement of the export credit agencies and the international banks means that these agencies and banks will maintain their own respective project documentation, often in the form of loan agreements.

The nature and form of the overarching partnership, however, vary according to contract type. Furthermore, as we shall see, often the contractual clauses are even more important than the contract type in defining the nature of the partnership. The basic contract types are the (1) modern concession, (2) production-sharing agreement, (3) joint venture, and (4) service contract. Although each will be discussed in turn, it is important to stress that the content of contracts is often less dependent on type and more on specific terms.

In a field in which nationalism and antiforeign sentiment are rife, the name attached to an agreement may be more important rhetorically than in practice. One must recognize that the contract type that a host government decides on will not necessarily be uniform throughout all projects within the country. Certain projects may carry great exploration risks and thus call for a certain contract type. Nonetheless, from a developmental perspective, service contracts arguably afford the most independence to the host state. They are often associated with Middle Eastern countries that have high levels of domestic expertise. Joint ventures are next along the spectrum, because they involve substantial host state participation, sometimes a majority equity stake. Such ventures are common internationally. Thus, it will be important to identify the nature of the venture, that is, the relative percentages of ownership and control over the overall enterprise.

Production-sharing agreements are presently sites of intense controversy. In the former Soviet Union, there is some dissatisfaction with them in retrospect. And, in the Iraq context, public interest organizations argued that they were not an optimal means of achieving development. At the same time, in situations in which a large exploration risk exists, they may be the best way to advance developmental interests. Regardless of the contract type chosen, from a developmental perspective, it is important to attend to the levels of taxes and royalties as well as to clauses stipulating technology transfer and local sourcing requirements, among other issues. Given the fact that contracts are rarely public and that conditions vary from country to country and from project to project, it is difficult to provide an estimate of normal revenue splits.

Furthermore, when assessing the development impact of the different contractual forms and clauses, it is important to stress that generalizations are difficult. Not only do countries vary in the quality of their resources and in their level of domestic expertise, but it is possible that, as we shall see in the Iraq case, different projects within a country call for different contractual types. However, it may be argued that contractual clauses that focus on national content, local training, host government control over key decisions, and state-owned corporation participation all advance developmental objectives. From human rights and environmental perspectives, it may also be that the involvement of public and private international banks – and of certain oil majors with relevant policies – influences such practices on a project-specific basis.

The overriding importance of contractual clauses in determining the nature of revenue sharing means that it is difficult to generalize about the relationship between contract forms and revenue sharing. That is, royalty and taxation rates will be contractually determined. This is one reason why one must exercise caution in generalizing which contract type is best for development and financial purposes. At the same time, a qualitative difference exists between concession, joint venture, and risk-sharing agreements, on the one hand, and service contracts, on the other. Under the former models, the company will have a share in revenue, although the extent will depend on contractual clauses and legislation. Under the latter model, however, the company will be compensated generally by the host government for services carried out. Under such an arrangement, companies may have no stake in revenue. In other words, the company is contracted to provide a set service. The government pays the company accordingly in cash. As a result, the benefits of the commercial productivity of the project do not accrue to the company.

Importantly, the evolution from the concession contract to the modern participation agreements shows how the types of activities that contracts govern have changed over time. A greater emphasis today is placed on the development of local capacity. For example, contracts might stress that the foreign company must, all things being equal, purchase local content. In addition, a host government is more likely to play a role in projects through a state-owned company than was the case in the past. Furthermore, human rights and environmental commitments are perhaps the most significant recent development affecting projects. These commitments are incorporated into project documentation at the impetus of multinationals, private investment banks, or international financial institutions. These areas receive greater attention in the next section on contractual clauses and, with regard to human rights and the environment, within the following section on such inputs.

Before discussing relevant national and international legal aspects of projects, it is important to underscore that the contract will be the most important instrument by which benefits from and responsibilities of projects will be distributed. Importantly, national legislative action may establish the enabling environment in which contracts are negotiated and carried out. National regulatory action may also force the renegotiation of key contractual terms. With regard to international legal action, it is important to note that international organization action may impact on the contractual relationships among parties, as well as establish new parties. For example, if the World Bank's International Finance Corporation lends money to a project company, then it will be important to ascertain the terms of the loan and the mechanisms for enforcing provisions.

Furthermore, if, for example, the bank's Multilateral Investment Guarantee Agency provides political risk insurance for a project, this might influence the allocation of responsibilities among project parties in a material way. Because projects pull on international resources in different ways and because national legislation varies from country to country, it is not possible to arrive at ironclad rules regarding the relative importance of different levels of legal action. Nonetheless, the identification of the actors involved in specific projects is an important starting point for gauging relative influence.

A. Contracts at the National Level

At the national level, laws, regulations, and contract types are all important. This section, however, focuses mainly on contract types. At the same time, it is important to recognize that the importance of laws and regulations relative to contracts may vary; that is, laws and regulations may be more significant than contracts in the metal mineral sector of certain countries. However, Daniela Barberis, a leading commentator, makes the following point about the mining sector, which is significant for our purposes: "Many governments in developed countries use the unilateral licensing/leasing approach, while many developing countries prefer the consensual approach and use mining agreements which are negotiated with TMC [transnational mining companies]."[8]

Perhaps the difference in this approach lies in the purpose of mining legislation itself, which Barberis argues is to act as a signal of the host government's position toward investment in the sector. In developed countries, an investor would assume that a legislative signal amounts to secure investment that is relatively free of legislative risk. However, in developing countries, investors are keen to contractualize commitments by the government, arranging a reliable dispute-resolution mechanism, for instance. Australia provides an example in which the licensing system predominates. On the other hand, in Papua New Guinea mining agreements are of primary importance.[9] Nonetheless, laws and regulations are important in setting out the general enabling environment in which contracts will be negotiated and executed. Often a state-owned company or government ministry acts as the negotiating arm of the government. In such cases, regulations might explicitly delegate such authority to the public entity, which itself may be created by legislation. Both laws and regulations will be important for reinforcing contractual relationships and, at times, for altering such relations. For example, they may be the instrument guiding contract renegotiations. Legislated changes may be in the form of increases in rates of taxation or outright nationalizations. Nevertheless, contracts are important in setting out the primary relationships among parties.

For this reason, this section will look mainly at the different types of contracts, pointing out their similarities and differences. In addition, attention will be paid to how different contracts are suited to various economic situations. National laws and regulations will be discussed later in the chapter in the context of nationalizations and contractual renegotiations. In these situations, a legal or regulatory change may gear itself toward redefining the contractually determined relationship between host government and investor. It should be noted, however, that although the different contract forms will be elaborated in the following in turn, in practice the types sometimes mix with one another.

1. Modern concessions. Although the traditional concessionary contract is now a relic, concessions survive and flourish in many parts of the world, albeit sometimes as the less politically charged "license" or "lease."[10] Fundamentally, what distinguishes these two generations of concessions is the shift from an unequal bargain-based model toward a partnership-based one. As the other main contractual forms are introduced in the following, the differences between the modern concession and the other forms will be discussed. This section will set out the features of the modern concession that underscore its use as a partnership-based model.

The new generation of contracts aims to fulfill national development and welfare goals as well as purely financial ones. For example, the contract between Indonesia and P.T. Stanvac Indonesia provides the following:

> PTSI will plan and conduct all operations under this Contract in the best manner possible for the sound and progressive development of the petroleum industry in Indonesia, will at all times give consideration to the aspirations and welfare of the people of the Republic of Indonesia and to the economic development of the nation, and will cooperate with the Government in promoting the growth and development of the Indonesian economic and social structure by assisting in making available information and technical data relating to enterprises and developments which would be of mutual benefit to the Government and to the operations being conducted by PTSI as contractor for PN.[11]

Just as with the first generation of concessions, today's contracts grant the company the right to explore, produce, and market resources. However, the latitude afforded to companies is relatively curtailed. Control over projects is premised on partnership, not dominance. Accordingly, leading commentators speak of the move from concession to participation.[12] The actual distance between the traditional and modern often depends on the natural attributes of the country.

The most important set of nations in this regard are those that make up OPEC. Countries like Saudi Arabia, Iran, and Iraq all renegotiated traditional concessions, replacing them with dramatically different profit-sharing regimes.[13] Nonetheless, the locus of control has invariably shifted along the continuum toward partnership. Unlike the production-sharing agreement discussed in the following, the terms of participation are mainly based on a grant for a specified period of time. In contrast, the main aim of the production-sharing agreement is to encourage a company to undertake the exploration risk and, in return, provide a flexible period to recoup sunk costs and capture profits.

In many countries, the transmutation of the traditional concession into the modern one happened through host government–initiated renegotiations and nationalizations. These contract amendments were most famously carried out in Latin America and North Africa. The terms of the modern contracts that emerged varied from country to country and from project to project. Although projects were renegotiated by each government, in the oil sector, OPEC played a significant role in pooling information on terms of renegotiation among member countries.[14] Most governments sought to modify contracts so as to address the excesses of the traditional concessions discussed previously.

If the main criticisms of the concessions related to degree of foreign control, geographical scope, duration, and financial compensation, then it is unsurprising that the new contracts sought to rebalance these terms. Governments might limit the acreage of the concession and the duration of the contract. Thus, no longer would companies be granted rights to an entire country. Furthermore, host governments are now keen to ensure that companies cannot leave areas unexplored for long periods of time. Hosts now have a say in when a company must hand control over unexplored land back to the government. An Indonesian contract between Indonesia and P.T. Stanvac Indonesia sets forth a minimum expenditure on explorations by the oil company over a number of years:

> a. PTSI must commence exploratory operations in the New Area under this Contract not later than six (6) months after the date the ratification of this Contract is promulgated. The minimum amounts to be spent by PTSI in conducting operations during the first eight (8) years following the date of the ratification of this Contract is promulgated shall, in the aggregate, be not less than hereafter specified for each of these eight (8) years as follows:

First Contract Year	U.S. 1,000,000
Second Contract Year	U.S. 1,000,000
Third Contract Year	U.S. 1,500,000
Fourth Contract Year	U.S. 1,500,000
Fifth Contract Year	U.S. 1,250,000
Sixth Contract Year	U.S. 1,250,000
Seventh Contract Year	U.S. 1,250,000
Eighth Contract Year	U.S. 1,250,000[15]

Likewise, in an agreement between Egypt, the Egyptian General Petroleum Corporation, and Esso Egypt Inc. (United States), the concession provides: "ESSO shall spend a minimum of forty-eight (48) million U.S. dollars on exploration over a period of twelve (12) years." It then goes on to break down amounts that must be spent on a yearly basis.[16] The literature does not provide evidence of whether countries like Indonesia and Egypt have benefited from these modern concession contracts or if it has been wise for Indonesia, for instance, to subsequently pursue production-sharing agreements. The main clauses found in concessions are set forth in the following. Of course, contracts pick and choose among such clauses and the specifics vary.

With regard to finances, royalties – which had previously been tied to volume of production – might be made sensitive to the market value of the resources. Similarly, taxation regimes might be instituted, eclipsing a legacy of either no or minimal taxation.

2. Production-sharing agreements. Indonesia was first to employ production-sharing agreements.[17] As we shall see in the following discussion, such agreements are at the heart of present-day controversies over oil extraction, from regrets over their use in post-Soviet Russia to their proposed use in postwar Iraq.[18] They are less common in mining.[19] Barberis argues that they are unusual in mining, "because the Government does not have a major interest in receiving the actual production of mining activities as it does with petroleum."[20] Commentators have not seriously considered whether production-sharing agreements should be used more fully in mining. In Indonesia there was a discussion about using this type of agreement; however, ultimately it was decided that such a preference would have an adverse impact on the ability to secure foreign investment insurance.[21] This type of agreement grants a company the right to explore for natural resources. If resources are not found, then the company loses the money it spent. However, if commercially exploitable resources are discovered, then the company has the right to recoup sunk costs and then share in the profits. This is the incentive for shouldering the risk of nondiscovery.

The production-sharing agreement differs from the concession in two main respects. First, the production-sharing agreement does not grant the company ownership rights in the resource. The significance of this is that the government may take a greater interest in technology transfer, preparing for the eventual turning over of the resources to its hands. Furthermore, unlike the concession, which grants the company rights to the resource for a specified period of time, the production-sharing agreement grants the company an interest in the resource that is tied to the recouping of sunk costs and, of course, to the garnering of a profit. A production-sharing agreement may be useful to a host government that is keen to encourage a company to undertake the risk of exploration. The company might find it more useful than a modern concession, for instance, in the situation in which a company is uncertain about its ability to recoup its sunk costs within the strictly definite time period provided for by the modern concession. John S. Smith and colleagues identify the three key issues that production-sharing agreements must address: "(1) the existence of a work program or minimum dollar contribution towards development; (2) the duration of the exploration and development phase; and (3) the sharing of benefits of production between the multinational and state oil company if production is achieved."[22] Importantly, during a successful postdiscovery phase of cost recoup and profit garnering, the government does take a share of the financial largess through taxation and royalty.

Production-sharing agreements have been roughly devised to encourage private investment in untested areas. Host governments appreciate certain attributes of private companies, as is indicated by the Agreement on the Exploration, Development and Production Sharing for the Shakh Deniz Prospective Area in the Azerbaijan Sector of the Caspian Sea, which was signed between the State Oil Company of the Azerbaijan Republic (Azerbaijan), on the one hand, and Socar Commercial Affiliate (Azerbaijan), BP Exploration (Azerbaijan) Limited (UK), Elf Petroleum Azerbaijan B.V. (France), Lukoil International Limited (Russia), Oil Industries Engineering and Construction (Iran), Statoil Azerbaijan A.S. (Azerbaijan), and Turkish

Petroleum Overseas Company Limited (Turkey), on the other hand: "Whereas, Contractor has the technical knowledge and experience, the administrative and managerial expertise, and financial resources to efficiently develop and produce the Petroleum resources of the Contract Area, and desires to contract with SOCAR for that purpose."[23] As a result, companies are given special financial incentives to invest, but they also must shoulder the risk that no resources will be found. Along these lines, the Azerbaijan contract grants the companies the "sole and exclusive right to conduct Petroleum Operations within and with respect to the Contract Area."[24]

To entice companies to seek out resources, the host government, on discovery of resources, allows companies to recoup sunk costs and to garner an agreed-upon profit. If the company does not succeed in finding resources, then it generally loses the money it spent. The Azerbaijan agreement, for instance, provides the following:

> 2.2. Except as expressly provided elsewhere herein, in the event production resulting from Petroleum Operations, upon completion of commercial production from the Contract Area at the end of the term of this Agreement, inclusive of all extensions provided in Article 4 is insufficient for full recovery of Contractor's Capital Costs and Operating Costs as provided hereunder, the Contractor shall not be entitled to any reimbursement or compensation for any of its costs not recovered.[25]

If a commercial discovery is made, then the company has the right to recoup sunk costs and an agreed-upon profit. For example, the Azerbaijan contract indicates,

> (a) Contractor shall be entitled to the recovery of Petroleum costs as follows:
>
> (i) All Operating Costs shall first be recovered from Total Production;
>
> (ii) All Capital Costs shall then be recovered from a maximum of fifty (50) percent of Crude Oil and fifty (50) percent of Non-associated Natural Gas remaining out of Total Production after Crude Oil and Non-associated Natural Gas required to recover Contractor's Operating Costs ("Capital Cost Recovery Petroleum"). (Final Consolidated Version 3/30/96: Article 11 Contractor's Recovery of Petroleum Costs and Production Sharing, 11.2 Cost Recovery (a)(i) and (ii))

Afterwards, according to this particular agreement, profit sharing between the host government and the companies kicks in, according to a profit-sharing formula.[26]

Under production-sharing agreements, in the partnership forged between governments and companies, the host maintains varying degrees of oversight over decision-making. The life cycle of the project is important in this situation. If a project will eventually shift to government control once the company has recouped costs and captured a profit, then the host must plan from the start for this eventuality. This means that decisional control is partially reserved for the government even during the period of robust private involvement. For example, in the Azerbaijan case, a steering committee was established to oversee the project:

> 5.1 Steering Committee for Project Management
>
> SOCAR and Contractor shall, not later than thirty (30) days from the commencement of the Development and Production Period establish the Steering Committee.
>
> The functions of the Steering Committee shall include but not be limited to:
>
> (a) overseeing Petroleum Operations;
> (b) examination, revision and approval of Contractor's Annual Work Programmes and Budgets;
> (c) supervising the accounting of costs and expenses in accordance with the Accounting Procedure;
> (d) establishing sub-committees of the Steering Committee and reviewing the work of such sub-committees;
> (e) reviewing, revising and approving training programmes;
> (f) review and approval of the abandonment plan and cost of abandonment operations pursuant to Article 14.2 (g).[27]

The government must also ensure that it has the knowledge and expertise necessary to eventually run the project. The attendant increased microlevel government participation is also in line with the overarching emphasis on partnership.

3. Joint ventures. Also in line with the partnership-based approach, under the joint venture arrangement, the foreign company does business with a national state-owned company. The venture may involve creating a jointly controlled project company. As with the concession and the production-sharing agreement, it is important to look to the specifics of the venture's legal arrangement to ascertain the extent to which control over the companies rests in foreign or domestic hands. As indicated, contract types often bleed into one another. Nonetheless, what is important about the joint venture, in distinction to the modern concession and production-sharing agreements in their purest forms, is that it provides a corporate-based, structured means for technology transfer and shared decision-making. Of course, such goals may be accomplished through other instruments; however, a corporate partnership may be the most strategically attuned means available.

Joint venture agreements can be found throughout the world. Contracts are not generally public, so it is not possible to conclude that they look the same everywhere. Nonetheless, it is fair to assume that the content of joint venture contracts is shaped by political exigencies everywhere. Thus, when the host government is in a particularly strong negotiating position, the local partner may have greater rights than in a situation in which the local government is weak. The politicized nature of these arrangements is evidenced by the recent controversy over the Russian government's intervention in the Sakhalin-2 project, a joint venture among Shell, Mitsui (Japan), and Mitsubishi (Japan).

Importantly, joint ventures may be incorporated into other contractual types, such as the production-sharing agreement. For example, the Azerbaijan contract involves mixed corporate participation. The relevant clause is set out in the next section. Likewise, the Camisea project discussed in Chapter 4 is a joint venture project. It is important to look at the specific clauses included in the joint venture agreement. Once again, this may be more a matter of picking and choosing the desired clauses than relying on a specific contract form.

Like the production-sharing agreement, the joint venture arrangement puts a premium on technology transfer. The aim is to foster eventual genuine independence by the state-owned company. Inevitably, the prospect of independence runs counter to the interests of multinationals. As a result, the extent of technology transfer built into the joint venture is negotiated and varies depending on the bargaining strength of the national government.

4. Service contracts. Often the government seeks to exert greater control over the exploration and exploitation of its resources. It may do this through service contracts, whereby private companies are brought in to accomplish carefully delimited tasks. Unlike modern concessions, production-sharing agreements, and joint ventures, service contracts are thought of as a device in which the host government exercises the greatest control over the project. That is, the host government contracts the foreign company only to achieve a carefully delimited service. The company does not generally share in the revenue produced. Thus, the host government does not cede control of the resource in a meaningful way. As might be obvious, under the service contract, a host government must have the requisite technological know-how and access to capital. Often this is not the case when exploration risk capital is required. It is also important to remember that a service contract might be for a minor task, in which case it is preferable to the other contract forms. The three main types of service contracts are the risk service contract, the pure service contract, and the technical assistance contract. They will be discussed briefly in turn.

a. Risk service contracts. Like the production-sharing agreement, the risk service contract addresses the situation in which a host government seeks to utilize private companies to bear the risk of exploration. Two scenarios are envisioned: either commercially exploitable resources are identified or they are not. If they are, then the company receives cash remuneration for its efforts, in addition to a possible stake in the subsequent enterprise. If resources are not found, then the company is out the money invested.[28] These types of contracts are generally out of favor.[29]

b. Pure service contracts. More straightforward is the pure service contract, whereby a company is brought in to fulfill a defined service and is compensated accordingly. Unlike the risk service contract, the host government shoulders all risks. Under this type of contract, the company also attains an interest in the extracted resource.[30]

c. Technical assistance contracts. The last main type of service contract is the technical assistance contract. Its scope is narrower. As with the other service contracts, the company is brought in to fulfill a defined task for which it receives a fixed compensation. However, unlike the other service contracts, the company has no possibility of attaining an interest in the resource.[31] Importantly, on its face, the technical service contract appears closest to a transnational public-private partnership in which the host government is the strongest party. Once again, it is important to recognize that contract choice is tied as much to rhetorical needs as to anything else. Ernest E. Smith explains, "The technical assistance agreement is one of several types of arrangements that can be used to take advantage of the multinationals' technological and managerial expertise and capital resources while allowing the host country to maintain at least the appearance that its state oil company has control and ownership."[32] Often, service contracts are held out as the ideal choice in situations characterized by nationalism. However, the value of a host country's natural resources may be more determinative of contract form choice. Nonetheless, as indicated previously, the meaning of the contract may ultimately lie in the content of the clauses.

5. Contractual clauses. As indicated previously, the choice of contract type might be less important than the content of particular contract clauses. Dzienkowski argues,

> As stated before, although one can attempt to offer conceptual and theoretical differences among the three [contractual types], in reality it may be difficult to classify petroleum agreements into one category. This difficulty may result from a harmonization of agreements whereby the parties are borrowing the best type of agreement to fit a particular situation.[33]

This section sets forth a number of important contractual clauses.

In a joint venture arrangement, a contract may specify the percentages held in the enterprise by the various contracting parties. So, for example, the Azerbaijan contract provides the following breakdown:

> 1.1 The Rights and Obligations under this Agreement of each of the Contracting Parties shall be held in the following respective percentage of Participating Interests as of the date this Agreement is executed:

CONTRACTOR PARTIES	PERCENTAGE
SCA	10.0%
BP	25.5%
Elf	10%
Lukoil	10%
OIEC	10%
Statoil	25.5%
TPAO	9.0%
TOTAL	100.00%[34]

The number of parties to such an agreement and their respective shares are, of course, project dependent.

Another important clause in a contract is the one setting out reimbursement for sunk exploration costs. In some cases, the project company will shoulder this risk, as under the production-sharing agreement. However, in other cases, the host government may cover all or part of this cost. Similarly, a clause might indicate the company's responsibilities during the exploration phase. This might include a commitment to spend a specified amount of money on exploration or to undertake an agreed-upon level of exploration. There may be a provision within the contract indicating the circumstances under which the company may be granted an extension of the time allotted for exploration.

A different set of provisions may govern the discovery phase. For example, the company will be obligated to notify the host government in the case of a discovery of a commercially exploitable resource. The Azerbaijan contract provides the following:

> 4.4 Discovery
>
> Before the end of the Exploration Period or if the Contractor enters the Additional Exploration Period then [sic] before the end of the Additional Exploration Period, Contractor shall notify SOCAR in writing of a Discovery and its commerciality, summarising relevant information relating to said Discovery, including but not limited to the following, to the extent same are available: location plan, geographical maps and interpretations, seismic and

> other geophysical data, drilling chapters, well logs, core samplings, lithographical maps and description of formations, drill stem tests, completion chapters, production tests including quantities of fluid produced, build-up/draw down tests and pressure analysis, and analyses of oil, gas and water samples and other information consistent with generally accepted Petroleum industry practice ("Notice of Discovery and its Commerciality").[35]

Moving forward, contractual clauses may set out the specific terms governing the production phase. This phase may last a certain number of years, and a clause may set out the conditions on which the phase may be extended. It may be important for the host government to set out specific commitments during this phase, because, as indicated earlier, it is possible that host government and company interests will diverge. That is, it might not be in the commercial interests of the company to fully exploit reserves within the time frame that the government desires.

As indicated in the previous section on production-sharing agreements, many of these decisions regarding the strategic exploitation of reserves may be governed by an oversight committee with representatives from the host government and companies. A mechanism for decision sharing may be a useful way of resolving conflicting commercial and political interests.

Contracts may also stipulate certain local content preferences. For example, a contract may include a clause indicating that the company is to employ local workers, so long as they meet certain qualifications. For example, the Azerbaijan contract provides the following:

> (b) Contractor shall require Operating Company to give preference, as far as is consistent with efficient operations, to employ citizens of the Azerbaijan Republic in the performance of Petroleum Operations to the extent reasonably practicable, provided that such citizens have the required knowledge, qualifications and experience. Such citizens shall be eligible for training in Accordance with Article 6.8.[36]

The host government might require that the company train locals. Likewise, a company may agree to source goods locally. For example, the relevant part of the agreement between Egypt, the Egyptian General Petroleum Corporation, and Esso Egypt Inc. (United States) provides the following:

> ARTICLE XXIII
>
> LOCAL CONTRACTORS AND LOCALLY MANUFACTURED EQUIPMENT
>
> (a) The Operator and its contractors shall: –
>
> (1) Give priority to local contractors as long as their prices and performance are comparable with International prices and performance. The Operator shall, however, subject to the preceding sentence, be

exempted from the provisions of Presidential Decree No. 1203 of 1961 as amended.

(2) Give preference to locally manufactured materials, equipment, machinery and consumables, however, such material may be imported for operations conducted hereunder if the price of locally manufactured material at Operator's stores is more than ten (10%) per cent higher than the price of the imported material at Operator's stores.[37]

It is also worth noting that contracts may require that the company keep certain records of its operations. Governments may find such provisions useful in determining taxation and royalty rates. Governments may not always have the expertise or capacity to enforce certain revenue schemes. Thus, such clauses may reduce the burden on the government.

Moving forward in the project cycle, a contract may provide for the transfer of control away from the company and to the host government. For example, a clause may provide that facilities will be transferred to the government as the company leaves the country. The clause may stipulate the condition of the facility.

And, lastly, as indicated in the following section on renegotiations, a contract will typically include a clause indicating how disputes, should they arise, will be resolved. That is, both the forum and choice of law may be stipulated in the contract.

In conclusion, it is important to note that one cannot generalize about revenue sharing and the prevalence of specific contract clauses within agreements. Such information is not publicly available. At the same time, one might ask whether it would be in the interests of developing countries to have such information published. At present, it is the sort of information that experienced countries and active law firms might hold privately.

B. Bilateral and Multilateral Agreements

Although this chapter focuses mainly on contract types, it is important to point to key bilateral and multilateral legal issues raised by the involvement of infrastructure banks. Because of space constraints, this section aims to point to key issues rather than providing a cursory survey. It first looks briefly at bilateral investment treaties and bilateral subsidy programs. It then turns to the multilateral level, looking at the subsidy programs of international financial institutions.

Parties to an investment agreement generally stipulate the choice of law and forum in which any contractual disputes will be heard. A dispute might be heard in an international arbitration tribunal or in the national courts. Parties might have to exhaust local courts before turning to the international tribunal. In situations of ambiguity, a relevant bilateral investment treaty between the governments of the respective parties may provide guidance. Otherwise, it is worth noting that legal scholars are presently debating the significance of bilateral investment treaties for development.[38] However, to date, legal studies have not isolated treaties relating to oil and gas or hard mineral extraction for study. Thus, given the early stage of these studies and the lack of relevant sector-specific published data, it is too early to generalize about the relationship between bilateral investment agreements, investment, and development in our area.

Many international projects rely on public and private sources of financing, and on financing from domestic, foreign, and international sources. In this section, we focus on the legal implications of foreign public sources of financing. National public banks and insurance agencies play a role in facilitating projects through subsidy programs. These subsidies range from the political risk insurance provided by the U.S Overseas Private Investment Corporation (OPIC) to the loans offered by the U.S. Export-Import Bank or the French Coface. These public subsidies are used by project companies to encourage private banks to invest in projects that are otherwise too politically risky. Importantly, developing countries increasingly have their own export banks, which play a role in facilitating South-South investment. Public banks may facilitate private investment through finance-sweetening insurance policies, loan agreements, and feasibility studies. They may also mitigate political risk through informal political intervention. In other words, their involvement may mean that the home state government of the multinational involved might be willing to step in, should a conflict arise with the host government, and use diplomacy to smooth the situation.

At the international level, subsidies similar to bilateral-based subsidies exist. Also, it is important to reference the Energy Charter Treaty, which advances sustainable and sovereignty-respecting development. The most important public subsidies are offered by the World Bank Group through its International Finance Corporation (IFC) and Multilateral Investment Guarantee Agency (MIGA). The Oil, Gas, Mining and Chemicals Department of the IFC is relevant.

For example, the Baku-Tbilisi-Ceyhan oil pipeline relies on a diverse set of public agencies. The pipeline part of this project runs through several countries, including Azerbaijan, Georgia, and Turkey. It is approximately 154 miles long. Among others, this pipeline is financed by seven export credit agencies, the European Bank for Reconstruction and Development, the IFC, and fifteen commercial banks.[39] Each bank, public or private, will have its own set of project documentation. This may mean multiple loan agreements, each with its own set of terms and conditions. At the same time, the actions of multiple public and private banks are often coordinated.

Importantly, these public agencies may attach certain conditions to their subsidies. For example, both OPIC and the Export-Import Bank often attach environmental and human rights conditions to their loans. Complying with these conditions may mean establishing special entities or hiring consultants to ensure that wishes are fulfilled. Importantly, they must be understood in tandem with international efforts through the IFC and MIGA. They must also be related to the initiative by the major private investment banks involved in the projects, the so-called Equator Principles.

IV. Conclusion

This chapter showed how partnerships have been asked to renegotiate the basic imbalances of colonialism and some of the inherent challenges faced. Next, we turn to a discussion of how renegotiations of partnerships to rebalance them can also pose serious empirical, normative, and policy challenges in practice.

12

Renegotiations

I. Introduction

For a number of chapters we have looked at infrastructure banks and partnerships, focusing on what they deliver in practice. Our aim has been to learn from experience when modeling our own domestic bank. This chapter looks at an important movement around the world that is under way right now. From Latin America to Africa, we live in a period of widespread renegotiations of extractive concessionary public-private partnership (P3) contracts. Almost universally, government-driven renegotiations are justified based on domestic demand. In other words, arguments are made by politicians, protestors, citizens, and others that the legacy of the privatization of natural resources represents a usurpation of ownership by a foreign entity over a national birthright. Claimants argue that foreign control over P3s is akin to neo-colonial rule. This argument harks back to the last period of renegotiations and cancellations – the initiation of the decidedly anticolonial New International Economic Order. The government thus acts as an instrument of the people to take back control of a national property.

This discussion of renegotiations highlights the fact that partnerships themselves can be dramatically reconfigured over time. Moreover, it is not always clear that shifts in the nature of partnerships result in more equitable outcomes. For this reason, as we revisit and reforge our own partnerships, it is important to benchmark them against both what has gone before and the types of issues that countries around the world have faced. This inequality that might inhere not only in partnerships but also in their renegotiation was also a persistent feature in the American nineteenth- and early-twentieth-century railroads.

Thus, when renegotiations do happen, the logical next question is whether the new contractual arrangement benefits the constituency in whose name the revision occurred. That is, do the renegotiated contracts distribute revenue domestically in an equitable manner that promotes sustainable development goals?

At the same time, when discussing government-driven renegotiations, it is important to note that this story of national repossession is not a universal one. For example, fully industrialized countries without a legacy of colonial occupation also renegotiate contracts. Moreover, many governments – for example, those of the United Kingdom and Brazil – are on the downside of renegotiations. Nonetheless, many renegotiations throughout the world result in increased government revenue share. This chapter discusses these government-driven renegotiations. Specifically, the concern is with how the benefits from these renegotiations are distributed within the country.

These renegotiations do not only occur with the legacy of privatizations. They also happen often in the context of the so-called natural resource curse. That is, countries with spectacular extractive resources are often mired in poverty and conflict. Furthermore, arguments often go one step further, claiming that it is the abundant resources themselves that cause the political and economic problems. Nonetheless, enormous energy is devoted to promoting sustainable development within resource-rich countries facing these problems. Just as explanations of the nature of the curse are multicausal, so too are policy prescriptions. However, an increasing consensus is emerging that transparency is an important step toward remedying the problem and putting governments on a path toward sustainability and growth.

To this end, in the extractives sector, a coalition comprising large numbers of public interest groups has mounted a campaign to increase transparency within resource-rich countries. This campaign is supported by many governments, intergovernmental organizations, and companies. The Publish What You Pay campaign was formed to promote the use of extractive revenue to achieve poverty reduction, economic growth, and sustainable development. The Revenue Watch Institute has been important. The campaign aims to counter the inequitable use of revenue leading to the exacerbation of conflict and encouragement of corruption. The premise of the campaign is that transparency in management and revenue use results in greater equity in decision-making.

These groups have made the case for transparency and produced tangible results, articulating agendas, defining issues, and advocating for processes. More than one country have agreed to produce reports on transparency in their extractive sector. Much of the success has been in establishing agenda-driven processes. Light has been shed on aspects of the revenue streams, particularly in flows between multinationals and governments. At the same time, the movement toward transparency is still in its infancy. With regard to the issue at hand within this chapter, information regarding how revenues are distributed domestically, very little is known. In the next section, a number of points will be made regarding the limitations inherent in measuring this phenomenon.

Although concrete successes have resulted from this extractives campaign, the debates over transparency and accountability within renegotiations are largely normative. Most agree that, regardless of the side one takes on the advisability of renegotiations, revenue streams generated from extractives projects should be channeled to productive domestic purposes in an equitable fashion. This chorus is sung by intergovernmental organizations, donor countries, transnational corporations, investment banks, civil society organizations, academics, and others. Given the low level of transparency with regard to where revenues go, the resultant discussion is largely prescriptive. For this reason, this chapter is careful to make explicit an analysis of the empirical basis for claims made about how revenues are distributed domestically. To put it mildly, the body of empirical data on this aspect of renegotiation is sparse.

This chapter attempts to cast light on how increased revenues are distributed domestically. The approach is comparative, qualitative, and evaluative, with reference to specific facts when reliable. The next section makes a number of points about measurement. Then, we turn to a brief overview of renegotiations. The fourth section presents a number of representative case studies. Given the partial record, focus is paid (1) to evaluating current practices of renegotiations at different stages (Venezuela and Bolivia), (2) to understanding how the processes by which renegotiations are pursued might determine outcomes (Congo), and (3) to understanding how resource revenues might be rechanneled to diversify economies more generally (Qatar). A number of concluding observations are then made.

II. Measurement Issues

Before presenting the case studies, given the transparency problems endemic in the renegotiation process, it is necessary to make a number of points about measuring resource distribution. These points are made to highlight the need to be skeptical about claims regarding the actual impact of renegotiations on domestic policies. At the same time, these points are also raised to (1) highlight what is measurable and (2) make clear what we would need to know to understand more fully the phenomenon under study.

First, the extractive sector of most countries is notoriously not transparent. A broad-based multi-stakeholder coalition has promoted the Extractives Industry Transparency Initiative, which aims to remedy this lack of transparency. The premise of this initiative is that lack of transparency exacerbates poverty, corruption, and conflict. Making information known about the nature of agreements will, it is argued, drive poverty reduction, economic growth, and sustainable development. In other words, a remedy of the so-called natural resource curse may be greater publicizing of revenue streams and use. Thus, this chapter must contend with the fact that this transparency does not currently exist and revenue streams are widely seen as captured by a small set of actors. That is, the lack of transparency makes measurement itself difficult.

Second, the nature of the underlying distribution of revenue from projects may be set forth within the contracts governing specific projects. In fact, efforts to renegotiate projects result in revision of material contract terms. However, the contracts themselves are rarely publicly available, as will be discussed in the Congo case study.[1] As a result, the specifics of revisions are not known, compounding accountability shortcomings. Moreover, as we shall see in the Venezuela case study, oil revenues are often channeled off of the balance sheet of the state. Because information on renegotiations is held away from regulatory environments and instead within privately held contracts, it is difficult to ascertain material commitments. As a result, it is difficult to ascertain whether parties are carrying out their commitments.

Third, renegotiations are sometimes part of larger regime change within countries such as Bolivia, Venezuela, and the Congo. A correlation may thus exist between renegotiations and a reallocation of government budgets toward a new set of priorities that bring a new government into power. At the same time, the nature of the causal nexus between renegotiations and redistribution may not be readily apparent. For example, as we shall see within this chapter, the renegotiation of oil projects has resulted in contributions into general development and poverty reduction funds. Disaggregating the source of funds is thus not always possible.

Fourth, many of the changes discussed in this chapter are recent or have not been extensively evaluated from the perspective of their impact on societies writ large. Much of the literature and public policy discussion are prescriptive. Moreover, given the importance of the underlying equity issue, the antagonistic nature of policy debates, and the amount of financial capital at stake, sharp disagreement exists over the factual record. The statistics are often government-produced and contested – a point made often with regard to the Venezuelan renegotiations and the difficulty of identifying reliable data. And many of the societal projects to which revenues are channeled are medium or long term in their expected return. For example, as we shall see with the Qatar case study, even a seemingly robust and promising societal plan may take time to reap rewards. Thus the nature and extent of benefits produced are not always readily and immediately ascertainable.

Fifth, because renegotiations often occur in association with spikes in commodity prices, it is not always clear whether benefits accrued result from price elevation generally or renegotiated terms specifically. The point is often made by transnational corporations that renegotiations may dry up pools of financial capital necessary to invest in exploration. Similarly, renegotiations may sever international ties essential to ensuring effective distribution networks and access to markets. These two points are made in the Bolivian context discussed in the following. Also, as we shall see in our discussion of Qatar, the most important point may be how one uses revenue from extractives. Of course, in places like the Congo where the pre-renegotiation revenue share is enormously unbalanced, it may be impossible to capture the benefits of commodity prices without renegotiation.

Sixth, although each of the case studies concerns itself with the use of revenues domestically, the international context is enormously important everywhere in determining the nature of this use. This is true not only in relation to the market and financial capital issue. It is also true for countries like Venezuela that seek to use renegotiations to redefine the country's role in the world.

However, even given these qualifications about our ability to measure the phenomenon under study, something nonetheless may be said about how the benefits of renegotiations are distributed domestically. Even more might be said if we broaden our inquiry slightly to ask how the elevation in commodity value affects internal development strategies in emerging economies generally. For this reason, this chapter makes a point of discussing how Qatar is channeling these upside benefits of commodity price elevations into grand societal plans. In addition, the chapter aims to give further texture to the transparency debate by asking what more we would like to know in order to understand the distribution of revenue domestically.

III. Overview of Renegotiations

Government-driven renegotiations are a by-product of the elevation of natural resources prices now under way. Rising commodity prices are attributed to a range of factors including economic growth in China, India, and elsewhere, resulting in a thirst for metals, minerals, and oil and gas. Another factor is conflict in the Middle East. After decades of a buyer-driven market, the demand for these commodities has returned us to a sellers' market, although it is unclear what the legacy of the financial crisis will ultimately be on commodity prices and renegotiations. As a result, buyer-oriented contracts are being reopened. A spate of renegotiations has resulted. Such government-driven renegotiations have occurred in Algeria, Angola, Argentina, Bolivia, Brazil, China, Congo, Denmark, Ecuador, Egypt, India, Indonesia, Kazakhstan, Libya, Netherlands, Nigeria, Pakistan, Russia, Sudan, Trinidad and Tobago, United Kingdom, United States, and Venezuela.

With the price of the underlying commodity substantially elevated, such renegotiations are entirely predictable. Governments seek to reopen contractual bargains that distributed the upside benefit of commodity price increases to transnational firms. It is important to remember that this allocation of benefits and risks resulted not only from low commodity prices but also often from the shouldering of exploration risks by companies. In renegotiating terms, governments make the argument that the original bargain disproportionately favored foreign interests.

Renegotiations are a genre of nationalization that has a long history. In the nineteenth century, infrastructure nationalizations in the rail sector were prevalent. In the twentieth century, infrastructure nationalizations were prolific across sectors. Extractive nationalizations impacted substantially on the distribution of power throughout the world.

Extractive nationalizations started before the Second World War with Mexican nationalizations of U.S. oil company property in the late 1930s. Many subsequent postwar nationalizations were tied to a period of decolonization and the reversal of what were seen as unequal and at times unconscionable deals. Nationalizations happened in Iran, Egypt, Chile, Bolivia, and elsewhere.[2]

The present-day renegotiation argument is often framed in the context of neo-colonialism. That is, a set of foreign interests controls a primary national source of wealth. Political independence exists in a context of international economic disparities that are sometimes extreme. Moreover, the neo-colonial critique has further resonance because it harks back to the last significant period of renegotiations that occurred in the wake of decolonization. Then too, contracts were reopened with arguments that the bargains that they represented were grossly lopsided. Furthermore, this previous wave of renegotiations occurred mainly during commodity price spikes that highlighted the inequities of the underlying bargain.

At the same time, although resonances to the last wave of renegotiation have rhetorical purchase, substantial differences exist that impact on the subject of the chapter. The main difference is that civil society actors, both domestic groups and international public interest organizations, play an increased role in defining the nature of the national public interest in the context of renegotiations. That is, during the previous wave, the New International Economic Order was premised on a right to development in which governments were the definers and guardians of the national interest. Even though the right to development was at times critiqued for this, in practice an alternative model was not obvious. Today, civil society, however uneven and critiqued, presents a secondary set of voices with a degree of legitimacy in claiming to speak for a national public interest.

Furthermore, the renegotiation itself is legitimized because government seeks terms that allocate benefits to the population writ large. In other words, if natural resources are the property of the people of a specific nation, then the government has a fiduciary duty to ensure the advancement of its domestic constituency. For this reason, governments conjure the national interest when pursuing renegotiations. For example, in Bolivia renegotiations were driven in part by protests, and in Ecuador protests impacted on bottom-line decision-making.[3] Likewise, Venezuelan president Hugo Chavez has made the case that state control over natural resources is popularly motivated.

IV. Case Studies: Domestic Distribution of Revenue

Discussions of renegotiations lump large numbers of countries together. In practice, although most governments justify renegotiation using common arguments about national birthright and foreign usurpation of control, the fact that countries vary dramatically in their natural resources, political composition, history, place in international commercial and political life, and stage of renegotiation means that discussions must attend to variation. Moreover, as was discussed in Section II, a range of measurement problems exists that affects our understanding of the renegotiation processes in different countries.

This chapter adopts a case study approach to understand renegotiation and the resulting distribution of domestic revenue. It offers representative cases. The first case, Venezuela, is a prominent case in which the government used the renegotiation process as a means of carrying out a massive reallocation of power within the country. Next, we turn to Bolivia. Like in Venezuela, the Bolivian case is a Latin American renegotiation in which popular demands were harnessed to drive renegotiation. However, Bolivia differs from Venezuela in that it has arguably less leverage. As a result, the terms of renegotiation that Bolivia can realistically dictate are more modest. Our third case study, the Democratic Republic of the Congo (DRC), looks at an early-stage renegotiation. As a result, not as much is known about the impact that renegotiations will ultimately have. Nonetheless, the case of the DRC is notable because of debates around the process of renegotiation itself. The Congo is a laboratory for understanding whether a carefully modeled process for carrying out renegotiations will result in a certain distribution of domestic resources. That is, do transparent renegotiations produce more equitable domestic revenue spreads? Our final case study, Qatar, does not explicitly address a situation of renegotiation. Instead, it asks whether benefits from commodity price spikes can be used effectively to reorient domestic agendas, leading to a diversification of the economy. In other words, does a legacy of extractive dependence constrain forward-looking economic decision-making?

A. Venezuela

In 2001, Venezuela passed a new hydrocarbons law reorganizing the sector and renegotiating the benefit spread between foreign investors and the government. The hydrocarbons law required that future investments in the country be 51 percent controlled by the state-owned entity, Petroleos de Venezuela S.A. (PDVSA). At the same time, the government has progressively renegotiated existing contracts to also conform to this 51 percent share. In 2007, by presidential decree, Hugo Chavez ordered the expropriation of projects on the Orinoco River Belt. In doing so, Venezuela formed mixed corporate entities charged with exploiting resources with PDVSA, holding a majority equity stake in them. In addition, the hydrocarbons law reapportioned royalty rates.

These renegotiations have occurred within a larger seismic shift in the role of government within the Venezuelan economy. The rise of the presidency of Chavez has been subject to much debate, and the impact of his policies on the society writ large and on foreign investment has been hotly contested. Investors have been sharply critical of the reallocation of resource revenues to domestic programs.[4] It should not come as a surprise then that an assessment of the impact of renegotiations on the internal distribution of resources is passionately discussed.

This section thus seeks both to set forth those aspects of the record on which consensus exists and to analyze divergent views on the nature and impact of renegotiations. Importantly, the transformation of the Venezuelan political landscape, the country's aspirations, and the role of natural resources therein are also tied to regional and international ambitions; however important, these developments are outside the scope of this chapter.[5]

1. The mechanics. PDVSA, a creature of state law (Organic Law Reserving to the State 1975), plays a central role in mediating the distribution of natural resource benefits within the country. It is a holding company comprising all of the state-owned entities in the sector. The Organic Hydrocarbons Law (2002) and the Organic Law of Gas Hydrocarbons (1999 and 2000) set forth the rules governing the company. The Ministry of Energy and Petroleum oversees PDVSA and controls its governance and operations. The companies gathered within the holding company participate under the strictures of private commercial law. The private nature of these companies makes them less amenable to study.

For our purposes, PDVSA is significant mainly because, under the two hydrocarbons laws, it must contribute to state-sponsored social programs. These contributions take a number of forms.

PDVSA and its component companies make direct financial contributions to government programs. They also offer managerial assistance. These social programs are far-reaching and include alternative energy, education, health care, infrastructure, job creation, regional economic development programs, and subsidized food distribution.

Although PDVSA efforts are generally discussed in terms of freestanding social development objectives, the company's aspirations are integrated into national plans. Figures vary widely in the amount of capital channeled to domestic programs by the company relative to other sources. Michael Shifter estimated in 2006 that twenty billion dollars had been directed over a three-year period.[6] In 2007, Mark Weisbrot argued that social spending had increased more than three-hundred-fold since Chavez took office.[7] At the same time, determining the extent of social spending originating from oil renegotiations is fraught with difficulty. Nonetheless, Weisbrot and Luis Sandoval estimate that the amount of social spending contributed by PDVSA amounted to 7.3 percent of the gross domestic product (GDP) in 2006.[8]

The PDVSA's role in national social and economic development was reformulated with the change in political regime that brought Chavez to power. The company was reformulated. The new government leadership argued for a shift away from oil management and production serving elite interests. Chavez also desired a shift away from PDVSA as an instrument of foreign concerns. Instead, the PDVSA would, according to Rafael Ramirez of the Ministry of Energy and Petroleum, be "at the service of the Venezuelan people, of our highest interests, which cover all sectors of the country." Ramirez placed the company into the broader Plan for Sowing the Oil, a strategic direction for the sector for 2005–2030. The plan seeks to ensure that national capacities are strengthened and the economic order itself is reconstructed to be fairer and more balanced through building capacities, promoting development, deconcentrating the population, and continuing to build the industrial sector.[9]

Sharp disagreement exists over the nature of the PDVSA initiatives and their impact on the alleviation of poverty. On the one hand, many commentators view the PDVSA funds as a device for establishing a patronage system within the country with dubious positive impact. On the other hand, some commentators argue that PDVSA programs have increased government revenues directed at tackling poverty and that a number of discernable significant outcomes have been produced. Before elaborating on this controversy, it is useful first to set out the activities of PDVSA. It is also important to put these controversies into perspective for our purposes: they generally are concerned mainly with revenues directed at poverty alleviation, whereas our concern is with the distribution of revenues domestically in a broader sense.

With regard to alternative energy, PDVSA has invested in ethanol production. In the short term, this production will feed into its gasoline products. Ethanol is envisaged as an environmentally sustainable energy source. Also, ethanol programs aim to reinforce agricultural programs within the country. This is part of a rural development strategy based on sugarcane and yucca.

Large amounts of money have either been promised or transferred to various social programs. Although some financial figures are available, how and whether PDVSA money has been spent is not transparent. Much of the money is off the balance sheet and government-controlled. Moreover, as discussed in the following, the impact of money promised and spent has not been subject to reliable analysis.

PDVSA funds reinforce a development strategy premised on community-based development. To do so, it supports Endogenous Development Nuclei, which are local empowerment organizations. PDVSA argues that it uses these organizations to promote self-sufficiency in a way that respects pluralism within the country. These efforts aim to eradicate poverty throughout the country and support minority group interests. In doing so, they promote a number of principles: (1) citizen empowerment and education aimed at increasing participation in all areas of national life, (2) formulation and implementation of national strategies and programs that integrate PDVSA activities with other initiatives, and (3) ensuring that PDVSA initiatives are in line with community interests and that channels of communication are open and productive between these initiatives and those interests.

The main PDVSA-controlled fund is Fondespa, the Fund for Social and Economic Development within the Country. Its mandate arises out of Article 5 of the Organic Law of Hydrocarbons. Fondespa is specifically devoted to redressing inequalities within the country and has been championed by President Chavez. It was formalized by the shareholders in 2004 "to fulfill the principles of a proper nexus between revenues coming from hydrocarbons and the national economy."[10] It does so through investments in social welfare, human capitalization, social and economic development, infrastructure, services, and promotion of financial improvements in the oil sector. In doing so, PDVSA seeks to address the natural resource curse – widespread poverty and inequality in the face of tremendous natural resource wealth. The fund is administered by Banco de Desarrollo y Social (BANDES), the Social and Economic Development Bank.

According to Ramirez, by 2005 PDVSA had placed $2.84 billion into Fondespa.[11] Whether the money has been spent or replenished subsequently is not entirely clear. Furthermore, disagreement exists over whether the money in Fondespa goes toward social programs or toward other investments related to currency hedging. One figure estimates not only that the fund holds $2.84 billion but that 80 percent of that has been invested in social and development programs. According to the government, the breakdown of expenditures is (1) 26 percent into electricity improvements, (2) 24 percent into roads and highways,[12] (3) 20 percent into development generally, (4) 13 percent into agriculture, (5) 9 percent into environment and communication, and (6) 8 percent into public services.

PDVSA also channels resources directly to community development and social missions. The community development programs are carried out through Palmaven. It contributes expertise to specific community-directed initiatives, helping to solve problems and build local institutional capacity. The social missions are envisaged as ambitious efforts to promote a rights-based development of marginalized groups. Missions take varying forms, including educational programs (e.g., Ribas Mission [high school diplomas], Sucra Mission [university construction and scholarships]), health care (e.g., Barrio Adentro Mission [full access in cooperation with Cuba]), food provision (e.g., Mercal Mission [subsidies]), naturalization (e.g., Identity Mission [right to identity through documents, citizenship, and electoral participation]), unemployment services (e.g., Vuelvan Caras Mission [technical training to form production and service cooperatives, student scholarships, instructors, supervisors, supply of materials, and supply of equipment to universities]), and indigenous rights promotion (e.g., Guaicaipuro Mission [guaranteeing agricultural and nutritional needs and sustainable development promotion]).

2. The evaluation. Sharp disagreement exists over whether the government's public commitments to channel increased oil revenues resulting from renegotiations (and the related rise in oil prices) are producing positive real-world outcomes. Shifter argues, "Available data of these measures' effect are mixed and not altogether reliable."[13] This point is seconded by Francisco Rodriguez, who argues against a tendency to rely on government figures.[14] In response to numbers suggesting an increase in poverty under Chavez, the government revisited the metric to take into account non–income entitlement schemes like heath care and education.[15] This revised metric was then adopted by Weisbrot.

A number of arguments are made on behalf of these initiatives, some exuberant, other measured. Perhaps the least controversial is the evaluation of the missions. These are generally credited with increasing service quality to poor people and increasing literacy.[16] Moreover, the mission successes are tied to what is viewed as a productive aspect of an international alliance with Cuba. In exchange for oil, Cuba provides teachers and doctors, producing local successes. Weisbrot and Sandoval credit Chavez with effecting a seismic shift in the scale of financial capital flowing to poverty reduction and in the results produced.

Critics of Chavez are, however, more numerous. As discussed previously, a main criticism of the arguments for successful poverty alleviation takes the form of disagreements over the metric. The most vocal detractor here is Rodriguez. Shifter argues, “Chavez’s policy ideas are mostly dubious. (Despite the record oil profits that are funding social spending, his initiatives have yielded only modest gains.)”[17] Second, opponents argue that Chavez is too concerned with using oil to position himself as an international political player to the detriment of serious domestic needs.[18] Third, arguments are made that Chavez is using this revenue to establish an unaccountable patronage system.[19] Fourth, an argument is made that Chavez is maintaining a mono-economy rather than using revenues to diversify economically.[20]

In evaluating the state of the secondary literature in this area, it is important to highlight the differences in metric, the concern of the author regarding either poverty reduction or national economic policy, and the absence of longitudinal data (for obvious reasons). We next turn to Bolivia, which shares much in common with Venezuela politically but is situated differently in terms of its wealth and international aspirations. In addition, the programs are less ambitious and the impact of renegotiations on domestic distributions less understood.

B. Bolivia

In Bolivia, the drive for renegotiation was public demand. In 2003, protestors took to the streets to claim national public ownership of natural resources. These mainly indigenous groups argued against a proposed distribution of revenues to the natural resource–rich provinces. Instead, the groups advocated a broader and more even distribution across the country. By 2005, Evo Morales was president and a contract renegotiation was under way. The issue for our purposes is what this popular mandate driving government renegotiations means in practical terms for the distribution of revenues domestically.

1. The mechanics. Under the auspices of the passage of the National Hydrocarbons Law and facilitated by Executive Decree 28701, ownership and control of natural resources were renegotiated through various legal techniques, transferring increased power to Yacimentos Petroliferos Fiscales Bolivianos (YPFB). Oil fields were militarized, renegotiations occurred, and the government found itself navigating the difficult maze of how to increase state revenues without alienating markets and shrinking the value of domestic oil resources.

The justification of the renegotiations in Bolivia is in line with the country's constitution. The constitution sets out, in Article 133, the purpose of the government economically. It speaks of "strengthening" "national independence and the country's development" through defense and the use of "natural and human resources." These are to be used for both "security" and "the Bolivian people's well-being." The constitution places this state purpose as more important than private interests. As a result, the renegotiations are designed to redistribute the use of revenues away from private firms' interests and toward these larger security-based economic and common good goals.

Bolivia has experienced several waves of renegotiations in its history. This recent wave is a direct response to the 1990s' privatizations.

These renegotiations have resulted in a number of shifts in revenue distribution. First, private firms are now required to satiate the domestic market's needs before exporting resources. Second, the government continues to be concerned with how to deploy domestic revenues to ensure that YPFB operates in a commercially advisable way. This preoccupation with the corporate governance of YPFB is a common theme in other renegotiations. If one purpose of renegotiations is to increase government revenue, then the state-owned companies have to operate so as to generate money. That is, focus goes to ensuring that YPFB will develop infrastructure, exploration, and production. Attention also goes to how to cultivate international connections necessary for distribution.[21]

2. The evaluation. Legally, the renegotiations were driven by the passage of the National Hydrocarbons Law. In 2006, the government passed Hydrocarbon Law 3058. This sweeping legislation sought to dissolve contracts of the state-owned enterprise, YPFB, into the heart of all agreements. The increased government revenue share would be distributed throughout the provinces.

Arguments have been made both for and against the renegotiations in Bolivia as instruments for more equitable distribution of revenues within the country. On the one hand, Joseph Stiglitz makes the case that the renegotiations are legitimately justified on a pro-poor policy basis. In fact, he sees the failure to pass the privatization of the sector through Congress as nullifying the agreements that the renegotiations seek to overturn.[22] However, Stiglitz's arguments go more toward a justification for renegotiations than toward whether they produce social development in practice. On the other hand, arguments are made that the renegotiations may lead to a new distribution of internal revenues that is ultimately detrimental to the local population – a net negative. First, renegotiations may decrease foreign appetite for investment in Bolivia, driving down efficiency and overall revenue into the country.[23]

Moreover, arguments are made that, by acting under the color of bilateral investment agreements, the foreign investors have agreed to promote domestic interests, and thus reform rather than renegotiation is in order. For example, the Agreement on Encouragement and Reciprocal Protection of Investments between the Kingdom of the Netherlands and the Republic of Bolivia is cited in this regard. This agreement is important because the main Brazilian company involved, Petrobas Bolivia, has its headquarters in the Netherlands:

> [T]he protection of foreign investments helps "to strengthen the traditional ties of friendship" and "to extend and intensify the economic relations" between the Netherlands and Bolivia. Both the Netherlands and Bolivia have recognized that the "agreement upon the treatment to be accorded to such investments will stimulate the flow of capital and technology and the economic development of the Contracting Parties and that fair and equitable treatment of investment is desirable."[24]

Here a justification of investment is its promotion of national economic development goals. Reformists argue that these investment regimes are capable of effective distribution of revenue benefits within the host state. Some argue that greater civil society participation in law-making is likely to remedy deficiencies, thus undermining the argument for renegotiation.[25]

In evaluating the record of renegotiation in relation to domestic distribution, it is important to highlight the normative nature of the arguments made. This genre of argument is made in part because the renegotiation process and its effects are ongoing. However, as a basis for drawing empirical conclusions, such arguments are of limited value. Furthermore, the opportunity costs associated with renegotiations make it difficult to benchmark the success or shortcomings of renegotiations.

Nonetheless, the Stiglitz argument shares a feature with the argument for greater civil society participation made by opponents: a focus on process-based measures and solutions for renegotiation. With this in mind, we turn next to the Congo, in which process is seen as a promising avenue for effective domestic distribution of renegotiation-produced revenue.

C. Congo

Renegotiations and cancellations of extractive sector contracts are under way in the Congo. The justification for these efforts are familiar: (1) a legacy of unequal bargains that effect revenue streams and (2) a need to have both the benefits accrued and the potential revenue streams from projects directed to national security, equitable distribution, and economic growth. The DRC is still in the early stages of renegotiations. For this reason, this section relates the current state of play.

1. The mechanics. The idea to pursue renegotiation of mining contracts within the Congo was introduced in 2007. As with the previous examples, the decision to renegotiate was tied to regime change, with a democratic election. Similarly, with the governance change came a new set of policy directives. Shortly thereafter, the Interministerial Commission for the Revisitation of Mining Contracts was constituted to review existing contracts.

The commission was greeted with widespread skepticism. However, a number of steps were taken to assuage concerns. Civil society campaigners played an important role in driving a more participatory process. Campaigners included both international and domestic players. The Carter Center also acted as an independent advisor, with the assistance of Columbia University Law School's Human Rights Clinic, bringing with it legitimacy and subject-specific expertise in both extractives and sustainability.

Specifically, the Carter Center has tried to introduce into the renegotiation process legitimacy, participation, sustainability, transparency, and a concern for human rights outcomes. If the DRC process is to be successful in channeling resources domestically in an equitable and productive fashion, then it is important to set out several of the innovations introduced by the Carter Center:

> The Ministry of Mines recognized the possibility that The Carter Center could help mobilize expertise to assist the review and, by monitoring the process, ensure and strengthen the legitimacy of the outcome. As a condition of its involvement, The Carter Center asked the Ministry of Mines to commit to: (i) public disclosure of all contracts in the sector; (ii) regular communication between Revisitation Commission and the public regarding the process, including an opportunity for civil society to submit its advice and have it considered; and (iii) full disclosure of the results of the Commission's work and its conclusion.[26]

The DRC has tremendous metal and mineral wealth. Many of its natural resources are essential sources of the basic commodities of the global high-tech economy, from cellular phones to computers. Extractives include cobalt, copper, and diamonds. However, only 2 percent of the revenue generated from extractive projects finds its way to the national budget. It is widely thought that a main impediment to the effective channeling of resources is a legacy of poorly conceived contracts governing projects. For this reason, the government and others have pushed for a review of these contracts with an eye toward how they allocate benefits and risks associated with projects.

2. The evaluation. Importantly, in the DRC the renegotiation of contracts is itself viewed as an exercise in reenvisioning the government itself and its domestic priorities. That is, the hope is that new contracts will set out terms that will prioritize specific development objectives, establishing the legal infrastructure for channeling revenue domestically in a sustainable manner. For this reason, the DRC renegotiations are a useful means for understanding how governments can use the process of renegotiation to set domestic priorities.

The aspiration of many involved is to make the process participatory and the resultant contracts transparent. The Carter Center, which is providing advice on the renegotiations, put the matter this way:

> The Carter Center views the review of contracts and the reform of the mining sector as essential to the consolidation of democracy in the DRC. The process is important in its own right because of mining's potential to contribute to development; but it is also important for what it represents. It is a major test of the will of the government to overcome the legacy of war profiteering and corruption, and respond to the widespread public demand for accountability and the rule of law.[27]

In other words, contract revision is a governance exercise in itself. If this experiment works, then it might meet some of the challenges to and skepticism concerning the Venezuelan and Bolivian experiences, in which transparency and accountability challenges cloud an evaluation of the nature and effect of revenue distribution domestically.

That said, although tremendous successes have occurred within the DRC, at the same time, the renegotiation process is still aspirational, an experiment in its early stages. As with other renegotiations, a transparent paper trail and an appropriately tailored accountability device are preconditions to evaluating how revenues are directed and to what end. The DRC's success in this regard may in part be measured by the carrying forward of best practices in the review process within the renegotiations and new contract formation. Although the government has made an effort toward endogenous good practice within the process, exogenous factors such as the role of independent advisors like the Carter Center and campaigns by public interest groups are also important.

The DRC faces a number of challenges in its renegotiations. For example, the legacy of conflict still affects the political process. This is compounded by the fact that the financial interests at play are enormous and that the intergovernmental international assistance in the renegotiation has not been as well resourced as those advisors acting on behalf of firms. Unlike in the Venezuelan and Bolivian cases, in which domestic participation is often advocated to the exclusion of external actors in order to achieve a more equitable domestic distribution, the Carter Center underscores the importance of international assistance:

> A successful review would give a powerful boost to the legitimacy of a government that the international community spent enormous sums to help put in place. It could also help ensure good will towards western governments, who are currently perceived to be complicit with companies that benefit from illegal or grossly imbalanced contractual arrangements. Most importantly, it is a necessary step towards ensuring that the mining industry benefits the people as a whole. Without a serious review, suspicion and distrust are likely to undermine the efforts of the government, the international community, and the companies involved.[28]

Moreover, even in countries with more stable governments, little knowledge exists about which contractual types are ideal for channeling resources to domestic concerns. Furthermore, the DRC has been hesitant to wholeheartedly embrace international law firm representation. This wariness results from dissatisfaction with the generation of contracts now being renegotiated, which were produced with such assistance. In addition, although efforts are being made to introduce transparency and participation into the process, some suggest that new contracts are being forged without public knowledge.

Whereas the DRC example concerns itself with process and assumptions about its correlation with good outcomes, we turn next to a large-scale societal initiative in which bold goals are the defining feature. In Qatar, a seismic shift away from a mono-extractives economy and toward a knowledge-based one is the aspiration. Qatar does not face as many immediate conflict-based legacies as the DRC. Also, in contrast to Bolivia and Venezuela, Qatar is attempting to integrate with the United States and others, although it is important to note that the U.S. market is important to Venezuela.

D. Qatar

In discussing how the revenues accrued from renegotiations are distributed domestically, the point has been made that it is difficult to disaggregate how the oil wealth of a country is spent generally from how renegotiation-generated oil wealth is spent. This point was made previously in relation to Venezuela. For this reason, it is useful to look at how countries productively channel oil wealth domestically into sustainable diversified economic growth strategies as a backdrop for understanding models that renegotiations might emulate. Here, we look at Qatar's efforts in this regard. As with development strategies generally, analysis of the successes and failures of Qatar in productively channeling extractive resources into sustainable domestic investments may not be clear for many years. Nonetheless, a number of lessons can be drawn from Qatar's efforts.

1. The mechanics. Qatar is now investing its oil and gas revenue into an ambitious development program aiming to transform the country into a knowledge-based economy. This program has many components. The creation of the Qatar Science and Technology Park is an important part of the program. This park is reinforced by the creation of Education City. Both are in part foreign-direct-investment schemes and national growth strategies. The aim is to attract leading high-tech firms into the park and to mobilize their resources to grow a domestic knowledge economy. A number of synergies will make this possible. Two important areas are technology transfer and the training of new economy laborers.

The high-tech firms will partner with Qatar entrepreneurs and companies in an effort to localize operations. Such a partnership not only integrates local firms into the foreign companies' operations; it also plays a role in growing a regional high-tech economy. By sharing knowledge and localization strategies, Qatar will be well positioned to take advantage of regional markets as they grow.

To play a meaningful role in the transnational company operations and in the global economy more generally, Qatar has established Education City. This ambitious initiative attracts world-class universities to locate offsite centers within Qatar. Universities with operations in Qatar include Cornell, Carnegie Mellon, and Georgetown. Education City is unusual in that these universities confer degrees that allow Qatar graduates within the offsite centers to meet stringent U.S. professional standards. For instance, medical degrees conferred by the Cornell Medical Center within Qatar are equivalent to the university's U.S. degree program. Furthermore, not only do these degrees confer international mobility on the graduates, they also help provide domestically trained workers that are valuable to foreign firms locating within the Science and Technology Park.

These efforts to stimulate growth within Qatar and to promote a regional economy are further reinforced through other national initiatives. For example, the Qatar Financial Centre uses the conservative revenue stream of extractive wealth to strategically channel capital into projects within the country and regionally. In other words, as with the sovereign wealth funds, national extractive capital is being used as an investment vehicle in a way dissociated from the origin of the revenue and also, in part, for domestic growth purposes.

2. The evaluation. Thus, Qatar represents an example of how extractive wealth is not necessarily a curse. Of course, wide variation exists among countries as to the impediments of effective domestic channeling of resources. Nonetheless, Qatar might offer not only a model but also a potential partner to countries seeking to channel domestic capital effectively. It may be that Qatar-based enterprises will increasingly seek their own international linkages with countries in Latin America and elsewhere.

At the same time, as with other efforts to diversify economies or to leapfrog development, it is important to devise criteria for assessing the impact of domestic channeling of resources on short-, medium-, and long-term bases. The more ambitious and forward-looking a project is, however, the less reliable the metric.

V. Concluding Observations and Prescriptions

In conclusion, we might draw a number of observations about renegotiations and domestic distribution. First, more primary research and secondary literature debate are necessary to ascertain the nature of flows and their impact. Second, more comparative work is necessary in order to understand the empirical record in terms of both commonalities and divergences. It is also useful for cross-germination of lessons that might be learned. Third, new metrics need to be developed to understand and assess forward-looking deployment of revenue. If the impact will not be felt for some time, then how does one determine whether a certain course is advisable? Fourth, attention needs to be paid to the issue of opportunity costs. In other words, are renegotiations the most effective way of channeling resources domestically? Or do they create inefficiencies and lead to flip-flopping with upturns and downturns in the market? Fifth, a cataloging of concrete policy prescriptions arising from a carefully designed research study that looks systematically, cross-nationally, and empirically at renegotiations is essential to move forward the debate.

As we think about recommendations for how government should approach partnerships in efforts to rebalance society-wide imbalances and to make the most of valuable natural assets, it is useful to turn next to the conclusion, wherein a number of overarching recommendations are made for the Obama Bank.

13

Recommendations

I. Introduction

This book has described how our efforts to establish an infrastructure bank to promote reinvestment in American domestic infrastructure through public-private partnerships (P3s) is based explicitly on a model that has been the cornerstone of our foreign commercial policy for the last several decades. In the policy debates, we have painted this model as an unqualified success. In doing so, we have focused on two aspects of this model. First, an infrastructure bank has the ability to leverage sizable amounts of private capital to invest in much-needed projects, filling the gap between what government can afford and what our society needs. Second, a bank has the appeal of making decisions about which infrastructure projects are best for society based on the merits of the projects rather than on politics. Although these are both essential and laudable goals for a bank, as this book has explained, the track record of international banks in both these areas has been mixed.

The leveraging function of banks has often obscured liabilities of projects and resulted in hidden costs and nonassessed risks being passed on to public institutions. As a result, in using companies to advance public interest goals, we have often geared our accountability mechanisms more toward ensuring private firm profitability than the stated purpose of the projects. This policy distortion has often meant that international infrastructure banks and P3s have been frequently critiqued as promoting projects that advance insider dealings that undermine merit-based decision-making.

That said, the Obama Bank, if properly conceived, can promote merit-based durable projects that advance our recovery and reinvestment. This book has focused not only on some of the real-world problems that international banks and P3s have faced in delivering on their promises, but also on many laudable qualities that should be emulated. Moreover, it has described how the ability of projects to produce public goods has been advanced throughout the world by civil society organizations and concerned citizenry generally. Both the institutional makeup of banks and their actual policies have evolved over time, largely in reaction to civil society demands. It is no exaggeration to say that international infrastructure banks and P3s have succeeded in promoting their public interest mandates largely because civil society has acted as a de facto instrument of accountability. Nonetheless, in creating our own domestically directed infrastructure bank, we have not sufficiently incorporated many of the resultant international best practices.

The Obama Bank will, like every other infrastructure bank, evolve over time, learning lessons from real-world experiences. If we learn real lessons from the experiences of international infrastructure banks at the outset, we are less likely to repeat some of their serious financial, social, and environmental problems. Moreover, our bank should not only reflect existing best practices, it should also learn lessons from international experiences that its sibling banks and their P3s have stubbornly avoided at high costs to the public interest. In order for our bank to live up to its aspirations, it must have an institutional structure and policy apparatus capable of carrying out its public mandates. At present, the bank is geared institutionally more toward raising capital and creating liquidity, both essential goals, than toward producing the public goods that are a prerequisite to achieving durable growth.

Throughout, this book has aimed at drawing many lessons from international experience. As a result, this conclusion does not catalog all of the points made. Instead, it offers a series of focused recommendations. Three areas receive particular focus. First, a number of cross-cutting thematic points about the bank are made. Second, recommendations are made regarding the institutional design of the bank. And, lastly, approaches to specific partnerships are addressed.

These recommendations build on earlier chapters and thus distill lessons rather than reiterating arguments already made with reference to international examples. Moreover, the aim here is to focus on areas that an evolving bank should address in order to learn lessons from actual international experience, rather than to provide prebaked solutions. The reason for this approach is that basic overarching institutional design and project conception decisions should be made in a participatory and deliberative way. Accountability arises from this, rather than only from expert briefs, financial or government wish lists, or partial accounts of a well-known track record, however well intentioned.

II. Overarching Recommendations

(1) A central lesson of infrastructure banks is that they evolve over time. The World Bank, for instance, was not initially established to promote P3s and yet, since the 1980s, it has dramatically reoriented itself to doing so. It has even created the Multilateral Investment Guarantee Agency to insure these P3s against political risks. As discussed previously, many of the basic features that make these banks accountable to their stated public interest purposes have also been created over time. Largely as a result of civil society campaigns, infrastructure banks review projects for

environmental and social impacts. We must thus not only see our own bank as likely to evolve, but also not view the international models as static.

(2) The Obama Bank will operate in numerous sectors, in many parts of the country, and will address a range of financial, legal, social, environmental, and other issues. As a result, the bank will need to develop special cross-cutting institutional expertise. For example, as the bank taps international financial markets, it will require special expertise in the risks and rewards involved. Also, a look at international infrastructure banks shows that subsidy systems have functioned poorly in practice. This poor track record does not apply only to corporate subsidies. Another main purpose of infrastructure banks is to deliver projects that redress inequalities. Poverty alleviation schemes such as take-or-pay clauses or cross-subsidy schemes have not functioned as planned.

(3) Similarly, because a central purpose of a bank is to address power disparities, it is important to develop an expertise in this area that learns from international experience. For example, the European Investment Bank, which has been advanced as the main model for the Obama Bank, has faced serious difficulties in rebalancing power disparities between long-standing members and newly acceding ones in Central and Eastern Europe. In fact, inabilities to address these disparities have effectively resulted

in projects falling apart at the concept stage, being renegotiated, or favoring environmentally polluting road systems over rail systems.

(4) Although civil society groups have driven international infrastructure bank accountability, every bank has resisted their participation. Infrastructure banks have excluded groups from governance decisions generally and attempted to exclude them from tendering decisions of specific projects. For example, the European Bank is not unique in its efforts to close out civil society groups from early stages of project development. Common practice among banks is to attempt to make key decisions before including civil society groups. Moreover, oftentimes groups are granted avenues for redress without real remedies attached. This has been true of most of the international banks. In addition, the Obama Bank should commission a study of the accountability measures, including transparency and participation practices, of existing banks with an eye toward adapting the best practices.

(5) One of the central features of the Obama administration has been a serious, unprecedented commitment to transparency and accountability. The Obama Bank will undoubtedly continue this. At the same time, the Obama Bank is an instrument that arises out of Obama's free market statist philosophy. Such a philosophy has generally pointed to a need to ensure that partnerships advance the public interest by looking at both the public and the private

sides. Accordingly, as the stimulus act has evolved, attention has been paid to lobbying and other aspects of the private side. However, the bond financing provisions have been excluded from these executive branch accountability measures. As a result, in many ways bond financing under the present administration has been accountability-exempt. Because the Obama Bank is in many ways a consolidation and advance of the bond and other subsidy-related measures first set forth in the stimulus, it must overturn the initial exemption from accountability. The Obama Bank itself should, along these lines, explore concrete ways of incorporating the Build America Bond program and private activity bond initiatives within its toolbox. For example, offering guarantees or insurance or subsidized interest rates for these existing bond programs makes sense. At the same time, strict public purposes just justify these sweeteners. The bank itself potentially offers an effective means of establishing an accountable leveraged liberalism.

III. Design Recommendations

(1) The Obama Bank should revisit its membership structure. Infrastructure banks generally include many governments, both hosts of projects and others, in their governance structure. This book does not advocate including foreign governments or international organizations. However, U.S. state – and possibly city – governments should be

included – and not simply as partners who bring projects to the bank for consideration. For projects to succeed, it is necessary to have meaningful local participation. Although such participation will no doubt happen partially through congressional representation and through our executive branch's structure as well as existing channels of input and coordination, the ability of regional projects to succeed depends on robust participation. As discussed previously, regionalization can only work with the buy-in of constituent political jurisdictions. International banks have faced substantial difficulties in this respect. Already, within the United States, citizens of certain states would be rightly concerned that infrastructure projects solve local needs, particularly when sacrifices are expected and costs substantial. This may run counter to regional and national aims. Front-end participation may cause some initial delays; however, projects are more likely to be durable.

At the same time, state and local governments are numerous. For this reason, the participation structure must be not only tiered but also representative and rotating. State governments may sensibly represent clusters within a region. The accountability feedback therein might be advanced through rotating representation. As our congressional system demonstrates, determining how to structure participation of states and cities requires much deliberation. The Obama Bank will reconfigure basic issues of federalism and separation of powers.

(2) International infrastructure banks invariably do a poor job of ensuring that projects actually produce public goods and, similarly, that they do not undermine the social and environmental rights of project-affected people. In fact, so substandard is this track record in U.S.-financed and internationally financed projects by infrastructure banks that a second linked institution should be created – a public interest unit. President Obama should charge the public interest unit with scrutinizing important bank decisions and specific projects to ensure that they promote the common good. This unit should have access to the bank's documentation. The job of the public interest unit would be to assess whether policies and projects produce public goods and how they impact on project-affected communities. It should actively engage civil society. Furthermore, we should have a public deliberative discussion about whether this public interest unit should have veto power over decisions and about the nature of its power vis-à-vis Obama Bank decision-making.

(3) Appointees to the bank should be subject to strict conflict-of-interest rules. Moreover, if appointees are exempted from such rules, then a detailed rationale should be given. In addition, every effort should be made to draw staff members from a range of sectors and backgrounds, including experience within civil society. In addition, attention should be paid to ensuring that the staff members have

a diversity of views toward models of promoting reinvestment. At all levels, attention should be paid to diversity in expertise, region, stakeholder background, and sector experience.

(4) Given the importance of pension funds in financing projects and the potential risks involved, the Obama Bank should include a distinct cluster of staff devoted to ensuring that projects advance the long-term interests of these funds. We are not only using government to leverage private investment, we are also using pension funds. International experience with projects shows that long-term durability is not as settled as assumed. For this reason, the Obama Bank should assist pension fund managers in conducting their requisite due diligence. We must use this also as an opportunity to have a realistic and grounded discussion of the due diligence standard in this area. Related to this expertise is the need to develop a critical capacity in renegotiations, which international experience demonstrates inevitably occurs but is not often appropriately approached or carried out.

(5) Given the wide scope of the Obama Bank, it should liaise closely with a number of relevant executive agencies, including Homeland Security, the Department of Labor, the Department of Treasury, and the Department of State.

(6) International infrastructure banks pursue varying approaches toward dispute resolution as it relates to both project-affected communities and foreign investors. The

Obama Bank should canvass these approaches and learn from best practices. It would be unrealistic to think that the default rules for dispute resolution are that our own domestic courts govern all aspects of our partnerships. If we desire such an approach, it must be forged.

IV. Project Recommendations

(1) Oftentimes the upside gains of partnerships are disproportionately enjoyed by private firms. Governments may take on too many downside risks. Moreover, public goods are often underproduced. Many renegotiations are driven by these features of partnerships. For this reason, the Obama Bank should engage in public deliberation over the pros and cons of taking ownership stakes in projects supported by it. This discussion should take place in the context of specific project decision-making. This is one of the main reasons for looking at international experience in the extractives sector, in which the nature of partnerships is often differently conceived. It may be more appropriate to view our economy as one with inherent untapped value, with risks of windfall profits, and with a serious need to enjoy a fair share of the upside gains of our reinvestment. We have for generations enjoyed the legacy assets of previous periods of sustained investments.

(2) Just like the earmark system that the Obama Bank seeks to move away from, infrastructure banks are prone

to supporting P3s with substantial conflicts of interest and tendencies toward insider dealing. As a result, the bank should develop a policy for how projects can be brought to it.

(3) The Obama Bank, a national institution, should conduct periodic reviews to ensure that it is financing projects with an equitable spread geographically. It may be that certain states are in a better position to petition the Obama Bank to support a project.

(4) Each project should have a wide range and an appropriately tailored assessment that goes beyond financial factors. It should pay attention as well to how the project might evolve over its life cycle. Additionally, even in making bond determinations, the bank should do due diligence into the particular banks and other service providers involved in a project to ascertain their track records, particularly when pursuing long-term projects.

(5) As discussed in the Introduction, our foreign affairs are inextricably interwoven with our domestic economy. The Obama Bank will be no exception. On the one hand, it aims to promote non-outsourceable American jobs, to wean us away from foreign oil, and to create a durable domestic recovery. On the other hand, the bank also is likely to seek out foreign investment to underwrite projects and also to attract overseas firms with complementary expertise. It is important to have frank discussions on the costs and benefits, risks and rewards of these decisions.

The Obama Bank is a vital institution for our economic renaissance. Financing a durable New Deal means taking into account more than the upside benefits of public-private partnerships. The Obama Bank's ability to learn from the vast publicly available information about the track record of international banks and partnerships will be one key measure of our ability to reinvest in a durable, equitable vision of America as we move away from a subprime mortgage–backed economy and toward laying a new foundation built on safe drinking water, accessible health care, clean energy, equal education, and other basic infrastructure.

Notes

Chapter 2. The Janesville Plan

1. These prefatory remarks did not appear in the prepared speech that was widely circulated.
2. Chris Matthews *Hardball* (February 14, 2008).
3. Jim Kuhnhenn "Clinton Plans Corporate Limits" *Ventura County Star* (February 15, 2008).
4. Council on Foreign Relations "Obama's Speech in Janesville Wisconsin" February 13, 2008, Speaker Barack Obama, available at http://www.cfr.org/publication/15492/%C2%A0.
5. "Obama's Speech in Janesville Wisconsin."
6. "Obama's Speech in Janesville Wisconsin."
7. David Rogers "Obama Plots Huge Railroad Expansion" *Politico* (February 17, 2009).
8. "President Barack Obama's Inaugural Address" (January 21, 2009), available at http://www.whitehouse.gov/the_press_office/President_Barack_Obamas_Inaugural_Address.
9. Sean Hannity "Interview with Rush Limbaugh" *Fox News* (January 21, 2009).

10. Greg Sargent "Times Reporter Defends Asking Obama If He's a 'Socialist'" *The Plum* (blog), available at http://theplumline.whorunsgov.com/political-media/times-reporter-defends-asking-obama-if-hes-a-socialist.
11. "CNBC Exclusive: CNBC Transcript: CNBC's Chief Washington Correspondent John Harwood Sits Down with Presidential Candidate Senator Barack Obama" CNBC (June 10, 2008), available at http://www.cnbc.com/id/25084346.
12. "President Barack Obama's Inaugural Address."
13. Quoted in Michael Likosky "Comment" in Matthew Gibney, ed., *Globalizing Rights: Oxford Amnesty Lectures* (Oxford: Oxford University Press 2003).
14. Michael B. Likosky *The Silicon Empire* (Aldershot: Ashgate 2005).
15. http://www.youtube.com/user/BarackObamadotcom.
16. Likosky 2005.

Chapter 3. A Bank of Our Own

1. Council on Competitiveness "Prioritize" *A 100-Day Energy Action Plan for the 44th President of the United States.*
2. *Id.*, 2.
3. *Id.*, 3.
4. United States Committee on Foreign Affairs *Foreign Assistance Act of 1969: Report of the Committee on Foreign Affairs together with Minority, Supplement and Additional Views on H.R. 14580: To Promote the Foreign Policy, Security, and General Welfare of the United States by Assisting the Peoples of the World to Achieve Economic Development within a Framework of Democratic, Economic, Social, and Political Institutions, and for Other Purposes* 91st Congress, 1st Session, House Report No. 91-611 (Washington, DC: United States Government Printing Office November 6, 1969), 3.
5. Quoted in *Foreign Assistance Act of 1969*, 11.
6. "Lawsuit Forces U.S. Financing Agencies to Account for Climate" *Environmental News Service* (February 7, 2009).

7. Michael C. Pollak "Making the Public Arteries Flow" *Record* (April 14, 1986) (on Giglio); Felix G. Rohatyn "Editorial: To Repair Our Nation" *New York Times* (December 17, 1989).
8. Rick Shaughghnessy "Hart Voices Support for Water Projects" *San Diego Union-Tribune* (December 4, 1986); "REVIEW & OUTLOOK (Editorial): Jesse's Juggernaut" *Wall Street Journal* (March 29, 1988); Joel Chernoff "Proposals Target Pension Money Infrastructure Financing Detailed" *Pensions & Investments* (November 9, 1992).
9. Jackson proposed a ten-year financing schedule for his bank, capitalized to the tune of sixty billion dollars. "Jesse's Juggernaut."
10. Milton Friedman "Preface" in Friedrich A. Hayek *The Road to Serfdom* (50th Anniversary Edition) (Chicago: University of Chicago Press 1994), xvi.
11. Lawrence A. Kudlow "Alice in Budgetland (Alice Rivlin Memo About Budget Causes Problems)" *National Review* 46(22) (November 21, 1994).
12. *Meet the Press* transcript for March 22, 2009 (New York City Mayor Michael Bloomberg, Pa. Governor Ed Rendell (D), Calif. Governor Arnold Schwarzenegger (R), Tom Brokaw, Erin Burnett (March 22, 2009).
13. The legislation in question was H.R.2521: To facilitate efficient investments and financing of infrastructure projects and new job creation through the establishment of a national infrastructure development bank, and for other purposes (introduced May 20, 2009).

Chapter 4. Leverage

1. "Obama's Speech in Janesville Wisconsin."
2. Lisa Lambert "US Senate Leader Cool to Infrastructure Bank" Reuters (March 25, 2009).
3. Gerald F. Seib and Joe Davidson "Campaign '88 – The Issues: Presidential Battle Spawns Strange Vocabulary – New Shorthand for Proposed Social Programs" *Wall Street Journal* (September 20, 1988).

4. Helen Huntley "Voters Will Be Deciding on Direction of the Economy Series: Campaign 1988: The Issues" *St. Petersburg Times* (October 19, 1988), 1.A.
5. David Lauter "Favors Problem-Solver Approach: Dukakis Believes America Seeks Activist Government" *Los Angeles Times* (September 11, 1988).
6. Joe Davidson "Campaign '88: Dukakis's Health Insurance Plan Would Face Bigger Fight on the Hill Than It Did in Massachusetts" *Wall Street Journal* (May 12, 1988), 1.
7. Dennis Farney and Jeffrey H. Birnbaum "Campaign '88 – Revamped Image: Democrats Repackage Liberalism, Proposing Cheaper Government – Washington Would Set Rules But States, Private Sector Would Execute the Policy – Will Public Back Bigger Role?" *Wall Street Journal* (April 25, 1988).
8. David Shribman "Campaign '88 – 'Frugal' Liberal: A Town Once Leery of Dukakis Observes Part of His 'Miracle' – But Some of His Ideas Flop, Others May Not Translate to the National Agenda – The Mess at Boston Harbor" *Wall Street Journal* (June 23, 1988), 1.
9. James Srodes "Contrasting Platforms (Interviews with Lawrence Summers and Robert Zoellick, The Candidates' Advisors)" *The Hard Choices: A Special Report on Government Spending* (October 18, 1988).
10. *Id.*
11. Ronald Brownstein "Divided Economic Vision Blurs Democratic Outlook Politics: Strategists See a Renewed Consensus as Vital to Targeting What Might Be the Only Chink in Bush's Armor" *Los Angeles Times* (July 1, 1991).
12. Seib and Davidson 1988.
13. Brownstein 1991.
14. *Id.*
15. Ronald Brownstein "The Conference CALLS: Dukakis Differs from the Old-Time Democrats" *Los Angeles Times* (July 17, 1988).
16. Joel Chernoff 1992.
17. *Id.*

18. Joan Pryde and Heather Ann Hope "White House Budget Memo Targets Deductions, Not Bonds' Tax Exemption" *The Bond Buyer* 310 (29514) (October 25, 1994).
19. "Clinton/Infrastructure Bank: Details to Follow" *Dow Jones News Service* (December 22, 1994).
20. "Opening Statement of Chairman Dodd: Condition of Our Nation's Infrastructure and Proposals for Needed Improvements" *State News Service* (March 11, 2008).
21. "Statement for Record by U.S. Senator Chuck Hagel: Condition of Our Nation's Infrastructure and Proposals for Needed Improvements" *State News Service* (March 11, 2008).
22. "Yarmuth Calls on House Speaker to Create Historic Infrastructure Bank" Congressional Documents and Publications (April 7, 2008).
23. *Meet the Press* transcript for March 22, 2009.
24. Lynne Marek "Growth of Privatization Deals Nets Big Fees for Firms: New Multibillion-Dollar Market Expected to Expand as Cash-Strapped Local and State Governments Look to Lease Public Assets" *National Law Journal* (June 16, 2008).
25. Richard Madris and Brian Greene "President Obama Proposes Creation and Funding of a National Infrastructure Bank" *Stroock Special Bulletin* (March 2009).
26. Marek 2008.
27. *Meet the Press* transcript for March 22, 2009.
28. For an elaboration of this definition with ample examples drawn from projects around the world, see Michael B. Likosky *Law, Infrastructure, and Human Rights* (New York: Cambridge University Press 2006).

Chapter 5. Free Market Statism

1. "The Democrats' March Toward Socialism" available from the Republican National Committee.
2. "RNC Resolution Recognizing the Democrats' March Toward Socialism" available from the Republican National Committee.

3. Republic National Committee.
4. For a treatment of the relationship between corporations and the Constitution, see David L. Ratner "Corporations and the Constitution" *University of San Francisco Law Review* 11 (1980–1981), 15.
5. *Dartmouth College v. Woodward* 17 U.S. 518 (1819).
6. *Santa Clara County v. Southern Pacific Railroad Company* 118 U.S. 394 (1886).
7. Ronald Reagan "First Inaugural Address" (January 20, 1981).
8. George H. W. Bush "Inaugural Address" (January 20, 1989).
9. William Clinton "1996 State of the Union Address" (January 27, 1996).
10. George W. Bush "President Honors Milton Friedman for Lifetime Achievements: Remarks by President in Tribute of Milton Friedman," available at www.whitehouse.gov/news/releases/2002/05/20020509-1.html.
11. "President-Elect Obama's Weekly Address" (January 10, 2009).
12. On railroads during the nineteenth and early-twentieth centuries, see Dorothy R. Adler *British Investment in American Railways 1834–1898* (Charlottesville: University of Virginia Press 1970); John Coatsworth "Railroads, Landholding, and Agrarian Protest in the Early Porfiriato" *Hispanic Historical Review* 54 (1) (February 1974), 48; Steven Salsbury *The State, the Investor, and the Railroad* (Cambridge, MA: Harvard University Press 1957); and Augustus J. Veenendaal *Slow Train to Paradise: How Dutch Investment Helped Build American Railways* (Stanford: Stanford University Press 1996).
13. Oscar Handlin and Mary F. Handlin "Revolutionary Economic Policy in Massachusetts" *William and Mary Quarterly* 4 (1) (3rd series) (January 1947), 3, 10.
14. *Lochner v. New York* 198 US 45 (1905). Justice Oliver Wendell Holmes wrote in a famous dissent, "The Fourteenth Amendment does not enact Mr. Herbert Spencer's Social Statistics." *Lochner* 75. A strong parallel exists between this *Lochner* position and present-day right to free trade positions. For a critique

of the latter, see Philip Alston "Resisting the Merger and Acquisition of Human Rights Law by Trade Law: A Reply to Petersmann" *European Journal of International Law* 13 (4) (2002), 815.

15. For a bibliography of legal literature on World War II defense procurement, see Law Branch, The Army Library *Bibliography on Government Procurement and Contractual Procedure and Related Materials* (Law Branch: The Army Library March 1953 [Revised March 1954]).
16. Morris R. Cohen "Property and Sovereignty" *Cornell Law Quarterly* 827 (1927–1928), 13; Morris R. Cohen "The Basis of Contract" *Harvard Law Review* 562 (1932–1933), 46.
17. Cohen 1932–1933, 562.
18. Cohen 1927–1928, 30.
19. Cohen 1932–1933, 565.
20. Robert L Hale "Coercion and Distribution in a Supposedly Noncoercive State" *Political Science Quarterly* 38 (1923), 470.
21. Robert L. Hale "Force and the State: A Comparison of 'Political' and 'Economic' Compulsion" *Columbia Law Review* (1935), 149.
22. Louis L. Jaffe "Law Making by Private Groups" *Harvard Law Review* 51 (1937–1938), 201, 220–221.
23. The adaptation of the Continental European free law doctrine was important here and not without controversy. See H. L. A. Hart *Essays in Jurisprudence and Philosophy* (Oxford: Clarendon Press 1983), 265–277 and Hermann Kantorowicz "Some Rationalism About Realism" *Yale Law Journal* 43 (1934), 1240. For more recent studies drawing on the insights of these Legal Realists, see Roderick M. Hills "The Constitutional Rights of Private Governments" *New York University Law Review* 78 (2003), 144 and Arthur J. Jacobson "Private Use of Public Authority: Sovereignty and Association in the Common Law" *Buffalo Law Review* 29 (1980), 603 ("Courts and legislatures have used the law of associations to distribute a portion of sovereignty to private persons," 601).

24. Charles A. Reich "The New Property" *Yale Law Journal* 73 (1964), 733, 764.
25. Reich 1964, 764.
26. Michael D. Reagan *The Managed Economy* (Oxford: Oxford University Press 1967), 190.
27. Don K. Price *Government and Science: Their Dynamic Relation in American Democracy* (New York: New York University Press 1954), 65–94. On how governments and universities intermingled during the Cold War, see Noam Chomsky, Laura Nader, Immanuel Wallerstein, Richard C. Lewontin, Richard Ohmann, Howard Zinn, Ira Katznelson, David Montgomery, and Ray Siever *The Cold War and the University: Toward an Intellectual History of the Postwar Years* (New York: New Press 1998).
28. Stewart Macaulay "Private Government" in Leon Lipson and Stanton Wheeler, eds., *Law and the Social Sciences* (New York: Russell Sage Foundation 1986).
29. *Id.*, 449.
30. *Id.*, 450.
31. Ernest F. Leathem "Defense Procurement – A Complex of Conflicts and Tensions" *Boston College Industrial and Commercial Law Review* V (1) (Fall 1963), 1.
32. On the renegotiations following the war and their use as a potential model today, see William E. Kovacic and Steven L. Schooner "A Modest Proposal to Enhance Civil/Military Integration: Rethinking the Renegotiation Regime as a Regulatory Mechanism to Decriminalize Cost, Pricing and Profit Policy" George Washington University Law School Public Law Research Paper No. 178 (December 2005).
33. President Dwight D. Eisenhower "The Military Industrial Complex Speech" (1961), available at http://www.yale.edu/lawweb/avalon/presiden/speeches/eisenhower001.html.
34. Leathem 1963.
35. Reagan 1967, 193.
36. Frederick T. Moore "Efficiency and Public Policy in Defense Procurement" *Law and Contemporary Problems* 29 (1964), 3, 4.
37. Reagan 1967, 193.

38. Price 1954, 65–94.
39. Reagan 1967, 194–195.
40. For extended discussions of the development of the public-private law divide and an assessment of the relevance of Legal Realist insights for privatization, see Likosky 2005, chapter 2. On the divide generally, see Alan Freeman and Elizabeth Mensch "The Public-Private Distinction in American Law and Life" *Buffalo Law Review* (1987), 237; Morton Horwitz "The History of the Public/Private Distinction" *University of Pennsylvania Law Review* 130 (1981–1982), 1423; Duncan Kennedy "The Structure of Blackstone's Commentaries" *Buffalo Law Review* 28 (1979), 205; and Duncan Kennedy "The Stages of the Decline of the Public/Private Distinction" *University of Pennsylvania Law Review* 130 (1982), 1349.

Chapter 6. A New Foundation

1. "President Barack Obama's Inaugural Address."
2. Louis Henkin *The Age of Rights* (New York: Columbia University Press 1990), 186.
3. American Recovery and Reinvestment Act of 2009 (2009) (ARRA).
4. Presidential Memorandum for the Heads of Executive Departments and Agencies (March 20, 2009).
5. ARRA Section 3.
6. Marriner Stoddard Eccles *Economic Balance and a Balanced Budget* (New York: Harper and Brothers 1940), 261.
7. Quoted in Wolfgang G. Friedmann *The State and the Rule of Law in a Mixed Economy* (London: Stevens and Sons Limited 1971), 56.
8. Franklin D. Roosevelt "The Four Freedoms" (Address to Congress January 6, 1941).
9. United Nations Charter (June 26, 1945).
10. Franklin D. Roosevelt "Address of the President Delivered by Radio from the White House in Connection with the Opening of the Fifth War Loan Drive" (June 12, 1944).

Chapter 7. P3s and Foreign Affairs

1. Dean Foust "The Swat Team from Washington: How a U.S. Treasury Trio Helped Contain the Asian Crisis" *Business Week* (February 23, 1998).
2. "Malaysians Are Enraged" *Straits Times Interactive* (November 18, 1998).
3. F. D. Lugard *The Dual Mandate in British Tropical Africa* (London: William Blackwood and Sons 1922), 617.
4. Lugard 1922.
5. J. S. Furnivall *Colonial Policy and Practice: A Comparative Study of Burma and Netherlands India* (New York: New York University Press 1956), 6.
6. W. J. Mommsen "Introduction" in W. J. Mommsen and J. A. de Moor, eds., *European Expansion and Law: The Encounter of European Indigenous Law in 19th- and 20th-Century Africa and Asia* (Oxford: Berg 1992), 1, 5.
7. United Nations General Resolution 1514(XV) (December 14, 1960), Article 7.
8. Gunnar Myrdal *Asian Drama: The Inquiry into the Poverty of Nations* (New York: Twentieth Century Fund 1968), 709.
9. Myrdal 1968, 715.
10. Myrdal 1968, 869.
11. Myrdal 1968, 728.
12. David L. Lewis, ed., *W. E. B. Du Bois: A Reader* (New York: Henry Holt and Company 1995), 564.
13. John Steinbeck *Of Mice and Men* (New York: Penguin 1993), 74.
14. Langston Hughes "A Dream Deferred" (1951).
15. Martin Luther King Jr. *I Have a Dream: Writings and Speeches that Changed the World* (James M. Washington, ed.) (New York: Harper Collins 1992), 155.
16. Milton Friedman 1994, ix.
17. Quoted in A. Basile and A. Germidis, *Investing in Free Export Processing Zones* (Washington, DC: Development Center of the Organization for Economic Cooperation and Development 1984), 20.

18. T. Takeo "Introduction" in *Free Trade Zones & Industrialization of Asia: Special Issue AMPO Quarterly Review* (Tokyo: Pacific-Asia Resource Center 1977), 1.
19. United Nations Industrial Development Organization *UNIDO BOT Guidelines* (Geneva: United Nations Industrial Development Organization 1996).
20. International Labor Organization and Centre on Transnational Corporations *Economic and Social Effects of Multinational Enterprises in Export Processing Zones* (Geneva: International Labour Office 1988).

Chapter 8. Companies as Policy Organs

1. For a useful guide with brief descriptions of many subsidy programs, see U.S. Department of Commerce *Export Programs Guide: A Business Guide to Federal Export Assistance* (Washington, DC: United States Government Printing Office 2003–2004).
2. Compiled in Cecil T. Carr, ed., *Select Charters of Trading Companies, A.D. 1530–1707*, Volume 48 (London: Selden Society 1913), 38. This clause echoed a similar one in a related earlier grant. Cecil T. Carr "Introduction" in Carr 1913, i, xxxviii. On chartered companies, see also W. H.-J. Leue "Legal Expansion in the Age of Companies: Aspects of the Administration of Justice in the English and Dutch Settlements of Maritime Asia, c. 1600–1750" in Wolfgang J. Mommsen and J. A. De Moor 1992, 129; M. F. Lindley, *The Acquisition of Government of Backward Territory in International Law: Being a Treatise on the Law and Practice Relating to Colonial Expansion* (London: Longmans, Green & Company 1926); R. Robert, *Chartered Companies and Their Role in the Development of Overseas Trade* (London: G. Bell and Sons 1969); R. E. Tindall, *Multinational Enterprises: Legal and Management Structures and Interrelationship of Ownership, Control, Antitrust, Labor, Taxation and Disclosure* (New York: Oceana Publications 1975), 1–8; and J. H. W. Verzijl *International Law in Historical Perspective Part II: International Persons* (Leyden: A. W. Sijthoff 1969).

3. For contra, see airlines such as United and Delta, which place flags on their planes.
4. This section limits itself mainly to the United States and the intergovernmental organizations of which it is an active member. However, other countries engage in similar behavior. For example, the European Union promotes its transportation companies in newly acceding states.
5. On this controversy, see Laura Dickinson "Public Law Values in a Privatized World" *Yale Journal of International Law* 31 (2006), 383; Naomi Klein "Pillaging Iraq in Pursuit of a Neocon Utopia" *Harper's Magazine* (September 2004); and Likosky 2006, chapter 4.
6. United States General Accounting Office *Report to Congressional Committees: Iraq Contract Costs: DOD Consideration of Defense Contract Audit Agency's Findings* (Washington, DC: U.S. Government Accountability Office September 2006), 4.
7. Steven Schooner "Contractor Atrocities at Abu Ghraib: Compromised Accountability in Streamlined Outsourced Government" *Stanford Law and Policy Review* 16 (2005), 549. See also the conference program of the event organized by the New York University School of Law's Institute for International Law and Justice: "Market Forces: Regulating Private Military Companies," available at http://iilj.org/documents/3-24-06PMC ConferenceProgram_000.pdf.
8. The subsequent carrying out of the reconstruction contracts has been controversial and the subject of scrutiny by both government and the popular press.
9. Several oversight reports have been issued on private contractors in Iraq, including audits by the Department of Defense's Contract Audit Agency of Kellogg and by the General Accountability Office. See, e.g., Coalition Provision Authority, *Federal Deployment Center Forward Operations at the Kuwait Hilton* (CPA IG Report No. 04-003); Department of Defense Contract Audit Agency, *Audit Report on Restore Iraqi Oil Task Order 5* (October 8, 2004); KPMG Bahrain, *Development Fund for Iraq: Report on Factual Findings in Connection with Disbursements for the Period*

from 1 January 2004 to 28 June 2004 (September 2004); United States Government Accountability Office, *Report to Congressional Committees, Rebuilding Iraq: Actions Needed to Improve Use of Private Security Providers* (July 2005); and United States Government Accountability Office, *Rebuilding Iraq: Fiscal Year 2003 Contract Award Procedures and Management Challenges* (2004).

10. Some commentators also argued that the decision to go to war itself was driven by the interests of private oil companies. The role of oil in U.S. national defense within the region dates back at least to the so-called Carter Doctrine, which was the subject of his 1980 State of the Union Address. President Jimmy Carter "State of the Union Address 1980," available at http://www.jimmycarterlibrary.org/documents/speeches/su80jec.phtml (January 23, 1980).
11. The oil-based infrastructure contracts were tendered in a second wave. This was an open tender, and Kellogg was awarded one of two contracts.
12. "Fixing Iraq's Infrastructure: U.S. Contractors Restored Power and Bridges while Repairing Neglected Water and Sewage Systems Vital to Iraqi's Health" in U.S. Agency for International Development *A Year in Iraq: Restoring Services* (May 2004), 5, 6. The subsequent tender was open, and Bechtel was awarded one of two contracts.
13. See 48 Code Federal Regulations 16.504 "Indefinite-Quantity Contracts"; Eric Aaserud "GSA Scheduled Contracts: Opportunities and Obligations" *Procurement Lawyer* 39 (Summer 2004), 4; D. Farriss "Checking Your Indefinite Delivery/Indefinite Quantity (IDIQ) IQ" *Construction Lawyer* 22 (Fall 2002), 24; David W. Lannetti "The Confluence of Convenience Terminations and Guaranteed Minimums in Government Contracts: What Is the Proper Remedy When the Government Fails to Order the Minimum Quantity Specified in an Indefinite-Delivery, Indefinite Quantity Contract" *Federal Circuit Bar Journal* 13 (2003), 1; Michael J. Lohnes "Note: Attempting to Spur Competition for Orders Placed Under Multiple Order and MAS Contracts: The Journey to the Unworkable Section 803" *Public Contract Law Journal* 33 (Spring 2004), 599; Denise B. Sirmons "Federal Contracting with

Women-Owned Businesses: An Analysis of Existing Challenges and Potential Opportunities" *Public Contract Law Journal* 33 (Summer 2004), 725; and Karen D. Thornton "Fine Tuning Acquisition Reforms Favorite Procurement Vehicle: The Indefinite Delivery Contract" *Public Contract Law Journal* 31 (Spring 2002), 383.

14. See both Bechtel contracts – Contract No. SPU-C-00-04-00001-00 between USAID and Bechtel National Inc. (January 5, 2004) and Contract No. EEE-C_00-03-00018-00 between USAID and Bechtel National Inc. (April 17, 2003).
15. General Services Administration, Department of Defense, National Aeronautics and Space Administration *Federal Acquisition Regulation* (March 2005), 16.306.
16. See www.publicintegrity.org/wow.
17. Representatives Carolyn Maloney and Henry Waxman have introduced legislation aimed to stem contracting abuses. See "Clean Contracting in Iraq Act" HR 3275. On Iraq reconstruction investigations, see http://www.democrats.reform.house.gov/investigations.asp?Issue=Iraq+Reconstruction.
18. Other forms of corporate aid exist, such as subsidies for farmers in the context of USAID grants. These grants are controversial when they promote genetically modified crops. Medical aid is another area that receives attention.
19. 46 USC 1283(a).
20. 46 USC 1281(a).
21. President George W. Bush "Presidential Memo on Marine War Risk Insurance" (December 12, 2001), available at http://www.whitehouse.gov/news/releases/2001/12/20011214-9.html.
22. See, e.g., Terrorism Risk Insurance Act of 2002.
23. Terrorism Risk Insurance Act Section 102(1)(A)(iii).
24. 42 USC 1651-4.
25. See, e.g., Contract No. SPU-C-00-04-00001-00 between USAID and Bechtel National Inc. (January 5, 2004) H15 SAFETY OF CONTRACTOR PERSONNEL.
26. Similarly, Gregory Shaffer looks at the relationship between governments and firms in the context of WTO disputes. His work

does not presume that governments and firms always have identical interests. Instead, he "evaluates how private firms collaborate with governmental authorities in the United States and the European Union (EU) to challenge foreign trade barriers before the WTO legal system and within its shadow." Gregory Shaffer *Defending Interests: Public-Private Partnerships in W.T.O. Litigation* (Washington, DC: Brookings Institutions Press 2003), 5.

27. See, e.g., Title 7 Subtitle B Chapter XIV Subchapter C "Export Programs."
28. See, e.g., Title 7 Subtitle B Chapter XV Part 1570 "Export Bonus Programs."
29. "Domestic International Sales Corporations" 26 USC 991-997.
30. On the SEC and its efforts to become a global regulator, see John Flood "Capital Markets, Globalisation and Global Elites" in Michael B. Likosky, ed., *Transnational Legal Processes* (New York: Cambridge University Press 2002), 114.
31. United States Agency for International Development *ADS 307* "Commodity Import Programs."
32. For the Department of Commerce's Trade Mission Policy, see U.S. Department of Commerce "Trade Mission Policy," available at http://www.ita.doc.gov/doctm/tmpol.html. The United States is not unique in this respect. In addition, government officials may travel to promote foreign direct and indirect inward investment.
33. On government-industry collaboration in the interests of private corporate actors with regard to government insurance programs covering expropriation risks, see Charles Lipson "The Development of Expropriation Insurance: The Role of Corporate Preferences and State Initiatives" *International Organization* 32(2) (1978), 351, 375.
34. 22 USC 2370a(b).
35. The Hickenlooper Amendments arose here. 22 USC 2370(e). The second amendment was a response to the Supreme Court ruling in *Banco Nactional de Cuba v. Sabbatino*, 376 US 398 (1964).
36. The relevant legislation is the Gonzalez amendments. Section 21 of the Inter-American Development Bank Act, P.L. 92-246; Section 12 of the International Development Association Act, P.L.

92-247; and Section 18 of the Asian Development Bank Act, P.L. 92-245 (March 10, 1972). On the Hickenlooper and Gonzalez amendments, see Richard W. Barrett "Avoiding the Expropriation Nightmare – Tax Consequences and Asset Protection Techniques" *University of Miami Law Review* 52 (1998), 831, 837–842. President Richard Nixon in 1972 stated that the government would follow through with retaliatory measures. See Richard Nixon "13-Statement Announcing United States Policy on Economic Assistance and Investment Security in Developing Nations" (January 19, 1972), available at http://www.presidency.ucsb.edu/ws/index.php?pid=3385 and Foreign Affairs Division, Congressional Research Service, Library of Congress *The Overseas Private Investment Corporation: A Critical Analysis: Prepared for the Committee on Foreign Affairs* (Washington, DC: United States Government Printing Office 1973), 103. See the Helms amendment in 1994 for its impact on the Hickenlooper and Gonzalez amendments.

37. For an early discussion of U.S. insurance programs for private national corporations, see Theodor Meron *Investment Insurance in International Law* (Dobbs Ferry, NY: Oceana Publications 1976).
38. Charles Lipson argues here that "the basic identity between corporate preferences, state initiatives, and policy outcomes" directs itself toward the goal of "private capital accumulation." Lipson 1978, 351, 375.
39. Foreign Assistance Act of 1948, Public Law 472, 60th Congress, Chapter 169, 2nd Session (S. 2202) (April 3, 1948).
40. Foreign Assistance Act of 1948, Section 111(b)(3) (providing up to fifteen million dollars in guarantees).
41. Lipson 1978, 354. At the same time, there was disagreement within the corporate community over whether these policies were appropriate. *Id.*, 357. These disagreements gave way to a more uniformly friendly position toward such insurance programs as they expanded their scope over time. *Id.*, 358–362.
42. Foreign Affairs Division 1973, 5.
43. Foreign Affairs Division 1973, 11 (discussing the implications of Executive Order 11579). On the subsequent evolution of political

risk insurance in the United States, see Kenneth W. Hansen "PRI and the Rise (and Fall?) of Private Investment in Public Infrastructure" in Michael B. Likosky, ed., *Privatising Development: Transnational Law, Infrastructure, and Human Rights* (Leiden: Martinus Nijhoff 2005), 105.

44. Lipson 1978, 365.
45. 22 USC 2194(d).
46. 22 USC 2191.
47. Many countries have modeled their overseas agencies on OPIC. These agencies vary in the emphasis they put on the aim of promoting corporate nationals overseas and the aim of promoting the interests of developing countries. Foreign Affairs Division 1973, 25, appendix C. However, related programs existed in the colonial context. For example, in 1946 the French government issued loans to its companies operating in colonial territories. Likewise, the British instituted a program in 1948 relating to the Commonwealth countries. Foreign Affairs Division 1973, 33.
48. 22 USC 2193(a).
49. 22 USC 2197(c).
50. United States Committee on Foreign Affairs *Foreign Assistance Act of 1969: Report of the Committee on Foreign Affairs Together with Minority, Supplement and Additional Views on H.R. 14580: To Promote the Foreign Policy, Security, and General Welfare of the United States by Assisting the Peoples of the World to Achieve Economic Development within a Framework of Democratic, Economic, Social, and Political Institutions, and for Other Purposes*, 91st Congress, 1st Session, House Report No. 91-611 (Washington, DC: United States Government Printing Office November 6, 1969), 3.
51. "Supplemental Views of Hon. John C. Culver, Hon. Benjamin S. Rosenthal, Hon. Edward R. Royball, and Hon. Jonathan B. Bhingham" in United States Committee on Foreign Affairs 1969, 179, 182.
52. Representatives H. R. Gross, Edward J. Derwinski, and J. Herbert Burke "Minority Views" in United States Committee on Foreign Affairs 1969, 192, 1934.

53. Quoted in Foreign Affairs Division 1973, 11.
54. On this office, see www.opic.gov/doingbusiness/investment.
55. Overseas Private Investment Corporation "Doing Business With Us: Worker and Human Rights," available at www.opic.gov/doingbusiness/investment/workersrights/index.asp.
56. 22 USC 2191a(a)(1).
57. 22 USC 2191a(a)(3).
58. 22 USC 2191a(a)(1).
59. 22 USC 2191a(c)(1).
60. 22 USC 2191a(c)(2).
61. Office of Accountability, Overseas Private Investment Corporation (brochure available at www.opic.gov).
62. 12 USC 635(a)(1). On the protection of workers' rights through international trade agreements, see Benjamin N. Davis "Note and Comment: The Effects of Worker Rights Protections in United States Trade Laws: A Case Study of El Salvador" *American University Journal of International Law and Policy* 10 (1995), 1167.
63. 12 USC 635(a)(2)(E).
64. 12 USC 635a(c)(8)(B).
65. 12 USC 635a(d)(2)(A).
66. 22 USC 2191(3)(c)(1).
67. William H. Becker and William M. McClenahan Jr. *The Market, the State, and the Export-Import Bank of the United States 1934–2000* (Cambridge: Cambridge University Press 2003), 3.
68. Becker and McClenahan 2003, 10–17.
69. Franklin D. Roosevelt "Executive Order 6581 Creating the Export-Import Bank of Washington" (February 2, 1934), available at http://www.presidency.ucsb.edu/ws/print.php?pid=14772.
70. Becker and McClenahan 2003, 17.
71. Becker and McClenahan 2003, 18–19.
72. Similarly, OPIC can work with foreign governments and multilateral institutions. 22 USC 2194(a)(2).
73. Becker and McClenahan 2003, 6.
74. On the Berne Union, see www.berneunion.org.uk.
75. The Export Credit Division. See http://www.oecd.org/department/0,2688,en_2649_34169_1_1_1_1_1,00.html.

76. World Trade Organization "Agreement on Subsidies and Countervailing Measures" *ILM* 33 (April 15, 1994), 1144, article 3 and annex I(j) and (k). See also "Brazil – Export Financing Programme for Aircraft: Report of the Panel" WT/DS46/R (April 14, 1999) (dispute between Canada and Brazil); Janet Koven Levit "The Dynamics of International Trade Finance Regulation: The Arrangement on Officially Supported Credits" *Harvard International Law Journal* 45 (Winter 2004), 65, 120–121; and Janet Koven Levit "A Bottom-Up Approach to International Law-Making: The Tale of Three Trade Finance Instruments" *Yale Journal of International Law* 30 (2005), 125, 144–173.
77. The agreement is the Arrangement on Guidelines for Officially Supported Export Credits. Levit 2004, 66; Levit 2005, 128.
78. www.eca-watch.org/goals/jakartadec.html.
79. 22 USC 262s-1.
80. On the history of MIGA, see Ibrahaim F. I. Shihata *MIGA and Foreign Investment: Origins, Operations, Policies and Basic Documents of the Multilateral Investment Guarantee Agency* (Dordrecht: Martinus Nijhoff 1988), 29–99.
81. Foreign Affairs Division 1973, 32.
82. Early feasibility studies situated MIGA within the context of national programs. See Shihata 1988, 49–50.
83. MIGA Convention chapter 1, article 2.
84. MIGA Convention chapter 3, article 11.
85. 22 USC 290k-2.
86. IFC Articles of Agreement, article 1.
87. IFC Articles of Agreement, article 1(i)–(iii).
88. For an argument that "third parties" should be able to bring claims against privatized international projects generally, see Carl S. Bjerre "Project Finance and Consent" in Likosky 2005, 221. Similarly, see the denial of standing by the International Centre for the Settlement of Investment Disputes to nongovernmental organizations in the context of a privatized Bolivian water project. *Aguas del Tunari SA v. Republic of Bolivia* (Case No. ARB/02/3), 15–18.
89. 22 USC 262d(a).

90. 22 USC 262d(a).
91. 22 USC 262d(c)(1).
92. 22 USC 262m-7(a)(2)(A) – amended by Public Law 105-118, Section 560(b)(2).
93. 22 USC 262m-7 – amended by Public Law 105-118, Section 560(b)(3).
94. 22 USC 262m-7.
95. Public Law 105-118 §560(b)(1).
96. Public Law 105-117 §560(b)(3).
97. "News Release: Ex-Im Bank Declines Financing Request to Back Peru's Camisea Gas Development Project" (August 28, 2003), available at http://www.exim.gov/pressrelease.cfm/49A54DF9-A3ED-883F-0CB97EF3DB2F5423.
98. On Camisea, see Likosky 2006, chapter 6.
99. Center for Strategic and International Studies *Guiding Principles for Strengthening American Infrastructure* (Washington, DC: CSIS March 27, 2006).

Chapter 9. Transparency

1. "Governor and U.S. Treasury Secretary Paulson Participate in Economic Roundtable to Discuss Trade," available at http://gov.ca.gov/index.php?/speech/8350/.
2. Presidential Memorandum for the Heads of Executive Departments and Agencies (March 20, 2009).
3. Louis D. Brandeis *Other People's Money and How the Bankers Use It* (New York: Frederick A. Stokes Company 1914), 92.
4. "Remarks of President Barack Obama on the Economy" (The White House Office of the Press Secretary January 28, 2009).
5. Brandeis 1914, 223.
6. Brandeis 1914, 96.
7. Brandeis 1914, 92.
8. Brandeis 1914, 92.
9. Rudolph von Jhering *The Struggle for Law* (Chicago: Callaghan and Company 1879), 1915.

10. Brandeis 1914, 92.
11. Arleen Jacobius “Public Funds Join Forces on Infrastructure Investing” *Pensions and Investments* (August 10, 2009).
12. “Bye-Bye Buyout; Hello Infrastructure” *Pensions and Investments* (June 1, 2009); Arleen Jacobius “Industry Heavyweights Revamp Businesses to Focus on New Area” *Pension and Investments* (June 1, 2009).
13. Brandeis 1914, 97.
14. Brandeis 1914, 101–102.
15. Correspondence (2009).
16. City of Chicago Department of Finance “Asset Lease Agreements,” available at http://egov.cityofchicago.org/city/webportal/portalContentItemAction.do?contentOID=537046395&contenTypeName=COC_EDITORIAL&topChannelName=Dept&entityName=Finance&deptMainCategoryOID=-536903914&blockName=Finance/Content&context=dept.
17. KPMG *The Changing Face of Infrastructure: Frontline Views from Private Sector Infrastructure Providers* (2009), 7.
18. Nicholas Bliss and Edward Braham *United Kingdom: Outlook for Infrastructure: 2009 and Beyond* (June 30, 2009).
19. KPMG 2009, 13.
20. David Snow “Don’t Do It Yourself” *Infrastructure Investor* (July 16, 2009).

Chapter 10. Contracts

1. Likosky 2005, 44–51; Likosky 2006, 36–42.
2. Hansen 2005, 105; Scott L. Hoffman *The Law and Business of International Project Finance* (3rd edn., New York: Cambridge University Press 2008).
3. Susan Rose-Ackerman *Corruption and Government: Causes, Consequences, and Reform* (New York: Cambridge University Press 1999); Susan Rose-Ackerman “Corruption and the Global Corporation: Ethical Obligations and Workable Strategies” in Michael B. Likosky, ed., *Transnational Legal Processes* (New York: Cambridge University Press 2002), 148; Likosky 2005.

4. Benjamin Esty *Modern Project Finance: A Casebook* (New Jersey: John Wiley and Sons 2004), 2.
5. Eric J. Woodhouse 'The Experience with Independent Power Projects in Developing Countries: Interim Report" (Presented at General Counsels' Roundtable Stanford University) (January 21–22, 2005).
6. Woodhouse 2005, 29.
7. Woodhouse 2005, 28.
8. Likosky 2005.
9. Frank Sader *Attracting Foreign Direct Investment into Infrastructure: Why Is It So Difficult?* (Foreign Investment Advisory Service 2000), 55.
10. Sader 2000, 58–59.
11. Van Mejia "NOTE: The Philippines Re-Energizes: Privatization of the National Power Corporation and the Red Flag of Political Risk" *Columbia Journal of Asian Law* 16 (2003), 355; Woodhouse 2005, 148.
12. Loren Page Ambinder, Nimali de Silva, and John Dewar "Essay: The Mirage Becomes Reality: Privatization and Project Finance Developments in the Middle East Power Market" *Fordham International Law Journal* 24 (2001), 1029, 1042.
13. Woodhouse 2005, 127.
14. Clifford Chance *Project Finance* (Clifford Chance 1999); P. Guislain *Privatisations* (Washington, DC: World Bank 1997); Hoffman 2008); Scott L. Hoffman *Law and Business of International Project Finance: A Resource for Governments, Sponsors, Lenders, Lawyers, and Project Participants* (Leiden: Kluwer Law International 2001); Scott L. Hoffman, "A Practical Guide to Transactional Project Finance: Basic Concepts, Risk Identification and Contractual Considerations" *Business Law* (45) (1989), 181; S. M. Levy, *Build, Operate, Transfer: Paving the Way for Tomorrow's Infrastructure* (New York: Wiley 1996); Sader 2000; Graham Vinter *Project Finance, a Legal Guide* (2nd edn., London: Sweet & Maxwell Ltd. 1998), 2–5; Don Wallace Jr. "Private Capital and Infrastructure: Tragic? Useful and Pleasant? Inevitable?"

in Michael B. Likosky 2005, 131; Don Wallace "Private Participation in Infrastructure and the Provision of Public Services – Inevitable and Difficult" *The Transnational Lawyer* 18 (2004), 117.

15. Tamara Lothian and Katharina Pistor "Local Institutions, Foreign Investment and Alternative Strategies of Development: Some Views from Practice" *Columbia Journal of Transnational Law* 42 (2003), 101, 120.
16. Stanford Global Projects First General Counsels' Roundtable 2005.
17. Likosky 2005.
18. Likosky 2006.
19. Likosky 2005, chapter 4.
20. Adapted from Sader 2000, 72–73; UNIDO 1996, 155; and author.
21. UNIDO 1996, 155; and author.
22. Stanford Global Projects First General Counsels' Roundtable 2005. This quotation draws on the following sources: Theodore Moran "Private Infrastructure for Development: Confronting Political and Regulatory Risks" paper presented at Private Infrastructure for Development Conference (September 8–10, 1999, Rome, Italy) and Frank Sader *Attracting Foreign Direct Investment into Infrastructure: Why Is It So Difficult?* Foreign Investment Advisory Service Occasional Paper No. 12 (Washington, DC: The World Bank and the International Finance Corporation 1999).
23. Luis Andres, Jose Luis Guasch, and Stephane Straub "Does Regulation and Institutional Design Matter for Infrastructure Sector Performance" (World Bank Policy Research Paper Series 4378).
24. Stanford Global Projects First General Counsels' Roundtable 2005.
25. J. Luis Guasch "Granting and Renegotiating Infrastructure Concessions: Doing It Right" (Washington, DC: World Bank 2004).
26. Flood 2002, 114.
27. Woodhouse 2005, 27–28.
28. Levy 1996, 22.

29. Lothian and Pistor 2003, 109.
30. David W. Eaton "Transformation of the Maquiladora Industry: The Driving Force Behind the Creation of a NAFTA Regional Economy" *Arizona Journal of International and Comparative Law* 14 (1997), 747; Likosky 2001, 2005; World Bank 1994.
31. Michel Kerf, R. David Gray, Timothy Irwin, Celine Levesque, and Robert R. Taylor (under the direction of Michael Klein) *Concessions for Infrastructure: A Guide to Their Design and Award* (Washington, DC: World Bank 1998), 9.
32. *Id.*
33. Sader 2000, 92.
34. Stanford Global Projects First General Counsels' Roundtable 2005.
35. Kathleen S. McArthur "Multilateral-Sponsored Municipal Bond Insurance: A New Approach to Promoting Infrastructure and Capital Markets Development in Latin America" *Law and Business Review* 12 (2006), 3, 6–8.
36. Barry Metzger "The Legacy of Failed Global Projects: Testing the Legal Paradigm" Stanford University Global Projects First General Counsels' Roundtable (January 21–22, 2005), 6.
37. Woodhouse 2005, 149.
38. See the work by Levitt, collaborators, and colleagues.
39. Moran 1999.
40. Kerf 1998, 9.
41. Sader 2000, 44.
42. Sader 2000, 34.
43. Woodhouse 2005, 130–131.
44. Van Mejia 2003, 355, 364–365.
45. Ambinder, de Silva, and Dewar 2001, 1035.
46. Ambinder, de Silva, and Dewar 2001, 1037–1038.
47. Paul R. Verkuil *Outsourcing Sovereignty: Why Privatization of Government Functions Threatens Democracy and What We Can Do About It* (New York: Cambridge University Press 2007).
48. Government of the Federated States of Micronesia "President Mori discusses reorganization of Compact Infrastructure Program Management Unit and is assured that goal to implement

$35 million per year in infrastructure development is on track" FSM Office of the President, Public Information: press, radio, video.

49. UNIDO 1996, 4.
50. The World Bank Group *The Private Sector in Infrastructure: Strategy, Regulation, and Risk* (World Bank 1997), 12.
51. Ashoka Mody, ed., *Infrastructure Delivery: Private Initiative and the Public Good* (Economic Development Institute of the World Bank 1996), xix.
52. World Bank 1997, 14.
53. World Bank 1997, 16.
54. Sader 2000, 76–77.
55. Barry Metzger "The Legacy of Failed Global Projects: Testing the Legal Paradigm" Stanford University Global Projects First General Counsels' Roundtable (January 21–22, 2005), 5.
56. Metzger 2005, 5.
57. Stanford Global Projects First General Counsels' Roundtable 2005, 30.
58. Felton Mack Johnston and Robert T. Wray "Insuring Arbitral Outcomes" *Political Risk Newsletter* 1 (2) (October 2005), 1, 3.
59. Wallace 2004, 2005.
60. Pedamon 2001, 1305.
61. Model Provisions 9–17, Recommendation 27.
62. Model Provisions 20–23, Recommendations 30–34.
63. Model Provision 29, Recommendation 41.
64. Model Provisions 28–51, Recommendations 40–70.
65. Carl S. Bjerre "Project Finance, Securitization and Consensuality" *Duke Journal of Comparative and International Law* 12 (2002), 411.
66. Stephen Wallenstein "Situating Project Finance and Securitization in Context: A Comment on Bjerre" *Duke Journal of Comparative and International Law* 12 (2002), 449.
67. Daniel D. Bradlow "Private Complaints and International Organizations: A Comparative Study of the Independent Inspection Mechanisms in International Financial Institutions" *Georgetown*

Journal of International Law 36 (2005), 403; L. David Brown and Jonathan Fox "Transnational Civil Society Coalitions and the World Bank: Lessons from Project and Policy Influence Campaigns" *IDR Report: A Continual Series of Occasional Papers* (Boston: Institute for Research 2000a); Jonathan A. Fox "The World Bank Inspection Panel: Lessons from the First Five Years" *Global Governance* 6 (2000b), 279; Jonathan A. Fox and L. David Brown, eds., *Struggles for Accountability: The World Bank, NGOs, and Grassroots Movements* (Cambridge, MA: MIT Press 1998); Likosky 2005.

68. Nan Zhang "NOTE: Moving Towards a Competitive Electricity Market? The Dilemma of Project Finance in the Wake of the Asian Financial Crisis" *Minnesota Journal of Global Trade* 9 (2000), 715, 735.
69. Likosky 2005; Lothian and Pistor 2003, 112–113.
70. Woodhouse 2005, 149.
71. Stanford Global Projects First General Counsels' Roundtable 2005, 7.
72. Kerf 1998, 34.
73. Irwin 1997, 37; Kerf 1998, 34.
74. Kerf 1998, 34.
75. Irwin 1997, 36; Kerf 1998, 34.
76. World Bank 1997, 37.
77. World Bank 1997, 37.
78. Pascual 2004, 110.
79. Ryan J. Orr "Investment in Foreign Infrastructure: The Legacy and Lessons of Legal-Contractual Failure" (Background Paper: Second General Counsels' Roundtable: The Collaboratory for Research on Global Projects, Stanford University, February 10–11, 2006).
80. Likosky 2005.
81. Proceeedings 2001.

Chapter 11. Emancipation

1. This taxonomy borrows from the three basic works in this area: Daniele Barberis *Negotiating Mining Agreements: Past, Present*

and Future Trends (Leiden: Kluwer Law International 1999); Yinka Omorogbe *The Oil and Gas Industry: Exploration and Production Contracts* (Lagos: Malthouse Press 1997); and Ernest E. Smith, John S. Dzienkowski, Owen L. Anderson, Gary B. Conine, John S. Lowe, and Bruce M. Kramer *International Petroleum Transactions* (2nd edn., Denver, CO: Rocky Mountain Mineral Law Foundation 2000).

2. Oil Concession of 1934 between the State of Kuwait and the Kuwait Oil Company Limited, a Great Britain firm, Article 3(d).
3. E. E. Smith "From Concessions to Service Contracts" *Tulsa Law Journal* 27 (1991–1992), 493, 495.
4. Oil Concession of 1934, Article 1.
5. Omorogbe 1997.
6. Oil Concession of 1934, Articles 2(a) and (b).
7. Likosky 2006.
8. Barberis 1999, 13.
9. *Id.*, 29–39.
10. Omorogbe 1997, 60.
11. Petroleum Working Contract Between Indonesia and P.T. Stanvac Indonesia 1964, Article 15.
12. Smith et al. 2000, 418–425; Note "From Concession to Participation: Restructuring the Middle East Oil Industry" *New York University Law Review* 48 (1973): 774.
13. Smith et al. 2000, 418–422.
14. *Id.*, 419.
15. Petroleum Working Contract Between Indonesia and P.T. Stanvac Indonesia 1964, Article 4(a).
16. Egypt – Egyptian General Petroleum Corporation – Esso: Concession Agreement for Petroleum Exploration and Production (December 14, 1974), Article IV; Egypt – Egyptian General Petroleum Corporation – Esso: Concession Agreement for Petroleum Exploration and Production (December 14, 1974), Article IV Work Program, Expenditures and Management of Operation (b).
17. R. Fabrikant "Production Sharing Contracts in the Indonesian Petroleum Industry" *Harvard International Law Journal* 16 (1975), 3030; T. N. Machmud "Production Sharing Contracts in

Indonesia: 25 Years' History" *Journal of Energy and Natural Resources Law* 11 (1993), 79; T. N. Machmud *The Indonesian Production Sharing Contract: An Investor's Perspective* (The Hague: Kluwer 2000).

18. M. A. Stoleson "Investment at an Impasse: Russia's Production-Sharing Agreement Law and the Continuing Barriers to Petroleum Investment in Russia" *Duke Journal of Comparative and International Law* (1996–1997), 677; V. Timokho "Recent Developments in the Russian Production-Sharing Agreement Law: Making the Law Work" *UCLA Journal of International Law and Foreign Affairs* 6 (2001–2002), 365.
19. Barberis 1999, 155.
20. *Id.*
21. *Id.*
22. Smith et al. 2000, 454.
23. Final Consolidated Version (March 30, 1996), preamble.
24. *Id.*, Article 2, Section 2.1.
25. *Id.*, Article 2 Grant of Rights and Scope, Section 2.2.
26. *Id.* Article 11 Contractor's Recovery of Petroleum Costs and Production Sharing, Section 11.5 Profit Petroleum.
27. *Id.*, Article 5 Steering Committee for Project Management and Annual Work Programmes, Article 5.1(a)–(f).
28. Omorogbe 1997, 63; J. S. C. Neto "Risk-Bearing Service Contracts in Brazil" *Journal of Energy and Natural Resources Law* 3 (1985), 114.
29. Smith et al. 2000, 511.
30. Omorogbe 1997, 63–64.
31. *Id.*, 65.
32. Smith et al. 2000, 512.
33. *Id.*, 472.
34. Final Consolidated Version (March 30, 1996), Article 1 Participating Interests, Section 1.1.
35. *Id.*, Article 1, Section 4.4.
36. *Id.*, Article 1, Section 6.7(b).
37. Egypt – Egyptian General Petroleum Corporation – Esso: Concession Agreement for Petroleum Exploration and Production (December 14, 1974), Articles XXIII(a)(1) and (2).

38. Z. Elkin, A. Guzman, and B. Simmons "Competing for Capital: The Diffusion of Bilateral Investment Treaties, 1960–2000" *International Organizations* 60 (2006), 811; S. Rose-Ackerman and J. Tobin "Foreign Direct Investment and the Business Environment in Developing Countries: The Impact of Bilateral Investment Treaties" *Yale Law and Economics Research Paper* No. 293 (2005).
39. http://www.bp.com/genericarticle.do?categoryld=9006669&contentld=7014358.

Chapter 12. Renegotiations

1. Likosky 2006.
2. Likosky 2006, chapter 2.
3. J. Kerr "Ecuador's New Energy Minister Calls for Renegotiation of Contracts, but Not Nationalization" *Global Insight* (January 22, 2007).
4. "Venezuela Makes Belated Payments to Private Oil Companies" *Oil Daily* (June 30, 2005). Criticisms have been tied to claims of lack of transparency domestically. "Ramirez; Q1 Net Oil Exports Were 2.14Mb/d" *Business News America – English* (May 18, 2005).
5. However, aspects of the Venezuela-Cuba relationship will be discussed as they impact the distribution of revenue from oil internally. Other important developments include the provision of heating discounts to poor families in the United States, providing oil to thirteen Caribbean nations, regional energy initiatives pursued with Argentina and Brazil, the purchase of Argentine and Ecuador bonds, support for Evo Morales in Bolivia, and wider hemispheric ambitions. Michael Shifter "In Search of Hugo Chavez" *Foreign Affairs* 85 (2006), 45, 50, 52–53.
6. Shifter 2006, 45, 50.
7. Mark Weisbrot "Progressive Change in Venzuela" *The Nation* (December 6, 2007).
8. Mark Weisbrot and Luis Sandoval "The Venezuelan Economy in the Chavez Years" *Center for Economic and Policy Research* 3 (July 2007).

9. Rafael Ramirez "The Plan for Sowing the Oil 2005–2030 in Context: PDVSA Is at the Service of the Bolivarian Republic of Venezuela" *The New PDVSA Contract: A Newsletter about Venezuela's National Oil Industry: Bolivarian Republic of Venezuela, Caracas* 3 (September–October 2005), 4.
10. Archived at http://www.pdvsa.com/index.php?tpl=interface.en/design/readmenuprinc.tpl.html&newsid_temas=39.
11. "PDVSA Deposits US$2.86bn Oil Revenue in Fondespa" *Business News Americas* (July 12, 2005).
12. For example, in 2004 allocations from Fondespa were made to the national railway and to road and highway projects (IAFE: $200 million, Moron-Boca de Aaroa-Tucacas road: $14.4 million, Antonio Jose de Sucre Cmana-Puerto Law Cruz highway: $58 million). "CVP to Allocate US$1.8bn in Infrastructure Funds" *Business News Americas* (November 15, 2004).
13. Shifter 2006, 45, 51.
14. Francisco Rodriguez "How Not to Defend the Revolution: Mark Weisbrot and the Misinterpretation of Venezuelan Evidence" *Wesleyan Economic Working Papers* No. 2008-001 (March 25, 2008).
15. Shifter 2006, 51.
16. *Id.*
17. *Id.*, 45, 46.
18. *Id.*, 45.
19. *Id.*, 51.
20. *Id.*
21. Larry B. Pascal "Summary of Oil and Gas Developments in South America" *Law and Business Review of the Americas* 13 (2007), 521, 533.
22. Joseph Stiglitz "Who Owns Bolivia?" *Daily Times* (June 22, 2006).
23. Caroline Jova "Nationalization in Bolivia: Curse or Blessing?" *LACC Working Paper Series* 12 (August 2006), 14.
24. Roberto Chacon de Albuquerquie "The Disappropriation of Foreign Companies Involved in the Exploration, Exploitation and Commercialization of Hydrocarbons in Bolivia" *Law and Business Review of the Americas* 14 (2008), 21, 46.

25. Wenhua Shan "Symposium on International Energy Law: Article: From 'North-South Divide' to 'Private-Public Debate': Revival of the Calvo Doctrine and the Changing Landscape in International Investment Law" *Northwestern Journal of International Law & Business* 27 (2007), 631, 664.
26. The Carter Center "Review of DRC Mining Contracts – Update and Recommendations" (November 30, 2007), 4.
27. *Id.*, 1.
28. *Id.*, 2.

Index